New

WITHDRAWN

W9-BUG-863

THE
1900s

Other books in this series:

THE
1900s

Myra H. Immell, *Book Editor*

David L. Bender, *Publisher*
Bruno Leone, *Executive Editor*
Bonnie Szumski, *Series Editor*
David M. Haugen, *Managing Editor*

Greenhaven Press, Inc., San Diego, California

AMERICA'S DECADES

Every effort has been made to trace the owners of copyrighted material. The articles in this volume may have been edited for content, length, and/or reading level. The titles have been changed to enhance the editorial purpose.

No part of this book may be reproduced or used in any form or by any means, electrical, mechanical, or otherwise, including, but not limited to, photocopy, recording, or any information storage and retrieval system, without prior written permission from the publisher.

Library of Congress Cataloging-in-Publication Data

The 1900s / Myra H. Immell, book editor.
    p.   cm. — (America's decades)
    Includes bibliographical references and index.
    ISBN 0-7377-0294-X (alk. paper) —
    ISBN 0-7377-0293-1 (pbk. : alk. paper)
    1. United States—Civilization—1865–1918. 2. Nineteen
hundreds (Decade). I. Immell, Myra H. II. Series.

E169.1 .A1124 2000
973.8—dc21   99-056322
                                                         CIP

Cover photos: (top) Archive Photos, (bottom) Corbis/Bettmann
Library of Congress, 18, 56, 71, 129, 157, 225
NASA, 171

©2000 by Greenhaven Press, Inc.
P.O. Box 289009, San Diego, CA 92198-9009

Printed in the U.S.A.

Contents

Chapter 1: The Onset of a New Century

Chapter 2: Daily Life in America: Dreams and Disasters

Chapter 3: Politics and Reform

trusts, pushed through reform legislation, struck a blow for conservation, made a mark in foreign affairs—and emerged as an all-time champion of national unity.

Chapter 4: Technology and Discovery

more when he began the Ford Motor Company and designed and produced the "Tin Lizzie," the first moderately priced automobile.

Chapter 5: Beyond American Boundaries

Chapter 6: The Eve of a New Decade

Foreword

In his book *The American Century*, historian Harold Evans maintains that the history of the twentieth century has been dominated by the rise of the United States as a global power: "The British dominated the nineteenth century, and the Chinese may cast a long shadow on the twenty-first, but the twentieth century belongs to the United States." In a 1998 interview he summarized his sweeping hypothesis this way: "At the beginning of the century the number of free democratic nations in the world was very limited. Now, at the end of the century, democracy is ascendant around the globe, and America has played the major part in making that happen."

As the new century dawns, historians are eager to appraise the past one hundred years. Evans's book is just one of many attempts to assess the historical impact that the United States has had in the past century. Although not all historians agree with Evans's characterization of the twentieth century as "America's century," no one disputes his basic observation that "in only the second century of its existence the United States became the world's leading economic, military and cultural power." For most of the twentieth century the United States has played an increasingly larger role in shaping world events. The Greenhaven Press America's Decades series is designed to help readers develop a better understanding of America and Americans during this important time.

Each volume in the ten-volume series provides an in-depth examination of the time period. In compiling each volume, editors have striven to cover not only the defining events of the decade—in both the domestic and international arenas—but also the cultural, intellectual, and technological trends that affected people's everyday lives.

Essays in the America's Decades series have been chosen for their concise, accessible, and engaging presentation of the facts. Each selection is preceded by a summary of the article's content. A comprehensive index and an annotated table of contents also aid readers in quickly locating material of interest. Each volume begins with an introductory essay that presents the broader themes of each decade. Several research aids are also present, including an extensive bibliography and a timeline that provides an at-a-glance overview of each decade.

Each volume in the Greenhaven Press America's Decades series serves as an informative introduction to a specific period in U.S. history. Together, the volumes comprise a detailed overview of twentieth century American history and serve as a valuable resource for students conducting research on this fascinating time period.

Introduction

At the turn of the century, the United States was a prosperous nation. Americans drew confidence from the fact that America was the world's leading industrial nation as well as the world's largest agricultural producer. Children in most states were required by law to attend school, and the population—a record-breaking 76 million people—was double what it had been just forty years before. The West had been won, and the American frontier, which for three hundred years had tempted the adventurous and land-hungry, was settled. For the first time, America was a world power, with territories outside of its continental boundaries and a growing interest and involvement in foreign affairs. Many people believed that this would be the American century.

The first decade of the century was characterized by innovation, change, and reform. Michigan engineer Henry Ford founded a motor company and ushered in the age of the automobile. Two bicycle manufacturers from Dayton, Ohio, Orville and Wilbur Wright, stunned the world with their first airplane flight. Millions of immigrants arrived, nearly 9 million between 1901 and 1910. They settled mostly in the cities, where they became an important new source of labor for burgeoning American industry. Cities grew, swelled by rural migrants and the increasing streams of immigrants seeking new lives and prosperity, and the once predominantly rural America began its steady transformation to an urban, industrialized society.

But with the changes and growth, the industrialization and urbanization, came many problems. The gap between rich and poor widened, and, in spite of government efforts and laws passed in the 1890s, huge trusts—corporations that control an entire market—grew and held sway, especially in such areas as steel, railroads, and financial institutions.

These political and societal issues and inequities were of particular concern to a group of reformers called Progressives, who firmly believed that their ideas would lead to progress and a better way of life for more Americans, not just those with money and power. Progressives set off a wave of reform across the country.

Reforming the Government

Above all, Progressives wanted honest and active government that would put some controls on big business. At the local level, they were confronted by a massive challenge: to reform urban political machines. The political machine was a well-organized group that controlled a political party's activities in a large area. The machine was dominated by one individual known as a political boss. Political bosses ran most city governments and, as a result, the cities themselves. The Progressives contended that nothing would change unless they could break boss rule and destroy the political machines. Journalist Lincoln Steffens confirmed this and captured the attention of the entire nation with his 1904 work *The Shame of the Cities,* which focused on corrupt practices in city government and the links between crooked politicians and big business.

Political bosses manipulated the choice of mayor and the city council. They made sure that the most important positions were held by their supporters, who had no misgivings about doing favors for businesses offering them "gifts" in the form of large sums of money. Machine politicians did what was expedient to stay in power, including stuffing ballot boxes, selling offices, receiving bribes, and stealing city funds. Some police officers resorted to extortion—that is, taking money to overlook or ignore illegal activities.

To make urban government more honest and efficient and eliminate the graft and corruption, the Progressives called for new forms of government that would take away power from politicians and give it to business and management experts. One such form of government was the commission, which put different experts in charge of different city departments. Individual reformers became mayors of some cities, including Detroit, Michigan, and Cleveland,

Ohio. They replaced the corrupt city officials with competent, honest men and paid close attention to what the people living in their cities wanted and needed.

Writers and reporters played an important role in this Progressive reform movement largely because they were in a position to gain widespread attention for social problems. Crusading writers went on the offensive in books, magazines, and newspapers, exposing America's social ills for the world to see. President Theodore Roosevelt dubbed these crusaders "muckrakers" after a character in the then-popular book *Pilgrim's Progress*.

Crusading American writers, journalists, and photographers increased Americans' awareness—and provoked their sense of guilt—describing conditions so dreadful that growing numbers of Americans reluctantly began to agree that things had to change. The muckrakers made sure that Americans were aware of the deplorable practices that were commonplace at the time. In 1906, for example, novelist Upton Sinclair's book *The Jungle* so shocked the public, including President Roosevelt, with the horrible conditions of Chicago's stockyards, the lives of stockyard workers, and the practices of the meatpacking industry that it led to passage of the first federal Meat Inspection Act. Over the decade, public commissions were formed to investigate and recommend changes in other areas as well, including child labor, working conditions, and housing.

Industrialization, Big Business, and Robber Barons

One of the targets of the Progressives was the small group of men who had started and built businesses into giant enterprises. These business entrepreneurs—men like Andrew Carnegie, Philip Armour, and John D. Rockefeller—had the ability and foresight to productively organize land, labor, and capital. They knew how to raise money and were not reluctant to adopt new technology. The profits they reaped made them millionaires and billionaires. At the same time, their relentless rise to power and the use of such ruthless business methods as artificially lowering prices to run other companies out of business earned these businessmen the appellation "robber baron." Critics argued that they were power- and money-hungry men bent on destroying anyone they perceived as competition, men who would do almost anything to further their own interests.

Journalist Ida M. Tarbell confirmed these accusations and set into motion the craze for reform journalism with her 1903 *History of the Standard Oil Company,* a scathing exposé of John D. Rockefeller's ruthless business practices in the Standard Oil Company. In this report, she made public Standard Oil's aggressive methods of getting rid of competition.

Yet the robber barons were also symbolic of the great American ideal: that anyone, even someone of humble origins, could prosper. Steel baron Andrew Carnegie, for example, was a Scottish immigrant who started out as a bobbin boy in a cotton factory, earning one dollar and twenty cents a week, and ended up in control of America's steel for a world market. American-born Philip Armour was a former farmer who revolutionized the meatpacking industry and, in the process, made himself a millionaire more than fifty times over. Native New Yorker John D. Rockefeller started out working for a trading company for fifteen dollars a week and came to totally control almost all aspects of the oil industry. Why shouldn't such men, using their ingenuity and business acumen, reap the rewards of their hard work?, asked some Americans.

Historians do not always agree with the robber barons' tactics. They do agree, however, that these titans of industry played a vital role in the changing American economy and influenced business and government well into the next century.

Reforming the Trusts

When Rockefeller consolidated his investments in mining, lumber, and transportation and created the Standard Oil Trust, he set a precedent that other entrepreneurs emulated. It was a precedent that led to protest, controversy, and political maneuverings that carried over into the 1900s.

At the heart of the controversy and legal ramifications was that Standard Oil and the other major trusts that were formed constituted monopolies—companies or groups with exclusive control over producing and/or selling commodities or services. Such exclusive control was illegal under some states' antimonopoly laws. Workers, consumers, and small business owners argued that trusts went against the democratic tradition of free enterprise. Early state and federal attempts to break the trusts and restrict big business, however, were blocked by the courts and remained a problem that gave impetus to the national push for reform in the 1900s.

The Progressives were convinced that the trusts were too powerful. They argued that, if not controlled, trusts would put small companies out of business. Afraid that monopolies were destroying competition, they worked for the regulation of business by all levels of government. They attacked giant trusts like Standard Oil and Andrew Carnegie's U.S. Steel and demanded that they be broken up.

Reform, however, was not easy to achieve and was relatively slow in coming. Then, in 1901, an assassin's bullet ended the life of President William McKinley, and Vice President Theodore Roosevelt ascended to the presidency. A national spokesperson for Progressives and reform, Roosevelt made progressivism a national creed. Using his executive powers, he ordered the Justice Department to use the 1890 Sherman Anti-Trust Act to prosecute the Northern Securities Company, a trust that financier J.P. Morgan and railroad potentate James J. Hill had created to control the activities of three powerful railroad companies. The Supreme Court ruled in 1904 that Northern Securities did violate the Sherman act and that it had to sell some of its assets. The case marked the first time that the federal government had taken an active role in regulating business.

That same year, Roosevelt was elected president. He promised the people a "square deal" and set out to push reforms through Congress. He got twenty-five indictments against trusts in the beef, oil, and tobacco industries, which earned him a reputation as a "trustbuster." Ironically, Roosevelt had not set out to destroy the trusts, merely to regulate them. He believed that the growth of big business, including the trusts, was a natural part of the economic system. As a result, he favored the government breaking up only those trusts that used unfair business practices.

The Immigrant Factor

Big business was not the only area in which Progressives worked for reform. At the start of the century, America was still an agricultural society—half of all Americans still worked as farmers—but that soon began to change. The development and growth of new industries, however, meant that many farmers—especially the younger ones—left their rural homes to seek industrial jobs in the cities. Their numbers were augmented by an influx of immigrants from other lands. America always had attracted people from overseas. But now even greater numbers of immigrants flocked to America, and most of them settled in the cities.

For most of these immigrants, America was the dream, the ultimate goal, the land of promise and opportunity, and they came in increasing numbers in the hope of escaping political or religious persecution, famine, and poverty. The result was large-scale foreign immigration, which proved to be a major contributor to urban growth. In the forty-year period from 1840 to 1880, about 9.5 million immigrants came to America, most of them white Anglo-Saxon Protestants from such northern and western European nations as Great Britain, Holland, Germany, and Scandinavia.

In the late 1800s, the nature of the immigration changed noticeably. Beginning in the 1880s, greater numbers of immigrants began to arrive, the majority of them from Asia and southern and eastern European countries like Italy, Poland, Russia, and Hungary. Most of these immigrants were Catholic, Jewish, or Eastern Orthodox rather than Protestant. The contrast between immigration prior to and following 1800 was so marked that historians have differentiated between the two, with the former referred to as "the old immigration" and the latter as "the new immigration."

While some of the immigrants gravitated to rural areas, most settled in cities. The overall result was that the cities grew and kept growing at an incredible rate, especially the cities of the industrial northeast. Between 1860 and 1900, the population of New York City more than tripled, and the populations of Chicago, Philadelphia, Boston, and Baltimore more than doubled. In 1860 less than 21 percent of the American population lived in small towns and cities of twenty-five hundred or more people. By 1900 almost 40 percent of the population was living in towns and cities of that size.

As they grew, cities began to spread outward, making urban sprawl a reality. Not too long before, hardly anyone had even heard of paved streets. City streets were uneven,

Immigrants from Antwerp, Belgium, huddle together on the deck of the Westernland *as they arrive at Ellis Island. During the 1900s, foreign immigration contributed to unprecedented growth in America's population.*

bumpy, and noisy because they were made of sand, gravel, wood blocks, bricks, or cobblestones. Then, asphalt was introduced; new modes of transportation appeared in the form of electric trolleys, subways, and elevated electric railways; and bridges were built across rivers and bays. All of these advances in transportation helped make travel more practical and more possible for many Americans.

When these transportation innovations were coupled with such improvements in communications as the telegraph and the telephone, the impact on cities was enormous. Factories, shops, and banks could congregate in one area without having to be concerned about being able to communicate with industries in other areas, and cities now had access to areas that had been difficult or impossible to get to before. People soon discovered that they could live in one place and work in another. Just because they worked in the city, they did not have to live there as well. With the paved roads, bridges, and new modes of transportation, they could move away from the downtown areas where most of the businesses and factories were located.

Cities spread out to include new housing areas away from downtown, changing the complexion of the downtown area currently known as the inner city. Middle- and upper-class Americans moved away from downtown, using the streetcars and trolleys to get to work. The poor and most of the newly arrived immigrants, however, had to live where they worked, which generally made the inner city populated with filthy tenements where unscrupulous landlords charged rent for run-down, unsanitary housing.

Reforming Urban Social and Work Conditions

In response to the poor housing conditions and general poverty of the city, some Progressives started establishing settlement houses to offer a wide range of services to the poor, including assistance in finding jobs, learning the English language, and receiving proper medical care. The first American settlement house was founded in 1884. By 1900 more than fifty settlement houses had been founded in

American cities, and more soon followed.

The plight of the poor served to make more obvious and less acceptable the income gap between the rich and the poor. While upper- and middle-class men had careers in public, professional, or business life and upper- and middle-class women stayed at home and took care of husbands and children or did volunteer work, the urban poor—men, women, and children—worked for meager wages as unskilled labor in meatpacking factories, steel plants, garment factories, and other urban industries. The rewards reaped by the upper and middle classes included status, power, and a high standard of living. In sharp contrast, the only "reward" reaped by the urban poor was a hard life in substandard housing in overcrowded, crime- and disease-ridden inner-city slums.

African Americans had a harder time than most. They lost many of the rights they had gained during Reconstruction, including the right to vote. Disgruntled southern state leaders found ways around the Fifteenth Amendment of the Constitution and denied African Americans that right. In the 1890s they required voters to pay a poll tax or pass a literacy test. But when they realized that this kept many poor whites from voting, they resorted to grandfather clauses in their state constitutions that gave the right to vote to those people whose father or grandfather had been allowed to vote prior to 1867. As most blacks were slaves then, they did not qualify as voters, which meant that their children and grandchildren did not qualify either.

In addition, African Americans were victims of segregation. In late 1897 the Supreme Court ruled that segregation in itself was not illegal and allowed a Louisiana law requiring railroads to have separate cars for blacks. The ruling had a profound effect for decades to come because it was interpreted as meaning that it was legal to practice segregation as long as "separate but equal" facilities were provided.

America Becomes a World Power

By the late 1800s America was economically sound and extremely productive. As far as food, the nation was raising more than it could use and producing more than it could consume. At the same time, raw materials such as rubber and tin were in short supply because of the increased industrialization. Some Americans saw these conditions as good reasons for America to obtain colonies overseas.

Another motive for expansion overseas was articulated by Congregationalist minister and writer Josiah Strong. He argued that the lands of the earth were limited and should be taken by the Anglo-Saxon race, which was superior to all other races. He pointed out that Anglo-Saxons and other Europeans already were dividing Africa into colonies, were about to do the same with China, and warned Americans not to fall behind.

In time the American desire for overseas empires became a reality. Between 1897 and 1909 Presidents William McKinley and Theodore Roosevelt took the first steps toward making the United States an imperial power. Under McKinley, expansionism began in earnest with Spanish-owned Cuba, which had been of interest to America since the early 1800s, when President Thomas Jefferson seriously considered annexing it. In the 1880s American capitalists began investing tens of millions of dollars in the island, buying up huge amounts of land to turn into sugar plantations.

In 1895 Cubans rebelled against the Spanish colonial government. American newspapers, which had a great deal of influence at the time, saw the minor revolt as a way to enlarge their circulation. They sent hundreds of reporters, photographers, and artists to Cuba to cover the revolt. It did not seem to matter that there really was very little to report. When artist Frederick Remington wrote his boss, tabloid newspaper publisher William Randolph Hearst, that there was no war and he wanted to come home, Hearst cabled him to stay there, telling him, "You furnish the pictures, and I'll furnish the war."

Hearst and others did, in fact, "furnish the war." Screaming headlines and sensationalized reports about Spanish-inflicted cruelty stirred the emotions of the American people. The newspaper coverage was the epitome of yellow journalism, the cheaply sensational and exploitive coloring of the news still favored today by some newspapers and members of the media.

A Splendid Little War

At the beginning of 1898, at the request of the American consul in Cuba, President McKinley sent the second-class battleship USS *Maine* to Cuba "to protect American interests." As the ship sat in the Havana harbor, a major explosion occurred, killing most of the *Maine*'s officers and crew. The American press exploited the explosion, blaming it on Spanish saboteurs. They published hundreds of editorials calling for revenge, inflaming the American people and inciting them to take action to protect the Cubans and avenge the deaths of the *Maine* officers and crew members. With Americans across the nation chanting the battle cry "Remember the *Maine*," the United States declared war on Spain, justifying the action under the guise of bringing peace to Cuba.

The war, which lasted only a little over three months, was fought both in the Caribbean and in the Philippines. Even before war had been declared, the Assistant Secretary of the Navy, Theodore Roosevelt, secretly had sent the American fleet in the Pacific to take over the Philippines in case the United States went to war with Spain.

Many historians believe that the war was unjustified. Nonetheless, they concur that by the time it was over, it had had a profound effect on America's status in the world. The United States emerged from the war as a world power, with possessions in the Caribbean and in the Pacific. Victory over Spain brought the Americans Cuba, Puerto Rico, Guam, and the Philippines.

During an interview at the White House, President McKinley justified his decision to lay claim to the Philippines:

> When next I realized that the Philippines had dropped into our laps, I confess I did not know what to do with them. . . .
>
> I walked the floor of the White House night after night until midnight; and I am not ashamed to tell you, gentle-

men, that I went down on my knees and prayed to Almighty God for light and guidance more than one night. And one night late it came to me this way. . . .

That we could not give them back to Spain—that would be cowardly and dishonorable.

That we could not turn them over to France or Germany, our commercial rivals in the Orient—that would be bad business and discreditable.

That we could not leave them to themselves—they were unfit for self-government, and they would soon have anarchy and misrule worse than Spain's was; and

That there was nothing left for us to do but to take them all, and to educate the Filipinos, and uplift and civilize and Christianize them and by God's grace do the very best for them, as our fellow men for whom Christ also died.

And then I went to bed and went to sleep, . . . and the next morning I sent for the chief engineer of the War Department (our map-maker), and I told him to put the Philippines on the map of the United States . . . and there they are and there they will stay while I am President!

McKinley's basic rationale was used over and over again from that time forward and into the 1900s to justify American expansion and empire-building, as the United States annexed the territory of Hawaii, added Wake Island and American Samoa to its overseas empire, and assumed the role of international policeman in world affairs.

Throughout the 1900s, under both Theodore Roosevelt and William Howard Taft, Americans actively supported the nation's aggressive foreign policy. Americans knew that President Roosevelt was a major advocate of American expansionism. He had made his position clear in 1899, advising Congress and the American people that Americans could not stay huddled within

our borders and avow ourselves merely an assemblage of

well-to-do hucksters who care nothing for what happens beyond. Such a policy would defeat even its own end; for as the nations grow to have ever wider and wider interests and are brought into closer and closer contact, if we are to hold our own in the struggle for naval and commercial supremacy, we must build up our power without our own borders. We must build the isthmian [Panama] canal, and we must grasp the points of vantage which will enable us to have our say in deciding the destiny of the oceans of the East and West.

Roosevelt set a course for America and Americans in the rapidly approaching new century:

The twentieth century looms before us big with the fate of many nations. Let us therefore boldly face the life of strife, resolute to do our duty well and manfully; resolute to uphold righteousness by deed and by word, resolute to be both honest and brave, to serve high ideals, yet to use practical methods. Above all, let us shrink from no strife, moral or physical, within or without the Nation, provided we are certain that the strife is justified; for it is only through strife, through hard and dangerous endeavor, that we shall ultimately win the goal of true national greatness.

Throughout the 1900s, Roosevelt sought to promote democracy and economic growth all over the world and to protect American interests in the Western Hemisphere. He had no qualms about using force or threatening to use it to achieve these ends. This was the crux of his "big stick" foreign policy modeled after one of his favorite West African proverbs: "Speak softly, and carry a big stick, you will go far." This policy led to American intervention in several international quarrels and earned America and its president recognition by historians as an international policeman.

The Panama Canal

The high point of Theodore Roosevelt's "big stick" policy—and of his presidency—was the building of the Panama Canal. Many historians consider it his most important accomplishment as president. With the building of the canal, Roosevelt finally had accomplished what he had set out to do: ensure that America had total control over a strategically vital waterway. He had argued for years for an isthmian canal across Central America. The canal would eliminate the trip around South America, shortening the voyage from New York to San Francisco by thousands of miles and lowering the cost of shipping. The canal also would make it unnecessary for America to maintain separate fleets in the Atlantic and the Pacific by enabling ships to move quickly between the two oceans.

Once it was decided to build the canal in the Colombian province of Panama, the United States set about acquiring the necessary rights to the land it wanted. When Colombia hedged about selling the rights, a revolt was secretly planned and financed in New York designed to make Panama an independent nation. The revolt proved successful. In 1903 Panama declared independence from Colombia, and in 1904 the United States began building the Panama Canal. Although the first trip through the canal was not made until 1914 due to building delays and work stoppages caused by the high incidence of fatalities among the workers from malaria and yellow fever, the building of the Panama Canal came to be lauded as one of the outstanding achievements of the 1900s.

The Accomplishments of a Decade

Throughout the 1900s Americans made valiant efforts to improve their government and the quality of life in their nation. They found their strongest and most influential advocate for reform in Theodore Roosevelt, who loomed larger than life for most Americans and became an icon of the times.

During the 1900s, Roosevelt used his magnetism and all of his powers, including those of his executive office, to push through major domestic reforms. As part of his "square deal" policy, he backed legislation to regulate the railroads, asked for legislation to correct some of the worst abuses in the meatpacking industry, and pushed for conservation legislation. During the same period, he set aside land for public forests, more than quadrupled the size of the natural forests, and worked to preserve other valuable lands as well.

Roosevelt's efforts withstanding, the reform movement set into motion by the Progressives was only partly successful during the 1900s in doing what it had set out to do. Ultimately, however, it went a long way toward giving the people a greater voice in their government and making government more responsible for the health, education, and security of all Americans. In addition, state and federal agencies started to standardize rules for business and end some of the worst business practices. The government broadened its role in both social and economic matters and took more responsibility for the well-being of all Americans, setting a trend that did not end with the Progressive Era.

The laws passed during the decade of the 1900s went a long way toward reforming inequities of American society. In addition to setting new government standards for food quality, laws were passed that placed hard-hitting restrictions on child labor, bettered conditions in factories, and weakened the power of corrupt politicians.

Theodore Roosevelt's successor to the presidency, William Howard Taft, carried on the legacy of reform. During his tenure as president, which began in 1908, Americans witnessed the breaking up of such industry giants as the Standard Oil Company and the American Tobacco Company, the passage of measures to ensure safety in mines and give accident insurance to workers hired on government contracts, and an increase in the number of civil service jobs under the merit system.

In the end, the Progressives of the 1900s left Americans a legacy that carried over into the next decade and helped them face the challenges of their first world war.

CHAPTER 1

The Onset of a New Century

AMERICA'S DECADES

America Comes of Age

David R. Contosta and Robert Muccigrosso

Academicians David R. Contosta and Robert Muccigrosso explain that most historians agree that many of the forces that shaped and transformed twentieth-century America originated in the late 1800s. The authors describe how industry, which they consider the fundamental force, made it possible for the United States "to become a great world power within the space of a single generation."

W̲hen did the twentieth century begin? Most will answer, "January 1, 1900," but in fact 1900 was the last year of the nineteenth century. Round numbers are impressive and the confusion is therefore understandable, but for historians the question of beginnings is more difficult, as historical movements have shown scant regard for convenient dates on a calendar. Diplomatic historians might well conclude that the twentieth century began in 1898 with the Spanish-American War, or even three years earlier over the Venezuelan crisis of 1895. Political historians will doubtless choose the crucial election of 1896, while the economic historian will want to focus on the financial panic of 1893 and the ensuing depression.

In truth, many of the forces that have shaped the twentieth century had their origins in the latter decades of the nineteenth century and particularly in the 1890s. Chief among them was industrialization. It was industry that at-

---

Excerpted from *America in the Twentieth Century: Coming of Age,* by David R. Contosta and Robert Muccigrosso (New York: Harper & Row, 1988). Reprinted with permission from the authors.

tracted natives and immigrants alike to the cities, that undermined the personal element in economic exchange, and that prompted most of the cries for social, economic, and political reform. It was industry that gave the United States the potential to become a great world power within the space of a single generation.

With rapid industrialization and urbanization had come numerous "growing pains" and the need for large-scale readjustment. While a handful of daring entrepreneurs had reaped undreamed-of fortunes, others were left behind in the wake or became hostages to the new machinery and industrial organization. And as more and more Americans came to depend on factories for jobs, economic depressions became increasingly severe and widespread. Loud protests and demands for governmental action understandably arose. Workers tried to organize and struck for better pay and safer working conditions; farmers formed granges, alliances, and finally the Populist party. Consumers and smaller businessmen demanded curbs on big business, while midwestern farmers and others dependent upon the railroads pushed for regulation of freight rates. Congress created an Interstate Commerce Commission in 1887 and three years later passed the Sherman Antitrust Act. Both were disappointing in many respects, but the way had been opened for more effective regulation in the future.

Politics were also in need of reform as the century came to a close. Most of the larger cities were in the grip of corrupt bosses and their attendant "machines." Although they often assisted the poor with jobs, patronage, and even gifts of food and fuel, they were unwilling and unable to provide systematic solutions for urban problems like crime, public health, or routine maintenance. And on the national level the country had seen a series of relatively weak presidents whose power had been sapped by Congressional patronage, political fragmentation, and the widely held belief that the federal government should remain neutral on economic matters. The election of William McKinley to the presidency in 1896 signaled a shift toward Republican predominance and the beginnings of a more effective executive branch, but few could appreciate the change.

A New Century Brings New Problems

The decision to annex an island empire following the Spanish-American War also proved difficult and controversial. Some believed that taking the Philippines in particular would provide a stepping stone to large markets in Asia, while others welcomed a chance to join the other colonial powers in uplifting the more benighted peoples of the earth. Yet many Americans feared that their presence in the Far East would only stir up friction and possibly war with the great powers, and there were those who saw the new imperialism as a betrayal of the nation's own revolutionary heritage.

In ideas and the arts the United States was likewise awash with change. The painter Thomas Eakins had been scandalizing the public for several decades with his controversial teaching methods and highly realistic canvases. Daring architects such as Louis Sullivan were beginning to create tall buildings with structural steel supports and permitting the interior skeleton to dictate exterior design. And while the skyscraper was being born, William James, John Dewey, and other philosophers questioned the existence of scientific and moral absolutes, setting off an intellectual revolution that would challenge some of the most basic tenets of Western life and thought.

For Henry Adams, a brilliant critic and descendent of two American presidents, the cultural and economic upheaval of the late nineteenth century was profoundly unsettling. Mankind confronted "a far vaster universe," he wrote, "where all the old roads ran about in every direction, overrunning, dividing, subdividing, stopping abruptly, vanishing slowly, with side-paths that led nowhere, and sequences that could not be proved."

Adams clearly believed that the twentieth century would be filled with unparalleled problems and anxieties. Coincidentally or not, these new difficulties arose as the United States settled its vast interior and began functioning as a mature member of the world community. At the same time, fast steamships, oceanic telegraph cables, and growing international trade were making all nations more interdependent, whether they liked it or not. Traditional American desires to stay out of foreign entanglements would not die easily, nor would the old idea that the United States was under a new and perhaps divine dispensation, but Americans were soon to find that they were not exempt from the common burdens of humanity. In this sense the United States would emerge from a kind of national adolescence and "come of age" as the twentieth century unfolded.

Yet most Americans greeted the twentieth century with great expectations. The depression of the 1890s had ended, business was booming, and the country had acquired an island empire at comparatively little cost in money and men. Admittedly, there were a number of outstanding problems, but most citizens thought they could overcome them without too much difficulty. Few could imagine the enormous challenges and responsibilities that lay ahead.

America in 1900

Frederick Lewis Allen

In this glimpse of turn-of-the-century America, popular so-cial historian Frederick Lewis Allen describes the manners, mores, and way of life in the year 1900. He paints a vivid picture of a life very different from the one most Americans know today. Allen illustrates the vast gap between the wealthy and the poor at the start of the twentieth century. America, contends Allen, was a nation on the brink of great change—change for which it really was not prepared.

A graduate of Harvard University, Frederick Lewis Allen was a longtime editor of *Harper's* magazine and the author of numerous articles for *Harper's, Atlantic Monthly, The New Yorker,* and *Life.* Lewis also authored a number of books, including three widely acclaimed social histories of America—*The Big Change: America Transforms Itself 1900–1950, Only Yesterday: An Informal History of the Nineteen-Twenties,* and *Since Yesterday: The Nineteen-Thirties in America.* His papers are housed in the Manu-script Division of the Library of Congress.

On the morning of January 1, 1900, there was skating for New Yorkers in Van Cortlandt Park, and presently it began to snow. But the sharp cold had not chilled the en-thusiasm of the crowds who, the night before, had assem-bled in Lower Broadway to celebrate either the beginning of the twentieth century or the beginning of the last year of the nineteenth: there was some disagreement as to the proper interpretation of the event, but none as to the size and liveliness of the gathering. . . . It had been a good year, and another one was coming.

In its leading editorial of January 1, the *New York Times* sounded an optimistic keynote. "The year 1899 was a year of wonders, a veritable annus mirabilis, in business and production. . . ." it proclaimed. "It would be easy to speak of the twelve months just passed as the banner year were we not already confident that the distinction of highest records must presently pass to the year 1900. . . . The outlook on the threshold of the new year is extremely bright."

Uptown, in the mahogany-paneled library of his big brownstone house at the corner of Madison Avenue and Thirty-sixth Street, John Pierpont Morgan, head of the mightiest banking house in the world and the most powerful man in all American business, sat playing solitaire as the old year drew to an end. During the next twelve months Morgan would buy paintings and rare books and manuscripts in immense profusion on a European trip; would have a temporary ballroom built beside his house to accommodate twenty-four hundred guests at his daughter's wedding, and would begin negotiations with Andrew Carnegie—the twinkling little steelmaster whose personal income in 1900 would be over twenty-three million dollars, with no income tax to pay—for the formation of the United States Steel Corporation, the biggest corporation that the world had ever seen. Morgan could not foresee all this now as he ranged the cards before him, but he was content. . . .

There were, to be sure, hundreds of thousands of New Yorkers for whom the city was hardly "a pleasant place in which to live." On the Lower East Side there were poverty, filth, wretchedness on a scale which to us today would seem incredible. And in many other cities and industrial towns of America the immigrant families were living under comparable conditions, or worse; for at a time when the average wage earner in the United States got hardly five hundred dollars in a year . . . most of the newcomers to the country scrabbled for far less. . . .

It was a time of complacency. Since the end of the depression of the mid-nineties the voices of protest at the disparities of fortune in the United States had weakened. Populism was dead; the free-silver agitation had petered out, the once angry farmers of the Plains States were making out so well that in 1899 a traveler commented that "every barn in Kansas and Nebraska has had a new coat of paint." Not yet had the oncoming group of journalists whom President Theodore Roosevelt, in a burst of irritation, labeled "muckrakers" begun to publish their remorseless studies of the seamy sides of American life. . . .

Morgan looked confidently forward to an era of stability and common sense, in which political leaders like Mark Hanna would see that no foolish equalitarian ideas got anywhere in government, and in which the regulation of American business would be undertaken, not by politicians, but by bankers like himself, honorable men of wealth and judgment such as he liked to see in his favorite clubs. . . .

Morgan . . . would have been bewildered had [he] been able to foresee what the next half century would bring to the nation. . . .

Means of Transportation

To understand the extent and nature of the big change that was to take place, we must first go back to 1900 and look about us—at the scene, the conditions of life, the people. . . .

In that year 1900 there were registered in the whole United States only 13,824 automobiles. . . . And they were really few and far between except in the larger cities and the well-to-do resorts. For in 1900 everybody thought of automobiles as playthings of the rich—and not merely of the rich, but of the somewhat adventurous and sporting rich: people who enjoyed taking their chances with an unpredictable machine that might at any moment wreck them. There were almost no paved highways outside the cities, and of course there were no roadside garages or filling stations; every automobilist must be his own desperate mechanic. Probably half the men and women of America had never seen a car. . . .

But horses were everywhere, pulling surreys, democrats, buggies, cabs, delivery wagons of every sort on Main Street, and pulling harvesters on the tractorless farms out in the countryside. . . .

It is hard for us today to realize how very widely communities were separated from one another when they depended for transportation wholly on the railroad and the horse and wagon—and when telephones were still scarce, and radios non-existent. A town which was not situated on a railroad was really remote. A farmer who lived five miles outside the county seat made something of an event of hitching up and taking the family to town for a Saturday afternoon's shopping. . . . A trip to see friends ten miles away was likely to be an all-day expedition, for the horse had to be given a chance to rest and be fed. No wonder that each region, each town, each farm was far more dependent upon its own resources—its own produce, social contacts, amusements—than in later years. For in terms of travel and communication the United States was a very big country indeed.

No wonder, furthermore, that the majority of Americans were less likely than their descendants to be dogged by that frightening sense of insecurity which comes from being jostled by forces—economic, political, international—beyond one's personal ken. Their horizons were close to them. They lived among familiar people and familiar things—individuals and families and fellow townsmen much of their own sort, with ideas intelligible to them. A man's success or failure seemed more likely than in later years to depend upon forces and events within his own range of vision. . . . The world at which he looked over the dashboard of the family carriage might not be friendly, but at least most of it looked understandable.

Well-Dressed and Respectable

Every grown woman in town would be wearing a dress that virtually swept the street; that would in fact actually sweep it from time to time, battering and begriming the hem, if its owner had not learned to hold it clear. From the high collar of her shirtwaist to the ground, the woman of 1900 was amply enveloped in material. . . . Even for country wear, in fact even for golf or tennis, the skirt must reach within two or three inches of the ground, and a hat—usually a hard sailor hat—must almost imperatively be worn. . . .

At any season a woman was swathed in layer upon layer of underpinnings—chemise, drawers, corset, corset cover, and one or more petticoats. The corset of those days was a formidable personal prison which did its strenuous best, with the aid of whalebones, to distort the female form into an hour-glass shape. . . .

As for the men, their clothes, too, were formal and severe by today's standards. Collars were high and stiff. The man of affairs was likely to wear, even under his everyday sack suit (of three-button coat, obligatory waistcoat, and narrowish trousers), a shirt with hard detachable cuffs and perhaps a stiff bosom too. If he were a banker or a businessman of executive stature he probably wore a frock coat to the office, and a silk hat instead of the less formal derby—except between May 15 and September 15, when custom decreed a hard straw hat (or, for the affluent, possibly a Panama). To go hatless, except in the wide open spaces, was for the well-dressed male unthinkable. If the weather were intolerably hot, he might remove his coat, and in certain informal offices—newspaper city rooms, for instance—he customarily did so. But his waistcoat *must not come off* (a rule which, considering the sort of shirt he was wearing, was not without aesthetic merit). The term "shirt sleeves" remains in our language as a survival of that custom.

In the country he might wear a blue serge coat with white flannel (or, more economically, white duck) trousers, or, under the proper circumstances, a tweed coat with riding trousers or knickerbockers. But when a man returned to the city, or a farmer put on town clothes for a visit to the county seat, he must invariably get into the severe three-piece suit, with starched collar and cuffs—even under a July sun.

These implacable costumes, male and female, reflected the prevailing credo as to the relations between the sexes. The ideal woman was the sheltered lady, swathed not only in silk and muslin but in innocence and propriety, and the ideal man, whether a pillar of rectitude or a gay dog, virtuously protected the person and reputation of such tender creatures as were entrusted to his care. If unmarried, a girl must be accompanied by a chaperone whenever she ventured out to an evening's entertainment in the city. If she were a daughter of the rich, a maid might take the place of the chaperone; it was never quite clear, under these circumstances, who was supposed to protect the maid's virtue. . . .

The chaperone was, to be sure, chiefly an urban institution. In the smaller places, especially west of the Alleghenies, and among city people vacationing in the country, the rules were greatly relaxed. . . .

But throughout these companionships one might almost say that an imaginary chaperone was always present. What was operating was in effect an honor system: these boys and girls knew they were expected to behave with perfect propriety toward one another, and only rarely did they fail to do so. . . . Under the code which they followed a kiss was virtually tantamount to a proposal of marriage.

The Working Woman

The idea of the sheltered lady was of course difficult to maintain in a country in which 20.4 per cent of the female population were engaged in working for a living. This unhappy fact of life caused the moralists of the day deep concern. If there was a steadily increasing number of women working in offices, it was understood that they were victims of unfortunate financial circumstance; their fathers, poor fellows, were unable to support them properly; and it was hoped that their inevitable contacts with rude men of business would not sully their purity. If women who had not had "advantages" worked by the millions in shops and factories—at wages as low as six or eight dollars a week . . . this was understood to subject them to appalling temptations. . . .

There were also servant girls innumerable; but in the cities they were mostly of immigrant stock, or colored, and therefore, it was thought, could hardly hope for a better lot. And anyhow they were protected from temptation by being given very few hours off. In the country towns the servant girls were likely to be farmers' daughters who would presently marry a clerk or a man in the railroad office and set up housekeeping—with, one hoped, their innocence still unimpaired. . . .

If unhappy circumstances forced a "nicely brought up" young woman to work for a living, a career as schoolteacher, or music teacher, or trained nurse was considered acceptable for her. If she had the appropriate gift she might become a writer or artist or singer, even an opera singer. Some went on the stage; but at the grave risk of declassing themselves, for actresses were known to be mostly "fast." (Always, in discussions of the economic status and opportunities of women, the effect of a woman's occupation upon her sexual virtue was recurrent.) There were pioneers who, with flaming intensity, took up other careers—as doctors, for instance—against every sort of opposition; but it was an unusual community in which they were not considered unfeminine cranks for doing so, and one of the most telling arguments marshaled against their decision was that a girl who set out to earn money was selfishly causing her father needless embarrassment: somebody might think that he couldn't support her. By common consent the best—and safest—thing for a girl to do was to sit at home and help her mother about the house and wait for the "right man.". . .

The Cities and Suburbs

You could not travel far . . . without noticing how much smaller the cities and towns were. For in that year the population of the continental United States was just about half what it would be fifty years later—a little less than 76 millions. . . .

Not only would the thinness of the Western population remind you how much farther east, in those days, was the center of gravity of American industry and American cultural institutions; even in the Eastern cities you would miss many of the commonplace features of modern city life. Skyscrapers, for instance: the tallest building in the country was the Ivins Syndicate Building on Park Row in New York, which rose 29 stories, with towers which brought its utmost altitude to 382 feet. Not yet did visitors to New York remark upon the "famous skyline." And in other cities a ten- or twelve-story building was a thing of wonder.

There was little electric street-lighting; a commonplace sight at dusk in almost any American city was the appearance of the city lamplighter with his ladder, which he would set against a lamppost and climb to turn on the gas street-light. Nor was there, as yet, much illuminated advertising. New Yorkers could marvel at the great Heinz sign on the site of the future Flatiron Building at Fifth Avenue and Broadway and Twenty-third Street, a fifty-foot sign, with a huge pickle represented by green light bulbs, and HEINZ written across it in white bulbs, and slogans such as "57 Varieties" flashing on and off below; but this was a pioneer spectacle. . . .

As for public transportation in the cities, there was only one completed subway, a short one in Boston, though in New York ground was broken for another during 1900; and if New York and Chicago had their thundering elevated railroads (New York was just electrifying its line, which had previously run by steam), most urban Americans got about town in trolley cars, the screaming of whose wheels, as they rounded a corner, seemed to the countryman the authentic note of modern civilization. Electric trolley lines were booming; the financial journals were full of advertisements of the securities of new trolley enterprises; to put one's money into street-railroad development was to bet on the great American future.

Each city had its outlying residential areas, within walking distance of the railroad or trolley lines: long blocks of single-family or two-family houses, rising bleakly among the vacant lots and fields; comfortable lawn-surrounded houses for the more prosperous. And there were many commuters who made a cindery railroad journey to work from suburban towns. But those outlying towns were quite different from what they were to become in the automobile age. For only if one could be met at the station by a horse and carriage—which was inconvenient unless one could afford a coachman—or was an exceptionally hardy pedestrian, was it practicable to live more than a mile or so from the railroad or trolley. So the suburbs were small, and backed by open country. . . .

Vacation Time and Leisure

As you traveled away from the cities into the countryside, one of the things that would have puzzled you . . . would have been the comparative shortage of city people's summer cottages. The rich, to be sure, had their holiday resorts . . . the overwhelming majority . . . in the northeast part of the country. . . .

In most of the leading resorts there were fine country houses; in some of them, opulent ones. There were also many prosperous families whose special taste for the wilds would lead them to buy large tracts of Adirondack woodland and build luxurious "camps"; or whose liking for the simplicities of Cape Cod, or the White Mountains, or the Lake Michigan shoreline, or the rugged Monterey coast, would lead them to build more modest cottages for a two or three months' stay. But their choice of places was limited by two things—accessibility to a railroad, and the limited holiday time available to all but a few. The boom in summer-cottage building was only just beginning. . . . It was still the heyday of the big summer-resort hotel, to which well-to-do vacationists would come for a short stay, ranging usually from a week to a month: the shingled hotel with towers and turrets and whipping flags, with wide piazzas and interminable carpeted corridors, and with a vast dining room in which were served huge meals on the American plan, with a menu which took one from celery and olives through soup and fish and a roast to ice cream, cake, and nuts and almonds, with sherbet as a cooling encouragement in mid-meal.

For those who could not afford such grandeur, there were boardinghouses innumerable, with schoolteachers rocking on the porch and a group of croquet players on the lawn; and, here and there along the seashore or the lakeside, crowded colonies of tiny shingled shacks, each labeled clearly with its sentimental or jocose name—"Bide-a-Wee Cottage," "Doocum Inn," or the like. But the overwhelming majority of Americans outside the upper income brackets stayed at home, through the full heat of summer. And being carriageless, they had to satisfy their holiday dreams by taking a special reduced-rate railroad tour by day-coach to Niagara Falls or Atlantic City; or, more likely, an occasional trip out of town in an open trolley car to the Trolley Park, an amusement park at the end of the line.

So there was still lots of room to play in America—thousands of miles of shoreline, hundreds of lakes and rivers, hundreds of mountains, which you could explore to your heart's content, camping and bathing and hunting and fishing without asking anybody's permission, if you could only somehow reach them. Already there were far-sighted conservationists pointing out that for generations Americans had been despoiling the land while subduing it; that forests were being hacked to pieces, farm land misused and overused, natural resources plundered right and left; and that national parks would be needed, both to conserve these resources and to give the people room to play. But to most people such warnings just didn't make sense. If lumbermen destroyed one forest, there were others to enjoy; if cottagers bought up one beach, there were others open to any bathers. The bounties of nature seemed inexhaustible. . . .

The Amenities: Few and Far Between

Most of the city houses of the really prosperous were now electrified; but the man who was building a new house was only just beginning to install electric lights without adding gas, too, lest the current fail suddenly. And the houses of the great majority were still lighted by gas (in the cities and towns) or oil lamps (in the country). . . . A regular chore for the rural housewife was filling the lamps; and a frequent source of family pride was the possession of a Welsbach burner that would furnish adequate light for a whole family to read by as they gathered about the living-room table.

Of course there were no electric refrigerators—to say nothing of washing machines and deep-freeze units. Farmers—and summer cottagers—had icehouses in which big cubes of ice, cut during the winter at a neighboring pond or river, or imported by ship from north to south, lay buried deep in sawdust. When you needed ice, you climbed into the icehouse, scraped the sawdust away from a fine hunk of ice, and carried it in your ice tongs to the kitchen icebox. If you lived in the city, the ice company's wagon showed up at the door and the iceman stowed a huge cube in your icebox.

For a good many years there had been refrigerator cars on the railroads, but the great national long-distance traffic in fresh fruits and vegetables was still in its infancy. . . . In most parts of the United States people were virtually without fresh fruit and green vegetables from late autumn to late spring. During this time they consumed quantities of starches, in the form of pies, doughnuts, potatoes, and hot bread, which few would venture to absorb today. The result was that innumerable Americans were in sluggish health during the months of late winter and early spring, when their diet was short of vitamins. . . .

By the turn of the century running water, bathtubs, and water closets were to be found in virtually all the town houses of the prosperous, though many a fine house on a fashionable street still held only one bathroom. But not only did factory workers and farmers (except perhaps a few owners of big farms) still not dream of enjoying such luxuries, but even in the gracious houses of well-to-do people beyond the reach of city water lines and sewer lines, there was likely to be no bathroom at all. They washed with pitcher and basin in their bedrooms, each of them pouring his dirty water from the basin into a slop jar, to be emptied later in the day; and after breakfast they visited the privy behind the house. . . .

At a luxurious hotel you might, if you paid extra, get a room with private bath, but not until 1907 did Ellsworth M. Statler build in Buffalo the first hotel which offered every guest a room and private bath at a moderate price. . . .

A Lack of Communications

Telephones, in 1900, were clumsy things and comparatively scarce; they were to be found chiefly in business offices and in the houses of such well-to-do people as enjoyed experimenting with new mechanical devices. . . .

As for the instruments of mass communication which, in the years to come, were to do so much to provide Americans of all classes and conditions with similar information, ideas, and interests, these too were almost wholly lacking. There would be no radio for another twenty years; no television, except for a very limited audience, for over forty-five years. Crude motion pictures were occasionally to be seen at vaudeville theaters, or in peep-show parlors, but the first movie which told a story, *The Great Train Robbery,* was still three years in the future. There was as yet no magazine with a circulation of over a million. . . .

Accordingly there were sharp limits to the fund of information and ideas which people of all regions and all walks of life held in common. To some extent a Maine fisherman, an Ohio farmer, and a Chicago businessman would be able to discuss politics with one another, but in the absence of syndicated newspaper columns appearing from coast to coast their information would be based mostly upon what they had read in very divergent local newspapers, and in the absence both of the radio and of newsreels it is doubtful if any of them—except perhaps the Chicago businessman—had ever heard with his own ears the silver voice of William Jennings Bryan. . . .

And if the instruments of mass communication were lacking, so also were many social institutions which today

Americans take for granted. A nation of individualists, accustomed to the idea that each person must fend for himself as an independent unit, was moving into an age of interdependence but was still slow to recognize the fact and slow to organize the institutions which such an age required. . . .

It seems to be a continuing characteristic of American life that communities perpetually fail to catch up institutionally with their own growth; at any rate, it was glaringly true that the American town of 1900 had failed to adapt itself to the necessities of the onrushing industrial age.

Immigrants in Industrial America

Steven J. Diner

More immigrants arrived in America during the last decades of the nineteenth century and early decades of the twentieth century than ever before or after. According to author Steven J. Diner, professor of history at George Mason University in Fairfax, Virginia, most immigrants were young, highly motivated, and willing to work as hard as necessary to gain a better life than the one they had at home. Diner goes on to explain that once in this country, most immigrants did not return home but amended their ways of life and traditions to adapt to their new environment.

In 1883, Emma Lazarus, a thirty-four-year-old Jewish poet and writer whose family had lived in America for several generations, wrote "The New Colossus," a sonnet inspired by her volunteer work with immigrant refugees at Ward's Island in New York. Years later, schoolchildren learning about their nation's historic mission as a refuge for the oppressed would recite her words, posthumously mounted on the pedestal of the Statue of Liberty in 1903. "With silent lips," Miss Liberty cries:

> *"Give me your tired, your poor,*
> *Your huddled masses yearning to breathe free,*
> *The wretched refuse of your teeming shore.*
> *Send these, the homeless, tempest-tost to me. . . ."*

Progressive Era crusaders on behalf of immigrants routinely echoed Lazarus' message, if not her poetry. Kate Holladay Claghorn, a professor at the New York School of Social Work, wrote of the immigrant's "sheer helplessness." Reform journalist Robert Hunter detailed the suffering of newcomers "drawn from the miserable of every nation."

A powerful metaphor indeed, but not accurate. Most of the immigrants who came to America between 1890 and World War I sought economic opportunity more than personal liberty; many intended to return home once they earned some money. Most immigrants, although poor, did not come from the poorest of the poor, and few lacked homes. Emigration cost money, a carefully calculated investment enabling the sojourners to earn in America the funds needed to increase their modest landholdings and possessions back home. They could hardly be described as tired. Young, ambitious, and accustomed to hard work, immigrants acted boldly and deliberately to gain control over their lives. These artisans and farmers, refusing to accept passively the negative effects of industrial capitalism in their homelands, came to America to find economic security for their families.

More immigrants arrived during the Progressive Era than before or after, fifteen million in the twenty-four years between 1890 and 1914, although the foreign-born *proportion* of the U.S. population remained nearly the same in 1910 (14.5 percent) as in 1860 (13.2 percent). The sources of immigration changed substantially, however. Before 1890, most immigrants had come from Great Britain, Ireland, Canada, Germany, Scandinavia, Switzerland, and Holland. Immigrants after 1890 came disproportionately from the Austro-Hungarian Empire, Italy, Russia, Greece, Romania, and Turkey. Eighty-seven percent in 1882 arrived from the countries of Northwestern Europe, but by 1907, 81 percent hailed from the South and the East. A majority of the "new" immigrants were not Protestants, and they spoke languages, such as Polish, Yiddish, Lithuanian, Czech, and Greek, that were completely unfamiliar to Americans.

To be sure, immigrants continued to come to America from Northwestern Europe. Between 1890 and 1920, 874,000 people entered from Ireland, 991,000 from Germany, 571,000 from Sweden, 352,000 from Norway, but they drew little attention when compared with the 3,807,000 from Italy, for example. Substantial numbers also came from outside Europe, particularly from French and English Canada, Japan (until excluded by diplomatic agreement in 1906), Mexico, and Syria.

These fifteen million souls left amidst diverse economic and social circumstances, moved all over the country, and held thousands of different kinds of jobs. Yet they shared certain goals. Like all workers, they struggled for the economic security of their families, whether back home or in America. They also demanded autonomy over their family lives, their communities, and their culture, selectively taking elements from the Old World and the New. Finally, many newcomers to America sought to enhance their social status. If, as outsiders and poor laborers, they could not hope to acquire prestige within the larger American society, they could still compete for respect and social position within the ethnic communities and institutions they built in America. . . .

Immigrant Enterprise

With family economic security foremost, immigrants adapted their traditional values to the necessities of their new country, making pragmatic choices at every stage. The vast majority of immigrants worked for wages, pooling the wages of men, women, and children and the money earned from home manufacturing, laundering, and boarders. During the Progressive Era, only a few recent immigrants could write and speak English well enough to qualify for white-collar office or department store jobs, and a modest number became independent farmers. Some chose another alternative and became peddlers or shopkeepers. Although department stores, chain stores, and catalogue companies offered a wide array of goods to more and more Americans, opportunities remained for petty merchants, which some immigrants seized. Peddling required little or no capital. A distributor, usually a fellow countryman, supplied a newcomer with goods which the peddler paid for after he had sold them. In cities with large immigrant populations, peddling did not even require a working knowledge of English, since one could sell to fellow immigrants from a pushcart or by going from apartment to apartment. Eastern European Jews, Italians, Greeks, Irishmen, and Armenians dominated big-city peddling.

The *New York Tribune* reported in 1898 that "recently landed immigrants are advised by their friends to take a pushcart until they can establish themselves in some business." A Jewish immigrant in New York went "to the factory where the tinware was made" and a man "gave me a basket filled with a variety of tinware. . . . I felt happy that I had become a businessman. I went back to my lodging feeling that I might become a big businessman—perhaps even a tinware manufacturer." Immigrant women and children also sometimes tended pushcarts.

Other immigrants peddled in small towns and rural areas across America, carrying goods purchased from a countryman on their backs or in horse-drawn wagons. In the mid-nineteenth century, Central European Jews dominated the trade. By the turn of the century, most peddlers were Syrian immigrants, even though as late as 1908 people reported encountering Irish and Swedish peddlers in the Prairie States. The daughter of Francis Abraham Modi recalled that her father's two-hundred-pound pack consisted of "dry goods, mostly cut yardage, and clothing, shirts, work clothing, socks, pants and underwear." He also carried "a hand grip, which held combs, thread, needles . . . shaving soap, straight razors, and just about all the non-toiletries the farm folks would need."

Experienced peddlers taught novices the trade, and shopkeepers provided the recent arrivals with goods on credit. An early Syrian immigrant, Salem Bashara, supplied new immigrant peddlers from his store in Fort Wayne, Indiana. One newcomer, upon arrival in New York, showed

Salem's name and address to an interpreter "who put us on the train. Salem met us." A relative remembered that "those who had been here a month or two would teach them a few words . . . to knock on a door and say, 'Buy sumthin', Maam,' or how to say they were hungry and needed a place to sleep." While distributors imported some of the goods from the old country, Syrian women in America sewed or embroidered many of the items sold.

Why did so many immigrants take up either city or long-distance peddling? Peddlers faced hard work and long hours. Established shopkeepers, who disliked the competition, condemned them; reformers complained that push-cart operators cluttered busy city streets. Police officers who enforced antipeddling ordinances shook them down, and thieves stole from them. Nonetheless, peddling offered economic opportunities for those who could sell. Many peddlers dreamed of opening a store, and some succeeded. Moreover, peddling offered greater autonomy than wage labor. Unlike factory workers, Jewish peddlers could observe the Sabbath and religious holidays without penalty.

Small businesses offered immigrants these same advantages on a greater scale. Numerous immigrant enterprises, including kosher butcher shops and bakeries, Irish and German saloons, and ethnic groceries, provided goods or services unavailable elsewhere. Immigrants often preferred to buy American products from countrymen. An early-twentieth-century study of immigrant adaptation noted:

> The Jewish woman in New York buys a steamship ticket for her sister in Russia from a ticket peddler who collects fifty cents a week; the Polish laborer deposits his money with the saloon keeper; and this peddler or saloon keeper will eventually become a joint steamship agent, banker, employment agent, real-estate agent, etc.

These ethnic businesses, protected from mainstream competition, made immigrant neighborhoods distinctive places where newcomers felt comfortable, enhancing the economic security and personal autonomy of the proprietor.

Sometimes, immigrant entrepreneurs, building on relationships with their countrymen, carved out a special niche in the American economy. Settled Norwegian immigrants, for example, owned and worked in Brooklyn businesses catering to Norwegian merchant ships. Greek immigrants opened confectionery shops and restaurants. A number of Eastern European Jews who worked in the garment industry became small clothing manufacturers.

Immigrants from Asia relied especially on small enterprise because white employers refused to hire them for all but the most menial jobs. Congress excluded almost all new Chinese immigrants in 1882, and hostility to Chinese laborers, who had initially worked in railroad construction, mining, and other activities in rural areas of the West, forced them to cluster in urban Chinatowns. About 40 percent of the San Francisco Chinese in these years worked as merchants and shopkeepers, serving both Chinese residents and outsiders who went to Chinatown for exotic foods and imported goods. Even in the smaller inland towns, Chinese shopkeepers ran restaurants, groceries, and laundries. Chinese laborers found work largely in these Chinese-owned service enterprises. By 1920, 58 percent worked in service occupations, compared with only 10 percent of white immigrants. A Chinese laundry worker explained that the work was "very hard" but "there is nothing else to do. . . . This is the kind of life we have to take in America."

Japanese immigrants worked initially as laborers when they began arriving on the mainland in the 1880s, but many quickly established small businesses. By 1909, between 3,000 and 3,500 Japanese immigrants in the West operated hotels and boardinghouses, restaurants, barbershops, poolrooms, tailor shops, supply stores, shoemaker shops, and laundries. Some also fished for abalone, a delicacy in Japan, drying and canning it for sale back home. Most Japanese immigrants became self-employed farmers, however. In the 1890s, some began cultivating sugar beets, beans, potatoes, hops, and other fruits and vegetables, initially for a fixed wage and then for a fixed share of the crop. Having earned a little money, they leased land and eventually bought it outright. In 1909, Japanese-run farms produced 18 percent of the value of Los Angeles County farm products on just 1.5 percent of the farmland, typically selling their produce to Japanese dealers. Nativists fearful of Japanese progress in agriculture and business won passage of the California Alien Land Act of 1913, prohibiting foreigners from owning land in the state. Since Congress had banned the naturalization of Asian immigrants, the authors of the new law expected it to keep Japanese immigrants from owning land. But Japanese parents circumvented the law by placing title to the land in the names of their children born on American soil, who became citizens at birth. In the seven years following the passage of the Alien Land Law, Japanese-owned land tripled.

For European immigrants, self-employment offered an alternative to wage labor in factories and mines. For Chinese and Japanese immigrants, largely excluded from those occupations, entrepreneurship remained the only significant avenue to economic security and autonomy.

A Prosperous, Growing Nation

Fon W. Boardman Jr.

Fon W. Boardman Jr. chronicles the changes taking place in America as the twentieth century gets underway. Although the country was not totally without problems, Boardman explains, Americans were confident and the nation prosperous. In Boardman's opinion, the Spanish-American War of 1898 changed the course of the country, making it a colonial empire and greatly influencing Presidents William McKinley and Theodore Roosevelt. A lecturer in English at Columbia University for a number of years and longtime affiliate of Oxford University Press, Boardman has authored a number of American history books for young people.

T he world's newest imperial power, the United States of America, greeted January 1, 1900, the beginning of the twentieth century, with confidence. It was a prosperous, growing nation whose flag flew over territory extending from islands in the Atlantic Ocean westward to the far side of the Pacific Ocean.

The Civil War had ended nearly thirty-five years before and a whole new generation had been born since the surrender at Appomattox. The veterans of that war, who had been young men in 1865, were now the middle-aged leaders of business and politics. Their organization, the Grand Army of the Republic, was influential at the highest levels, and in the North thousands of persons still voted for the

Excerpted from *America and the Progressive Era, 1900–1917,* by Fon W. Boardman Jr. (New York: Henry Z. Walck, Inc., 1970). Reprinted with permission from the author.

Republican Party because "they saved the Union, didn't they?" Even so, North and South had been reconciled and events of the postwar years had brought the nation together again.

The country was still very rural and old-fashioned in spirit, even though there were many signs of change. Independence Day was celebrated with fireworks and parades in every small town. Ice-cream parlors did a good business after the band concert in the village square. Most town houses were still lighted by gas, and refrigeration was achieved with the aid of the iceman and the large cakes of ice he brought. Horses were everywhere, pulling all kinds of carriages and wagons, but already there were nearly 14,000 automobiles and the number was growing. Wages were low by later standards, but so were prices. Sofas were advertised at $9.98, turtleneck sweaters were eight cents each, and a man could buy a good quality suit for under $11.00.

The population of the United States reached 76,000,000 in 1900, double what it had been in 1870. By 1910 there would be more than 90,000,000 Americans. . . .

A Period of Change and Tensions

An important part of the nineteenth-century growth in population resulted from immigration: from 1870 to 1900 nearly 12,000,000 persons came to America's shores, mostly from Europe. Such newcomers were continuing to arrive at an average rate of about 1,000,000 a year.

At the same time, a much larger proportion of the American people—native and immigrant alike—was living in urban rather than rural areas. In 1870 there were only seven cities in the whole broad country that could boast of 200,000 or more inhabitants; in thirty years this number grew to nineteen.

Changes in the economic life of the country were as great and even more significant than population growth. The last decade or so of the old century marked the end of one era and the beginning of another. The frontier, which had moved steadily westward for generations, disappeared about 1890. Industry, for the first time, became more important than agriculture, and also became more dependent on machinery than on skilled labor. It was organized in ever larger units while the "trusts" and the holding companies began to dominate one field of enterprise after another. By 1900 there were 185 large industrial combinations whose total capitalization of $3,000,000,000 represented one-third of all the capital in all the nation's manufacturing enterprises.

The middle years of the 1890's had been a period of business depression, but conditions began to improve in 1897 and most Americans were optimistic as the new century dawned. This was true in spite of the fact that class and economic distinctions were steadily—and some thought dangerously—increasing. Almost all the wealth of the country was controlled by about 20 per cent of the people. Working men, who labored in units of hundreds and thousands, no longer had any direct contact with those who owned or controlled the enormous factories. Then, too, more and more of the actual control was exercised by bankers and financiers rather than by industrialists and factory managers. The farmers of the West and South felt themselves going down in both economic and social status. They loudly blamed the bankers and the railroad owners for their troubles, claiming that they could borrow money only at exorbitant rates of interest, and that the railroads were charging them far too much to transport their products.

Certainly the country was entering a period of increased tension among its member groups, in both economics and politics. The new century might look enticing, but it brought with it terrifying problems in adjusting to the new urban industrialized world. There was the need to absorb the masses of immigrants, most of whom lived in poverty in the large cities; to bridge the gap between the new gaudy rich and the landless factory hands; to bring up to date the antiquated political machinery so that a continent and its large cities could be governed honestly and efficiently.

American Empire

No event of the last years of the old century did more to change the world for Americans than the Spanish-American War in 1898. What started out for many well-meaning people as a struggle to free Cuba and the Cubans from oppressive Spanish rule ended as a war of conquest that presented the United States with a colonial empire. In ten weeks in the spring and summer, American naval and military strength toppled Spain as a world power, and made for this country a place in the ranks of imperial glory. The peace treaty that followed confirmed the American democracy as ruler of Puerto Rico in the Atlantic, and of the Philippine Islands in the Pacific, with their native and Spanish cultures and languages. In a separate and peaceful transaction the Hawaiian Islands were annexed in 1898 and became a territory in 1900. By agreement with Germany and Great Britain, seven islands in the Samoan group in the Pacific became United States property in 1899.

The Puerto Ricans preferred American to Spanish rule, but many Filipinos felt otherwise. Those who had been fighting the Spanish regime expected the United States to give the islands their freedom, as it was doing in Cuba, and they declared their independence in early 1899. The men in authority in Washington did not think the Filipinos were as yet capable of self-government, and saw the native government as an insurrection. Before the bloody struggle that followed was ended, American forces in the islands amounted to 74,000 men, and there were unpleasant charges of atrocities on both sides. In 1900 William Howard Taft was sent to the Philippines to establish a civil government, but it was 1902 before the war could be officially ended and a basic law for the islands passed by Congress. . . .

McKinley—Twice a Victor

The nation's leader at the opening of the twentieth century was William McKinley, born in Niles, Ohio, in 1843. He was a veteran of the Union Army in the Civil War, from which he had returned a major. After serving in Congress and as governor of Ohio, with the Cleveland industrialist and chairman of the Republican National Committee Mark Hanna as his chief supporter, he easily won the Republican nomination for the presidency in 1896. In one of the noisiest and bitterest campaigns ever staged, he defeated young William Jennings Bryan (1860–1925), the Democratic candidate. . . .

Once in office, McKinley had to turn his attention chiefly to foreign affairs. He made sincere efforts to settle the Cuban rebellion without American intervention, but the pressures on him became too great. He eventually advocated armed intervention against Spain, and when the war ended in complete American victory he decided, after

President William McKinley

some soul-searching, that the Philippines should be annexed. In 1900 he was renominated and defeated Bryan by a greater margin than before. . . . In this election Bryan chose to make anti-imperialism his main issue. Although he sternly denounced the acquisition of the former Spanish colonies, the majority of the people did not agree. The Republicans stuck to their theme that the nation was prosperous because of Republican rule. With business booming and with farmers doing somewhat better than usual, the party in power had little trouble in staying there.

Early in his second term, in September, 1901, President McKinley went to Buffalo, New York, to make a speech at the Pan-American Exposition. There, on September 6, he was shot twice by a young anarchist, Leon Czolgosz, who stood in the receiving line at a reception with a pistol concealed in a handkerchief. When he reached the President, he pulled the trigger, firing point-blank into his abdomen. For a few days McKinley seemed to be recovering, but he took a turn for the worse and died on September 14. The assassin was tried, convicted and electrocuted before the end of October.

The career of the last veteran of the Civil War to be president ended with an assassin's bullet. A handsome, kindly, genial man, McKinley was anxious to do the right thing and what was best for the country; and he firmly believed that this goal could be achieved by following established Republican policies. If the nation stayed on the gold standard, if tariff rates were kept high, and if the businessmen and financiers were allowed to operate the economic machinery as they thought best, the nation would prosper.

The New Generation—Theodore Roosevelt

McKinley's successor was Vice-President Theodore Roosevelt, not quite forty-three years old and the youngest man ever to become president of the United States. He represented a new generation. . . . Roosevelt was born in New York City on October 27, 1858, to a well-placed, well-to-do family. His childhood was easy and pleasant except that he was not a strong boy. His eyes were weak and he had asthma. He was determined to overcome his physical frailty and in the course of the years he succeeded in living a strenuous athletic life.

While still at Harvard he began writing his first book, which was published in 1882—a sound, favorably reviewed book, *The Naval War of 1812*. In the meantime, in 1881, he entered politics, which not many young men of his social class did at that time. He won election as a Republican to the New York State Assembly and served from 1881 to 1884. At first he caused some amusement with his "dude" clothing and his high-pitched voice, but his energy and determination made him an effective legislator. The constant activity, the voice, and, most of all, the enormous grin that seemed to reveal innumerable teeth became his trademark and a priceless gift to the newspaper cartoonists. . . .

In 1895 Roosevelt was appointed a commissioner of the Police Board of New York City and was elected its president. In effect, this made him police commissioner. He took to prowling the streets late at night, wearing a dark cloak and a hat pulled down over his face in an attempt to hide his famous teeth, while he sought policemen who might be neglecting their duty. Two years later the new president, William McKinley, somewhat reluctantly appointed Roosevelt assistant-secretary of the Navy. It was a post he greatly desired, but already his saber-rattling remarks in favor of American expansion had the peaceable McKinley worried.

Death of an American President

William McKinley was the third American president to be assassinated. His death left the American people stunned—and revengeful, as related in this excerpt from an article that appeared in a September 1901 Atlantic Monthly *magazine.*

For the third time within the memory of men who still feel themselves young, the President of the United States has been struck down by an assassin. Each of these crimes was as wanton as it was remediless. No shadow of excuse or palliation—except upon the charitable presumption of insanity—can be found. . . . The circumstances of President McKinley's assassination have been such as to cause even more general and poignant sorrow to the nation as a whole. United as never before, enjoying an era of political good feeling, and universally attracted by the lovable personal qualities of their President, the citizens of the United States, without regard to sectional or party differences, have been stunned and sickened by his murder.

The behavior of our people during the days that intervened between the firing of the fatal shot and the death of the President has been thoroughly characteristic. The first shock and amazement were followed by an outburst of anger against anarchists of

Those worries were well-founded. In February, 1898, when the Secretary of the Navy was absent from his office, Roosevelt took it upon himself to send instructions to Commodore George Dewey to make sure his Asiatic Squadron was ready to fight the Spanish Navy in the Pacific Ocean the moment war was declared. The eventual result of this action was the naval victory in Manila Bay on May 1. When war came, a desk job in Washington was too tame for Roosevelt. He received permission, along with Colonel Leonard Wood under whom he was supposed to serve, to form a volunteer cavalry regiment. Although it

---

every stripe. Even the clergy, upon the first Sunday after that ill-starred Friday, made use of ill-considered appeals to the mere spirit of revenge. This mood passed with calmer second thoughts, and with those swiftly mounting expectations—American-like in their optimism, but alas, how futile!—of the President's recovery. Then came the sudden change for the worse, the abandonment of hope, the hours of hushed waiting for the end. . . . His quiet courage and simple trust were contagious, and upon Sunday, the 15th, the public's mood had changed from one of blind anger and dismay to faith in the perpetuation of our system of self-government and faith in God.

But that the situation is in some respects very grave is generally realized. So far as the American people can protect the life of their Chief Magistrate against the common enemies of all governments, no effort will be spared to do so. A stricter enforcement of existing legislation, possibly new legislation looking to the closer supervision of the speech and action of suspicious elements in the community, is likely to follow. A blow directed against our President is a menace to each one of us, and we have full right to take every precaution against the foes of established order.

(No author given), "The Death of the President," *Atlantic Monthly,* September 1901.

had a formal designation, the unit was soon known as the Rough Riders, and Roosevelt was its leading spirit. The regiment was made up of an undisciplined mixture of cowboys and Indians from the West and Ivy Leaguish young men from the East. The Rough Riders had to leave their horses behind, but they were soon in the thick of things in Cuba. On July 1, 1898, Roosevelt got his chance to lead his men in a charge up San Juan Hill. Roosevelt performed bravely and became a national hero.

The Republican leaders of New York State decided that a war hero was just what they needed, and they made Colonel Roosevelt their candidate for the governorship that same year. Roosevelt won, but by fewer than 18,000 votes. He was such an ambitious governor, especially in his zeal to root out corruption, that in 1900 some Republican leaders were only too happy to have him nominated for the vice-presidency, in which it was normal for a man to disappear from public view.

Roosevelt Takes the Helm of Reform

Now, not much more than a year later, the Harvard educated, rough-riding cowboy with the squeaky voice was president of the United States. The public soon showed genuine fondness for their first exciting presidential personality in many years. . . .

Roosevelt was well prepared by his background, his education and his interests to deal with the new problems facing the recently industrialized and imperialistic nation. By nature, he saw all public issues, whether domestic or foreign, in moral terms. At the same time, he owed his political success to the Republican Party which was dominated by big business interests. Thus, while he was at heart in sympathy with the reform mood of large numbers of people, he was not ready to push for drastic changes; nor was he in a position to do so as chief of a Republican administration with a majority in both houses of the Congress. His first message to that Congress, in December, 1901, seemed conservative enough. However, he did say flatly that the existing laws and attitudes concerning great wealth and monopolistic business were "no longer sufficient." He was trying to express his beliefs and objectives, while still recognizing that he could not get a conservative Congress to go very far along his chosen path all at once.

Domestically, Roosevelt's biggest problem was that posed by the growing concentration of industrial and financial power: to what extent, if any, should the Federal government control or regulate—or dissolve—this new type of business organization popularly known as a "trust"? In foreign affairs Roosevelt was happy to play the role of chief of a mighty nation concerned with peace and war in Europe and Asia.

A particular field of possible achievement that interested him was that of the conservation of natural resources. Although a small start had been made a dozen years before, by setting aside some Federally owned land as forest reserves and parks, it was Theodore Roosevelt who first brought conservation to the nation's attention and who put a comprehensive policy into effect. Roosevelt's interest stemmed from his love of the outdoors and from his experiences in the West. With his strong support, the Newlands Act became law in 1902. This law authorized the government to build irrigation projects in sixteen Western states, and to use the proceeds from the sale of such irrigated land for further projects. A forest conservation program was consolidated and pushed by the dedicated Gifford Pinchot, the first American professional forester. When Roosevelt took office there were about 45,000,000 acres of land in the government reserves. During his time as president he added almost 150,000,000 acres. At one point, faced with a bill from Congress that would require that body's approval before any more forest reserves were created in certain states, Roosevelt gleefully established or increased thirty-two such reserves just before signing the bill into law.

At Roosevelt's urging, a Department of Commerce and Labor was established by law in 1903, and it included a Bureau of Corporations with authority to investigate the conduct of corporations engaged in interstate business. This was the first step in the president's program for dealing with the new business giants.

By 1904, when it was time for another presidential election, Roosevelt had achieved wide popularity with the people and had consolidated his power within the Republican Party. He was easily nominated. . . . The energetic incumbent was elected by an unprecedented margin of popular votes. . . . He was now president in his own right. He was also the most prominent leader of the progressive movement, whose program and activities determined the tone and temper of American politics until domestic reform, partly achieved, was eclipsed by the turmoil of World War I.

Theodore Roosevelt and the progressive movement had much in common. Both the President and the leaders of the progressives thrived on idealism and moral struggle, while in both cases the goals sought were clearer to them than the practical methods necessary to achieve those goals. Some aspects of the movement were inherited from the Populist agitation of the latter years of the nineteenth century. This was chiefly a southern and midwestern agrarian revolt against industry and finance. It was also, in its unspoken ideals, a nostalgic desire to turn back the clock, to keep America simple and rural. The progressives, while they sought the support of this same agricultural America, were urban-oriented and were concerned primarily with the problems of industrial monopolies, corruption in government, assimilation of the new immigrants, and the relief of the poverty that accompanied the new industrial order.

Unfortunately, they were not as forward-looking as they believed they were. They were honest beyond doubt, they were disinterested and sought nothing for themselves—except, perhaps, that some of them thought they deserved to rule over their less-favored neighbors. They did not believe the new industrial revolution could be denied, but they hoped to solve the problem of too much power in the hands of the great corporations by breaking those giants up into smaller units.

While in some measure they sought a better lot for the worker, at heart they feared labor unions almost as much as they did corporations, and for the same reasons: they too might become powerful and monopolistic. They wanted also to "Americanize" the immigrants so they would be better citizens, but in truth they looked down on the foreign-speaking, badly dressed, uneducated men and women who were arriving in large numbers every year from Europe. They did believe in democracy and they did believe that human nature could be changed by education. They believed in progress, but it was a progress that had as its goal a world in which all would emulate their manners and morals as well as behave like good citizens in political affairs. . . .

As president, Roosevelt was looked to for leadership in the fight for progressive goals, but he sometimes disappointed his followers. He did get more radical as time went on. Toward the end of his second term he proposed that the stock market be regulated; argued that the laboring man should get "a larger share of the wealth" he produced; and denounced "the speculative folly and the flagrant dishonesty of a few men of great wealth." A start was made, and some specific steps taken, but Roosevelt's chief contribution to the cause is generally conceded to be the publicity he gave it. . . .

But while the progressive movement, with the aid of some political leaders, was opening this twentieth-century battle for reform, American industry and finance were daily growing in wealth and power in the new economic world.

CHAPTER 2

Daily Life in America: Dreams and Disasters

AMERICA'S DECADES

Racism: A Reality of Life for African Americans

Judy Crichton

Racism was a fact of life for most African Americans during the early years of the twentieth century, as distinguished documentary writer, producer, and director Judy Crichton illustrates in the following article. The young poet Paul Laurence Dunbar, Crichton writes, was one of a small number of Americans that managed to move back and forth across the color line. According to Crichton, in 1900 an entire legal system was built in the South, home to most African Americans, to ensure that they were kept out of the mainstream of public life. Crichton describes the "get educated, work hard, wait and see" philosophy of African American leader Booker T. Washington and the dilemma that attitude presented to other African Americans like academic W.E.B. Du Bois. Judy Crichton has won numerous awards for her writing and journalism, including four Writers Guild Awards and five Emmys. As executive producer on the Public Broadcasting System (PBS) history series *The American Experience*, she worked on one hundred historical documentaries.

B y April, 1900, the daffodils were blooming in the park land facing the White House, and down by the water's edge there were thousands of iris. The rituals of

---

spring had resumed—winter carriages and sleighs sent off to be refurbished, lap robes packed away. At the Andrew Joyce Carriage Company customers were picking up their victorias. New models of these small open carriages were selling for $850. Better to have the old ones repainted and reupholstered. At the Capitol, where the hard winter had taken a toll, carpenters were repairing the leaky roof over the press gallery, which had been so bothersome for months.

On every pleasant day Mlle Marguerite Cassini, the beautiful young "niece" of the Russian ambassador, could be seen driving her new steam phaeton. It was quite like Marguerite to own her own automachine. In the warming sun, Washington society was taking to the streets. At noon, Secretary of State John Hay could be seen hurrying across Lafayette Square to his mansion opposite the White House for a frugal lunch of buttermilk and hoecake. Hay, literate and charming, had recently bought a Botticelli and was said to lie awake nights fearing it might warp.

Nearly every afternoon, a squad of Supreme Court justices walked down the south side of Pennsylvania Avenue, blocking traffic. On occasion, Justice John Marshall Harlan, the most liberal member of the Court and the most athletic, appeared in full golf costume. For Harlan, golf was not a sport but an obsession. President McKinley, too, was taking his daily constitution. Shoulders back, head high, arms swinging at his side, journalist William Allen White said the president looked as though he "was destined for a statue in the park, and was practicing the pose for it."

From McKinley's perspective things were going pretty well, except for the damnable war. Four soldiers from Massachusetts had been captured by guerrillas and tortured to death, the anti-imperialists were in an uproar, and the newspapers never seemed to let up. But the president was hoping that with General Arthur MacArthur taking over the command, the war would quiet down before the fall elections.

A Curious Literary Figure

As the weather softened, the papers reported that the popular young poet Paul Laurence Dunbar had returned to the capital from the mountains of Colorado. Dunbar was in rare spirits that spring. There was enough money, at least for the moment; his wife Alice and mother Matilda were at ease with each other; and his consumption seemed to be under control. He was coughing less and the hemorrhaging had stopped. The mountain air had proved better for his lungs than his own home remedy—a bedtime snack of raw onion with salt and a bottle of beer.

The Dunbars settled into their home on Spruce Street, in what was known as "the camp," a black settlement on the edge of Howard University. The pleasant house was now decorated with Navajo blankets and rugs, and Pueblo pottery Paul had bought out west. A delicate man of enormous grace and charm, in 1900 he was one of the best known African Americans in the country and one of America's most popular poets. His seventh book had just been published, the eighth was under way, and Alice was handling more requests for reading engagements than Paul had breath to fill.

Dunbar was a curious literary figure with a devoted following on both sides of the color line. He wrote in what amounted to two distinct languages, black dialect and classic white English. When he was still a regional poet skirting the edge of both obscurity and hunger, living with his mother in Dayton, Ohio, many of his readers had no idea whether he was white or black.

A doctor had written to say, "I learned that in a biblical sense, God Almighty had placed the stamp of Cain upon you, or in other words, your skin is black. Enclosed a check for five dollars (send me the number of poems that this amount will buy)." In 1896, when he was invited by a young classics professor at Wilberforce University to "come over . . . and read to us," the professor, W.E.B. Du Bois, who was familiar with Paul's work, "was astonished to find that he was a Negro."

A few months later William Dean Howells, the most influential literary critic in the country, devoted an entire column in *Harper's Weekly* to Dunbar's writing. "The world is too old now," Howells wrote, "and I find myself too much of its mood, to care for the work of a poet because he is black, because his father and mother were slaves, because he was, before and after he began to write poems, an elevator-boy. These facts would certainly attract me to him as a man, but when it came to literary art, I must judge it irrespective of these facts, and enjoy or endure it for what it was in itself.

"Still it will legitimately interest those who like to know . . . the sources of things, to learn that the father and mother of the first poet of his race in our language were negroes without admixture of white blood. In more than one piece he has produced a work of art." The review appeared on the morning of Paul's twenty-fourth birthday. Within days he had signed with a New York publisher, Dodd, Mead, received a $400 advance, and was being handled by the lecture bureau that represented Mark Twain.

Poetry with an Edge

Dubbed by the press the Black Robert Burns, Dunbar was now an international celebrity, with admirers turning up uninvited at his door. It was said that he walked about at home with a black chicken on his shoulder, probably not true, and that when he had a few drinks he would break into a war dance, which was more likely. In the spring of 1900 Paul was at the top of his form—except for his health. Tuberculosis was a pernicious disease without any cure; his mother watched him like a hawk, arguing with Alice over his care. His coughing spells had returned and he was forced to cut back on the readings he had always found such fun.

He brought to those engagements a musical bluesy sensibility, interacting with the audience, calling on them to participate, to join him in the choruses of his better-known poems:

Life

A crust of bread and a corner to sleep in,
A minute to smile and an hour to weep in,
A pint of joy to a peck of trouble,
And never a laugh but the moans come double;
And that is life!

. . . And never a laugh but the moans come double. . . . And that is life!

Dunbar's writing was easygoing but often had an edge that black audiences identified with. White audiences left his concerts feeling they had eavesdropped on a world they barely knew:

We wear the mask that grins and lies
It hides our cheeks and shades our eyes. . . .

In an increasingly segregated country, Paul Laurence Dunbar was one of a small group of Americans moving back and forth across the color line. From his perspective it was a logical way to live. He had grown up moving between the world of his parents, both former slaves, and Dayton's almost all-white public schools. At home he had absorbed tales of plantation life, told and retold in black southern talk, and in school he had read Shelley and Keats, Tennyson and Poe, and learned to speak and write in traditional Western cadence. His best friend was an outgoing fellow named Orville Wright. The boys appeared together in their class photograph, and at graduation marched down the aisle to an anthem Dunbar had written.

The Washington, D.C., of the African American

Critics were forever trying to wedge Paul into some tidy cultural niche, but he would have none of it. He defined himself as a cultural hybrid—a black man, an American, and a writer. Others might be confused about his identity, but Dunbar was not. On a scrap of paper found after his death he had written: "It is one of the peculiar phases of Anglo-Saxon conceit to refuse to believe that every black man does not want to be white."

In Washington, the Dunbars lived primarily within a large and congenial black community. Looking at photo stories of the city that year, one would assume the capital was an all-white town, except of course for the inevitable doormen, coachmen, and the black woman with a basket on her head. But there were ninety thousand African Americans living in Washington by 1900, and a large and prosperous middle class.

Black men and women were working for all the government agencies; Paul had worked as an assistant in the Library of Congress when he first came to town. In an essay published in *Harper's Weekly* in January, he had written about the postwar generation of dark-skinned doctors and lawyers and members of the board of trade and government clerks, "smoking as good a cigar as an Eastern Congressman." There were good schools and social clubs, churches and Howard University, and a gossipy black paper called *The Washington Bee*.

But for black Americans the capital was also a city of unmet promises, of dismal back alleys tourists never saw, jammed with the poor, the failed, and the damaged—southern rural people ill-fit for city life. The crime rate was up, the jails overfilled. And racial snubs, rudeness, and condescension were as much a part of the black experience here as anywhere else. Dunbar didn't mention it—he didn't have to, it was such a part of daily life. "Taking it all in all," he wrote, "Negro life in Washington is a promise rather than a fulfillment."

Those Americans, like Paul's parents, who had emerged from slavery with such a profound sense of hope, found themselves and their children trapped in a hostile and ever-narrowing world. In the thirty-five years since emancipation there had been progress to be sure, 60 percent of black children were now in school, 20 percent of black Americans owned their own homes, and there were five thousand businessmen, grocers, barbers, plumbers, and real estate men.

The Color Barrier Still Stands

Dunbar's old friend W.E.B. Du Bois, now a professor of sociology at Atlanta University, was producing the first extended analysis of African-American life, and his findings were not reassuring. Of the nine million black people in the country, Du Bois wrote, most were "still serfs bound to the soil or house servants." Moving up the American ladder was far more difficult than black Americans had hoped. Novelist Sutton E. Griggs wrote of the torment and frustrations of a southern black man who "would have made an excellent sales man, clerk, cashier, telegraph operator, conductor—but the color of his skin shut the doors so tight that he could not even peep in."

In the South, where 90 percent of black Americans still lived, not only were most white-collar jobs off limits, but an entire legal system was being constructed to isolate

W.E.B. Du Bois

black Americans from the mainstream of public life. Trains, trolleys, hotels, schools were being segregated by a growing and intricate body of law. Casual contact between the races was in some ways more limited than it had been in the days of slavery. Possibilities for advancement were being cut off in every direction.

In Mississippi, the state legislature was proposing to divide school funds in proportion to the real estate taxes paid in the white and black districts, all but guaranteeing that black school systems would remain penniless. T. Thomas Fortune, the black newspaper publisher in New York City, argued it would be "vastly cheaper to build schoolhouses than jails." Du Bois wrote: "Race antagonism can only be stopped by intelligence. It is dangerous to wait, it is foolish to hesitate. Let the nation immediately give generous aid to southern common school education."

But Du Bois was not hopeful. The most sensible suggestions were rejected with such contempt, and even hatred, that retaining one's equilibrium was proving difficult. After receiving a Harvard Ph.D., Du Bois had hoped to carve out

One Man's Credo

Academician W.E.B. Du Bois was a cultured and respected African American educator and leader. Du Bois had strong beliefs, which he expressed in this credo, published in The Independent *in 1904.*

I believe in God who made of one blood all races that dwell on earth. I believe that all men, black and brown and white, are brothers, varying, through Time and Opportunity, in form and gift and feature, but differing in no essential particular, and alike in soul and in the possibility of infinite development.

Especially do I believe in the Negro Race; in the beauty of its genius, the sweetness of its soul, and its strength in that meekness which shall yet inherit this turbulent earth.

I believe in pride of race and lineage and self; in pride of self so deep as to scorn injustice to other selves; in pride of lineage so great as to despise no man's father; in pride of race so chivalrous as neither to offer bastardy to the weak nor beg wedlock of the strong, knowing that men may be brothers in Christ, even tho they be not brothers-in-law.

I believe in Service—humble reverent service, from the blackening of boots to the whitening of souls; for Work is Heaven, Idleness Hell, and Wage is the "Well done!" of the Master who summoned all them that labor and are heavy laden, making no distinction between the black sweating cotton-hands of Georgia and the First Families of Virginia, since all distinction not based on deed is devilish and not divine.

a quiet academic life for himself and for his wife, Nina, but was now at the center of a profound American controversy: how to move a nation hip-deep in racism to fulfill its most basic promise—justice for all. He was being urged to join Booker T. Washington, the most powerful black leader in the country, at Tuskegee Institute but was uncertain about the effectiveness of Booker T.'s philosophy.

I believe in the Devil and his angels, who wantonly work to narrow the opportunity of struggling human beings, especially if they be black; who spit in the faces of the fallen, strike them that cannot strike again, believe the worst and work to prove it, hating the image which their Maker stamped on a brother's soul.

I believe in the Prince of Peace. I believe that War is Murder. I believe that armies and navies are at bottom the tinsel and braggadocio of oppression and wrong; and I believe that the wicked conquest of weaker and darker nations by nations whiter and stronger but foreshadows the death of that strength.

I believe in Liberty for all men; the space to stretch their arms and their souls; the right to breathe and the right to vote, the freedom to choose their friends, enjoy the sunshine and ride on the railroads, uncursed by color; thinking, dreaming, working as they will in a kingdom of God and love.

I believe in the training of children black even as white; the leading out of little souls into the green pastures and beside the still waters, not for pelf or peace, but for Life lit by some large vision of beauty and goodness and truth; lest we forget, and the sons of the fathers, like Esau, for mere meat barter their birthright in a mighty nation.

Finally, I believe in Patience—patience with the weakness of the Weak and the strength of the Strong, the prejudice of the Ignorant and the ignorance of the Blind; patience with the tardy triumph of Joy and the mad chastening of Sorrow—patience with God.

Professor W.E. Burghardt Du Bois, "Credo," *The Independent*, October 6, 1904.

Washington was urging his followers to pull themselves up by their bootstraps and practice patience. He would not publicly press for voting rights or social equality. He put his faith in vocational training, convinced that in the long run only economic success would lead to acceptance. The Reverend J.A. Jones, in Chattanooga, Tennessee, concurred: "When the Negro opens a first-class drugstore just across the street from the white man's . . . and every other form of business, prejudice will take wings." In time the marketplace would resolve the race problem. But everything in Du Bois's own experience argued against such reasoning.

Just the year before he'd been witness to a ghastly incident. A mob of two thousand people had assembled in Atlanta for the lynching of Sam Hose, accused of killing his employer in an argument over money. After Hose was tortured and burned at the stake, newspapers reported men, women, and children fighting over pieces of his charred flesh. Du Bois had seen Sam Hose's blackened knucklebones on display in the local drugstore. Historian David Levering Lewis writes, "Numbed by the horror Du Bois turned away from his work. From that moment forward he recognized that 'one could not be a calm, cool and detached [social] scientist while Negroes were lynched, murdered and starved.'"

Racism Runs Rampant

In the spring of 1900, Du Bois was torn. He could leave Atlanta with all its ugliness and tension for a well-paying position at Tuskegee Institute, or stay in the city and ally himself with the more radical forces fighting for black rights. In an article in the *Atlantic Monthly* a few years back, he had asked, "What, after all, am I? Am I an American or am I a Negro? Can I be both? Or is it my duty to cease to be a Negro as soon as possible and be an American? If I strive as a Negro, am I not perpetuating the very cleft that threatens and separates black and white in America?" As the cleft widened, conciliation did not seem possible.

The capricious nature of racism was exhausting. It was

not only those searing and horrific events—and there were more of those than many psyches could stand—but it was managing the most ordinary everyday encounters, to measure one's every gesture by another man's sensibility: to smile or not to smile, to make eye contact, to step aside or walk apace or modulate one's voice. Du Bois wrote with weariness, "In a world where it means so much to take a man by the hand and sit beside him, to look frankly into his eyes . . . in a world where a social cigar or a cup of tea together means more than legislative halls and magazine articles and speeches—one can imagine the consequences of the almost utter absences of such amenities between estranged races."

In 1900 those who daily banged up against the race wall were learning to walk the walk and wear the smile and mask their eyes. They bought Ozonized Ox Marrow, the Magnetic Comb to straighten their "Knotty, Nappy, Kinky Hair," and Imperial Whitener to bleach their skin—*every bottle guaranteed.* But there was not an ounce of compromise in Will Du Bois. He carried his independence in the set of his shoulders and the arc of his cane. He would reject Booker T.'s offer.

Like Frances Benjamin Johnston, Du Bois had also been asked by Thomas Calloway to contribute material to the Negro Exhibit in Paris. Calloway was an old college friend from Fisk; together they had waited tables and sung in a glee club at a summer resort on Lake Minnetonka, Minnesota. Now, at Calloway's request, Du Bois had embarked on assembling a "brief but comprehensive history of the Negro people," pulling together a collection of books by black writers and military histories on black soldiers going back to the Revolutionary War.

In February, he had agreed to attend a meeting in Savannah, Georgia, on Exposition business. He boarded a night train in Atlanta, wearing his standard conservative three-piece suit. A small and quiet man with an elegant manner, he requested a berth in a sleeping car but was forced instead to spend the night sitting in the filthy, crowded, soot-covered "colored" car in back of the engine.

Du Bois argued with the conductor, a train man, and a porter that the Jim Crow laws did not apply to interstate trains. The legal niceties of his argument were not heard. Later, he would file a formal protest but that, too, would come to naught.

He arrived in Savannah the following morning tired and grimy and raging at the railroad, and then proceeded to work on an exhibit heralding the progress of black citizens in America.

Living in Small-Town and Rural America

John W. Dodds

Growth and change typified the urban areas of America throughout the first decade of the twentieth century, but urban life was not the norm for most Americans. More Americans still lived on farms or in small towns than in big cities. According to John W. Dodds, author and longtime academic at Stanford University in Palo Alto, California, Americans thrived in the smaller towns. Dodds describes the routine and pace of a life infinitely simpler than that of today. Small-town America, Dodds argues, moved in the "regular channels of its own insularity" and was able to see the world "in comfortable terms of black and white."

L ife on the farm in the first year of the twentieth century was more like 1860 than 1940. In the first place, the majority of the people lived there. The population of the United States in 1901 was 77,585,000, and of this 60 percent was rural. The rhythms of daily life, set by the sun, had changed very little over the years, whether in the larger spaces of the great plains or on the smaller farms of the East and South. Horsepower and manpower were still the units of energy for the spring planting of the crops, the summer cultivating, the autumn harvesting, and for a multitude of other daily duties. Some reaping of grain was still

Reprinted from *Everyday Life in Twentieth Century America*, by John W. Dodds. New York: G.P. Putnam's Sons, 1965.

done by hand with the scythe or "cradle," though the horse-drawn McCormick reaper had changed all this in most communities.

The cows were milked by hand and the milk was put in large pans and placed in a cool structure. Sometimes the structure was called a "milk house," but if it could be located over or alongside a spring it was a "springhouse." There the cream would rise to the surface to be skimmed and churned—for all farmers made their own butter, or rather their wives and children did. Sometimes the more mechanically minded had a "dogpower" churn, turned by a set of gears activated by a dog walking on a treadmill. Farm families baked their own bread and of course raised their own fruits and vegetables and slaughtered their own meat. The occasional Saturday trips to the nearest general store were to get such staples as flour, navy beans (white kidney beans), molasses, oatmeal, and for the winter diet, dried prunes or peaches. And sometimes, for the children, candy—"jawbreakers," or long beltlike strips of licorice. Farmers had to be largely self-sufficient. Even as late as 1955 they had an average annual family income, from the farms themselves, of less than $1,000. In 1900 it would have been less than half of that.

People on the farms, then, lived much like their fathers and grandfathers before them. They rose before dawn most of the year and went to bed at night by kerosene lights and cooked their meals on wood or coal stoves. . . . There was no plumbing; they drew water from springs or wells, bathed in a washtub in the kitchen, and made treks to an outhouse which could hardly be called a sanitary "convenience." The roads connecting the scattered villages and farms were drifted with snow in the winter, bogged with mud in the spring, and deep with dust in the summer. Children walked to the one-room country schoolhouse . . . , where the teacher, if she represented the national norm, received an annual salary of $325.

Children had their own delights, of course: picking chestnuts or hunting in the woods on crisp October mornings, fishing and swimming in nearby "cricks," gathering wild blackberries or blueberries, finding the first trailing arbutus under the snow in the early spring, listening to sleigh bells on a tingling winter night.

The Simple Pleasures

Any community activity was largely a neighborhood one: picking up the rare mail and the weekly paper at the village post office (farmers were not given to extensive correspondence); talking politics across the line fence with a neighbor; getting dressed up in store clothes to go to the rural Sunday school and church services. The local minister often had two parishes some miles apart, and often he did some farming during the week. Sometimes there were Sunday school picnics or "strawberry festivals" in the churchyard or evening "socials" at the schoolhouse, with orations, selected literary readings and even debates—both children and parents nodding sleepily in the hot little schoolroom after a hard day's work. There was a good deal of "neighboring" when larger tasks required joint effort, such as the raising of a rooftree for a new barn. At harvest time steam threshing machines made the rounds from farm to farm and "thrashing day," with the women preparing gargantuan meals for the hungry farmers, was always a great community event.

Occasionally families enjoyed something in the nature of a celebration. Sometimes a one-ring circus would visit the county seat, and everyone would pile into a wagon (or even at times take the "hack" that ran between towns) for a day's outing. The annual county fair was a great event, too—an exciting mélange of horse-cattle-pig exhibitions, prize-winning pies and canned fruits and vegetables, horse races, lots of popcorn and soda pop, and a sort of carnival sideshow which parents inspected critically before allowing the children to attend.

Pleasures were for the most part simple, and the life very close to the soil. People talk today about getting back to the land. Most of them have little idea of what it meant to be on the land in 1900, the really hard life it represented. . . .

The Routines of Small-Town Living

If the rhythms of farm life in the early nineteen hundreds were different from today, those of urban life were even more different. Nearly half of all the people in towns and cities were in places of under 10,000. The small town was in many ways the heart of America. It has been written about, sung about, satirized, dramatized, and has become the symbol (sometimes even the sentimentalization) of the American way of life almost a century ago. The cities were growing, burgeoning—frequently with people who were fleeing the farms, and they in turn were becoming the focus of the new industrialization which was the hallmark of the U.S.A. But the industrial cities were still strange conglomerate masses of people, more and more foreign as they became swollen, after the 1870's, with the floods of immigrants from central and southern Europe who were manning the factories and mills. . . . The great continuities of the American tradition could be more easily identified in the smaller towns.

Life moved slowly in these places, and before World War I changes came slowly, too. To be sure, new motorcars came to town and snorted, smoky and smelly, up and down the brick or cobblestone streets. Many homes had gas, though not yet electricity, and except for the poorer districts, bathrooms and plumbing. Central heating was still something of a luxury; coal or gas stoves kept people warm, and many who were youngsters then can still remember the beautiful frost crystals inside the windowpanes on cold winter mornings. There were other remembered things, too: the rich smell of buckwheat cakes that came up the back stairs early in the morning; cutting and dragging in the tall Christmas tree from the nearest woods through the December snow and decking it with strings of popcorn and tinsel and puffs of white cotton; the long winter evenings when children did their homework around the dining-room table while mother darned socks and long black cotton stockings and father read the paper under the fishtail gaslight—or perhaps under a glaring Welsbach gas mantle which flooded the whole room with hissing brilliance.

No one thought of life then as being "stylized," but it was eminently predictable and its patterns rested upon a comfortable recurrence. Monday was always washday; Tuesday ironing day; Wednesday baking day; Friday cleaning day, and so on. Not infrequently the big sprawling kitchen was the center of much of the family life. People not only ate many of their meals there, but small children played there under the mother's eye. It was a kind of all-purpose room which architects and families of the later mid-century were to rediscover with delight.

Houses were set well back on roomy lots with lots of trees for youngsters to climb and with room for a sizable vegetable garden. Each house had its front porch where on summer evenings the adults would sit in porch swings and hold long conversations with friends and neighbors who came over to "visit." Everybody knew everybody else in the early-century American town; most of the families had lived there all their lives. The doctor was your friend as well as your physician. You knew the grocer and the dry-goods store owner and the schoolteacher, as well as the plumber and the carpenter—each of whom, incidentally, took pride in being a *good* plumber and a *good* carpenter. They shared the hymnbook with you in church and it never entered their heads that they weren't just as dignified—in the sight of man as well as in the sight of God—as anyone else.

The American small-town Sunday was really a day of rest then, for the codes in many places were such that almost any non-pious activity was frowned on. It was not a day for picnics, sports, or frolic, or even for reading that was not edifying. Father might take a long afternoon snooze, but the children, before they were released to read *The Youth's Companion*, might well have to study the *Shorter Catechism* and read a chapter in Wayland's *Elements of Moral Science*. Some towns took pride in having persuaded the railroad not to run local trains on Sunday, and others even banished the Sunday papers from the newsstands. The Puritan Ethic made Sunday something to be endured even for those who did not question its premises. But no one returned to work Monday morning tired out!

The All-Important Sears, Roebuck Catalog

Some of the best reading for one who wants to capture the tangibilities of life as it was lived in country and town during the first third of the century is in the pages of the Sears, Roebuck catalogs. Here is the record of what people actually bought and used, from farm machinery to clothes to books to household equipment—bought at a price which seems fantastically low today. At the turn of the century you could get oak well buckets for 36 cents each, potbelly stoves at $2.40, wood-or-coal kitchen ranges for $7.00; five-pound tubs of apple butter for 40 cents, maple syrup for 67 cents a five-gallon jug. A 30-volume set of the *Encyclopaedia Britannica* sold for $29.50. (It was true, of course, that the average hourly wage in industry was 29 cents. Farm laborers received a dollar a day.) . . .

A Hodgepodge of Houses

If you had been dropped into the residential section of an American town in the early part of the century you would have found most houses neither notably beautiful nor abysmally ugly. Most of them were squarish brick or wood boxes, set in a sizable yard and shrouded gratefully by trees which softened their harsher contours. Typically they had big front porches where the family could sit in rocking chairs on a warm summer's evening and watch the horses and buggies, and an occasional Ford, go by. Each had its own back porch and a big attic and cellar. These houses had no pretension to architectural style; they sprang from a book of plans or a builder's brain. There were, to be sure, various layers of architectural or regional differences. Some houses would be clean Colonial or Cape Cod, others would be architectural monstrosities surviving from the period after the Civil War when "Carpenter's Gothic" was the rage—a confusion of pointed towers, useless turrets, and eccentric dormer windows, all ornamented by jigsaw scrollwork and grotesque decoration, a sort of nightmare architecture. Sometimes you would find a surviving "Queen Anne" house, a relic of what the builder thought was "quaint" or "picturesque" in the later nineteenth century, dressed up with "ornamental" chimneys and swallowed by a rash of cornices and bulging excrescences.

Other sections of town might represent a hodgepodge of builders' choices in the *beaux-arts* style popularized by the Chicago World Fair of 1893—a mixed grill of Greek, Roman, and Renaissance. Any kind of purity of style was overwhelmed by a random eclecticism ranging from "Egyptian" to "Byzantine" cottages to "Italian" villas. People were trying to be comfortable, or stylish, in the surroundings of a past that never really existed. There was, however, one kind of organic architecture that came in, as it were, by the back door. Infiltrating the Middle West and the East was an importation from California called the "bungalow," a wooden cottage marked by big overhanging eaves, cobblestone chimneys, and big windows. Though it frequently became degraded in the builder's hands, it gave to the early century a new kind of freshness and honesty. As a matter of fact, though, the most eccentric creators of pseudo-Gothic or Queen Anne houses always prided themselves on the "sincerity" of their architecture—sincerity being a strangely ambiguous term.

Child Labor in the Southern Cotton Mill

Jacquelyn Dowd Hall, James Leloudis, Robert Korstad, Mary Murphy, Lu Ann Jones, and Christopher B. Daly

In the 1970s, staff of the Southern Oral History Program at the University of North Carolina at Chapel Hill interviewed more than two hundred textile workers and eventually used what they learned as the basis for a publication. The following excerpt explores the controversial issue of child labor in the cotton mills during the late 1800s and early 1900s, before child labor laws were enacted. According to the authors, the textile industry's profits and the survival of many families depended on the labor of children. The authors explain that efforts by reformers to impose restrictions on the employment of children often were not successful. Often, write the authors, mill work was not inflicted on children by their parents or other outside pressures. For some, it was a source of pride, of money, and of fun and, even with the long hours and hard work, children themselves chose the mill over school or staying at home.

At the time the excerpt was published author Jacquelyn Dowd Hall was professor of history and director of the Southern Oral History Program. James Leloudis, Robert Korstad, and Mary Murphy were doctoral candidates in American history at the University of North Carolina. Lu Ann Jones was an independent scholar at the National Mu-

Excerpted from *Like a Family: The Making of a Southern Cotton Mill World,* by Jacquelyn Dowd Hall, James Leloudis, Robert Korstad, Mary Murphy, Lu Ann Jones, and Christopher B. Daly. Copyright ©1988 by the University of North Carolina Press. Used by permission of the publisher.

seum of American History, and Christopher B. Daly was Boston Statehouse bureau chief for the Associated Press.

First-generation workers in southern mills had more to learn than just the mechanics of a new job. On the farm they had chosen and ordered their tasks according to their needs and the demands of their crops. Now they drove themselves to the continuous pace of a machine. Whereas most men, women, and children had once worked together and enjoyed the fruits of their own labor, now they were "hands," working under a boss's orders and for someone else's profit. Farm work, to be sure, had been hard, but mill work took a different toll. Millhands rose early in the morning, still tired from the day before. For ten, eleven, or twelve hours they walked, stretched, leaned, and pulled at their machines. Noise, heat, and humidity engulfed them. The lint that settled on their hair and skin marked them as mill workers, and the cotton dust that silently entered their lungs could eventually cripple or kill them. At best, mill work was a wrenching change. . . .

Reliance on the family labor system meant that the southern textile industry's growth was based to a large extent on the labor of children. Between 1880 and 1910 manufacturers reported that about one-quarter of their work force was under sixteen years of age, and many more child workers went unreported. Indeed, in the industry's early years, youngsters of seven or eight commonly doffed, spun, and did all sorts of casual labor. Originally the official definition of "children" applied to youngsters up to age eight but later rose to age twelve, then fourteen, and finally sixteen; nevertheless, young people remained crucial, both to the industry's profit margins and to their own families' survival.

Child labor was by no means unique to the South. The textile industry, wherever established, tended to rely on the labor of women and children. But the technical breakthroughs that enabled the South to enter and eventually capture the market in cotton goods also encouraged a particularly intense exploitation of the young. Women and children led the first wave of migrants to the region's mills, and manufacturers matched them with the low-skill jobs created by the advent of ring spinning. A study of women and children laborers conducted by the U.S. Bureau of Labor in 1907–8 found that half the spinners were under fourteen and 90 percent were under twenty-one. As [worker] Naomi Trammel put it, "That's where they put the children. You could run a frame where you couldn't run anything else."

Technology made child labor practical, but not necessary. The practice spread primarily as a solution to problems of labor recruitment and as a system of socializing and controlling a prospective labor force. South Carolina industrialist William Gregg, founder of Graniteville, the Old South's premier cotton mill, had hoped to attract the daughters of impoverished farmers. Young single women failed to show up in large numbers, but Gregg continued to believe that the "large class of miserable poor white people among us . . . might be induced to place their children in a situation in which they would be educated and reared in industrious habits." His words captured the industry rationale: children made up a large portion of the surplus labor in the countryside; the lure of wages for everyone in the family could induce hard-pressed farmers to cast their lot with the mills; all children who went to work at an early age would eventually grow into efficient, tractable, long-term workers.

Opposition to Child Labor

Critics of child labor were not hard to find. In the 1880s and 1890s the opposition was led by the Knights of Labor and the National Union of Textile Workers (NUTW), who complained that the low wages paid to children held down the earnings of adults. But after the turn of the century a new group of middle-class social reformers took up the banner of the child labor crusade. Educational and religious leaders such as Alabama's Edgar Gardner Murphy and North Carolina's Alexander J. McKelway organized opposition at the state level and then helped form the National Child Labor Committee (NCLC). These reformers worried that the mills' unlettered children would one day become a blight on the body politic. "In a democracy," McKelway argued, "the people all rule. Also, the people are ruled. And when it comes to the people's ruling us by their votes, electing our governors and presidents, initiating and vetoing legislation, taxing our incomes, we grow mightily concerned over the intelligence and independence of the electorate. We do not like to trust our interests now and the lives and fortunes of our children to a mass of voters who have been deprived of all opportunity for an education . . . who have been embittered by the robbery of their childhood, who are the material for the agitator, and the prey of the demagogue."

Mill men themselves were divided on the issue of child labor. Some firmly believed that hard work, commencing at a young age, was the best education available. Others championed the practice as a necessary evil in the natural progress of society. Daniel Augustus Tompkins traced the problem to the poverty caused by the Civil War, particularly to the resultant lack of educational opportunities. "In the absence of schools, the discipline of the mill and its training down to twelve years of age is much better for children than idleness and no discipline or training. . . . It would be far better to have ample school facilities and compel all children to go to school ten months in the year, and give them the other two months for vacations and recreation. But in the absence of such facilities, the discipline and training of the mill is best for the children of working people." Whatever the personal feelings of mill men, their duties to their stockholders demanded that they oppose restrictions on the employment of children. The fact of the matter, as the president of the American Cotton Manufacturers Association admitted to McKelway, was that without the labor of boys and girls under the age of fourteen, Piedmont mills simply could not operate.

Bit by bit, reformers chipped away at the opposition. By 1913 North Carolina, South Carolina, Alabama, and Georgia had laws that prohibited the employment of children under twelve and restricted the hours of labor for those below fourteen. Exemptions and lack of enforcement, however, enfeebled state regulations. The 1907–8 Bureau of Labor study found that an astounding 92 percent of the mills in South Carolina and 75 percent of those in North Carolina ignored child labor regulations. Flora McKinney's boss was one of those who paid little attention to the law. Her family moved to Lando, South Carolina, when she was nine or ten, and she soon followed her father into the mill. "When I got old enough, well, I really weren't old enough, but they'd take children to work then. We were supposed to be twelve years old before we could go to work, but I've hid from inspectors a lots of times. They'd come through and the section in front of us would send word to hide the kids, and we'd run to the water house. Then we'd all cram in there 'til they left."

Given the inadequacy of state legislation, members of the NCLC felt the need for federal action. To mobilize public opinion against child labor, the NCLC devised a highly effective propaganda campaign. Key to this effort were the photographs of Lewis Hine, which poignantly revealed the youthfulness of southern workers. Hines's images—of little girls dressed in long skirts and aprons and little boys wearing their workingmen's caps and suspenders, all swallowed up in rows of towering machines—became the crusade's symbols of the worst evils of industrialization. . . .

A Family Affair

Child labor involved more . . . than the exploitation of youth. There were stories behind the expressions captured on film by Lewis Hine, stories that fit neither the rationalizations of mill owners nor the fears of reformers. Mill work was a source of pride as well as pain, of fun as much as suffering; and children made choices, however hedged about by their parents' authority and their bosses' power.

For mill children, life was paced from the outset by the ringing of the factory bell. Working women, who often had to return to their jobs within a few weeks of childbirth, adapted their nursing schedule to breaks in the workday. "People used to go out," recalled Ada Mae Wilson. "They didn't have bottle babies like they do now. They nursed the breast. A lot healthier children. You'd come out at nine o-clock, and then at twelve you'd come home for lunch. And then at three they'd let you come back, and then you'd be off at six." If labor was scarce, a woman who had neither relatives nor older children at home might take her baby to the mill. Jessie Lee Carter had a neighbor with a nursing baby who would "take a quilt and lay that baby in her roping box while she worked. And she'd bring her baby down and keep it in the mill all day long."

As children got older, the mill was like a magnet, attracting their youthful curiosity and, all too soon, their labor. Until the 1920s no barbed wire fences, locked gates, or bricked-in windows separated the factory from the village. Children could easily wander in and out of the mill, and their first "work" might be indistinguishable from play. After school and in the summers, Emma Williams accompanied her mother to the mill. "I'm sure I didn't work for the money. I just wanted to work, I reckon. Oodles of kids. All of us used to do it together. [We] didn't do much, and it was real fun. I guess maybe one reason that it was fun was because that was the only time we got with other children. When we stayed home, well, we stayed home."

Most children first learned about factory labor when they tagged along with a parent or sibling, carried hot meals to the mill at dinnertime, or stopped by after school. But this casual contact had serious consequences, for on such visits relatives began teaching children the skills they would need when they were old enough for jobs of their own. Ethel Faucette carried lunch to her sister. "While she was eating," Faucette explained, "I learned how to work her job. I was already learned when I went to work." Geddes Dodson's father gave him specific chores during his daily visits. "When

God Must Work in Some Other Mine

During the early 1900s, child labor was common in many industries. In this excerpt, writer John Spargo describes the grueling work performed by children in the coal mines.

Work in the coal breakers is exceedingly hard and dangerous. Crouched over the chutes, the boys sit hour after hour, picking out the pieces of slate and other refuse from the coal as it rushes past to the washers. From the cramped position they have to assume, most of them become more or less deformed and bent-backed like old men. When a boy has been working for some time and begins to get round-shouldered, his fellows say that "He's got his boy to carry around whenever he goes."

The coal is hard, and accidents to the hands, such as cut, broken, or crushed fingers, are common among the boys. Sometimes there is a worse accident: a terrified shriek is heard, and a boy is mangled and torn in the machinery, or disappears in the chute to be picked out later smothered and dead. Clouds of dust fill the breakers and are inhaled by the boys, laying the foundations for asthma and miners' consumption.

I once stood in a breaker for half an hour and tried to do the work a twelve-year-old boy was doing day after day, for ten hours at a stretch, for sixty cents a day. The gloom of the breaker appalled me. Outside the sun shone brightly, the air was pellucid, and the birds sang in chorus with the trees and the rivers. Within the breaker there was blackness, clouds of deadly dust enfolded everything, the harsh, grinding roar of the machinery and the ceaseless rushing of coal through the chutes filled the ears. I tried to pick out the pieces of slate from the hurrying stream of coal, often missing them; my hands were bruised and cut in a few minutes; I was covered from head to foot with coal dust, and for many hours afterwards I was expectorating some of the small particles of anthracite I had swallowed.

I could not do that work and live, but there were boys of ten and twelve years of age doing it for fifty and sixty cents a day. Some of them had never been inside of a school; few of them could read a child's primer. True, some of them attended the night schools, but after working ten hours in the breaker the educational results from attending school were practically nil. "We goes fer a good time, an' we keeps de guys wot's dere hoppin' all de time," said little Owen Jones, whose work I had been trying to do. . . .

From the breakers the boys graduate to the mine depths, where they become door tenders, switch boys, or mule drivers. Here, far below the surface, work is still more dangerous. At fourteen and fifteen the boys assume the same risks as the men, and are surrounded by the same perils. Nor is it in Pennsylvania only that these conditions exist. In the bituminous mines of West Virginia, boys of nine or ten are frequently employed. I met one little fellow ten years old in Mt. Carbon, W. Va., last year, who was employed as a "trap boy." Think of what it means to be a trap boy at ten years of age. It means to sit alone in a dark mine passage hour after hour, with no human soul near; to see no living creature except the mules as they pass with their loads, or a rat or two seeking to share one's meal; to stand in water or mud that covers the ankles, chilled to the marrow by the cold draughts that rush in when you open the trap door for the mules to pass through; to work for fourteen hours—waiting—opening and shutting a door—then waiting again—for sixty cents; to reach the surface when all is wrapped in the mantle of night, and to fall to the earth exhausted and have to be carried away to the nearest "shack" to be revived before it is possible to walk to the farther shack called "home.". . . It is easy to believe what miners have again and again told me—that there are hundreds of little boys of nine and ten years of age employed in the coal mines of this state.

John Spargo, *The Bitter Cry of Children*. New York: Macmillan, 1906.

I was a little fellow, my daddy was a-working in the Poinsett Mill. He was a loom fixer. He'd run the weavers' looms through the dinner hour so they could go eat their dinner. We lived about a mile and a quarter from the mill, and I'd carry his lunch every day. He'd tell me to come on in the mill, and he made me fill his batteries while he run the weavers' looms—and I was just a little fellow. See, I knew a whole lot about the mill before I ever went in one."

"Helping," then, was a family affair, a form of apprenticeship by which basic skills and habits were transmitted to each new generation. But helping was also a vital part of the family economy and the mill labor system. A child's help could increase a parent's or older sibling's piecework earnings or simply relieve the strain of keeping up production. An Englishman who reported on the American textile industry visited a mill in South Carolina where weavers who had their sons or little brothers helping could take on two additional looms. Besides with parents working twelve-hour days in the mills, children often had no place else to go. Owners profited from such family needs. Early child labor legislation in the Carolinas only prohibited "employing" children under certain ages, so owners could stay within the letter the law by "permitting" or "suffering" underage children to "help." A story related by a federal investigator in Georgia illustrated the system's coercive potential. "A woman reported that her little daughter ten years old worked every day helping her sisters. The child quit for a while, but the overseer said to the mother, 'Bring her in; the two girls cannot tend those machines without her.' The mother asked that the child be given work by herself, but the overseer replied that the law would not permit it."

Family Pressures Lead to Mill Work

Given the laxity of enforcement, mill owners could essentially set their own policies according to individual conscience or the bottom line of profit and loss. Allie Smith provided a child's-eye view of the confusion that often resulted. Shortly after Allie's birth, her family moved to Saxapahaw, a community in Alamance County on the Haw River. By the time they left for Carrboro, in neighboring Orange County, when Allie was eleven, she knew how to spin from having helped an older sister. But Julian Shakespeare Carr, owner of the Carrboro mill, believed that mill men should voluntarily avoid child labor in order to stave off government interference. "When we moved to Carrboro," Allie recalled, "I thought I could go in and help her, and I did. But Mr. Carr owned this cotton mill, and I hadn't been over here long when he came over and said I couldn't come in and help. I would have to be on the payroll, so they put me on the payroll. And I worked there, I don't know how long—several months—and they said I couldn't work unless my father signed me up for being twelve years old. Well, he wouldn't do it. He said he didn't want me to work. They put me out and wouldn't let me work. And then when I got to be twelve, I went in and went to work."

Playing and helping could thus shade into full-time work. But getting that first official, full-time job was a major turning point. Managers, parents, and children themselves influenced the decision. Occasionally, mills openly dictated the age at which a child had to begin work. In 1904 the owners of a South Carolina mill mandated that "all children, members of a family above twelve years of age, shall work in the mill and shall not be excused from service therein without the consent of the superintendent for good cause." More often, pressure came from supervisors, who were personally responsible for keeping a quota of workers on hand. Jessie Lee Carter was four in 1905 when her family left their Tennessee farm for the Brandon Mill in Greenville. Six of her older brothers and sisters went to work right away; eight years later Jessie joined them. "When I got twelve years old, my uncle [who was a second hand in the spinning room] come to my daddy, and daddy let me quit school and go to work." During slack times children like Jessie Lee could be sent back to school, then called in again when the need arose.

For a large family with many mouths to feed, outside

pressure was often unnecessary. Lela Ranier's parents took her out of school when she was twelve and sent her to the mill. "Ma thought it was time. They thought maybe it would help 'em out, you know. They was making such a little bit. And they thought the little bit I made would help." Lacy Wright's father asked him to quit school when he reached twelve because his two oldest sisters had married and Lacy's father could not support the family on $1.25 a day. Other children realized the importance of their labor to the family's well-being and took it upon themselves to get a job. This was particularly true in families where the father was dead or disabled. Grover Hardin, for example, dropped out of school after the second grade. "I started out in the mill—the main reason—to help my mother. She wanted me to go to school until I got in the fifth grade. I told her, 'You need the help worse than I need the education, because I can get it later on, or I can do without it.' And so I went to work as quick as I possibly could. I started in as a sweeper."

Young People Want to Work in the Mill

Many parents wanted their children to stay in school, but youngsters often had their own plans. Ila Dodson insisted on quitting school when she was fourteen. "I wanted to make my own money. I done had two sisters go to work, and I seen how they was having money, and so I couldn't stand it no longer. My parents wanted me to go on to school, but I couldn't see that. Back then, didn't too many children go on to high school. It was just a common thing that when they'd get old enough, let them go to work. I like to worried them to death." Finally, Ila's parents relented and agreed to sign her worker's permit, required at that time in South Carolina for children under sixteen. But, she recalled, "Mama wouldn't even take me to town to get it, and my daddy wouldn't go with me. I said, 'Well, give me the Bible and give me a dime and I'll go get it.' A nickel streetcar fare up there and a nickel back, and I [took] the Bible because I had to prove my age."

Alice Evitt and Curtis Enlow also preferred mill work to schoolwork. "They'd let you go in there seven, eight years old," Alice recalled. "I'd go in there and mess around with my sisters; they'd be spinning. I liked to put up the ends and spin a little bit, so when I got twelve years old, I wanted to quit school. So I just quit and went to work, and I was twelve years old!" Both of Curtis's parents and two of his sisters worked in the card room at a Greenville mill. During summer vacation Curtis joined them there. "I was about thirteen years old, and I decided I would go to work. Well, I went to work, and my dad says if I quit when school started, he'd let me work. I went back to school, but I wasn't learning nothing—I didn't think I was. So I went and told him, and he says, 'All right, you ain't learning nothing. Well, you can go back to the mill.'"

Mamie Shue's parents had better luck keeping her in school. Although North Carolina's compulsory education law at the time required attendance only until age fourteen, Mamie's folks used it to frighten her into staying in school until she was sixteen. "I hated school all my life. But my parents told me if I didn't go to school, they'd put my daddy in jail. And I loved my daddy to death. So I went to school 'til I was sixteen." She did, however, start working after school in the spooling room. "I was fifteen when I started doing that. So when I was sixteen years old, they just give me a job, 'cause I could spool as good as the rest of them."

Young People Learn Quickly

Learning to "spool as good as the rest of them" was often a by-product of helping in the mills, but for those who had not started out as helpers—and even for some who had—learning constituted a memorable initiation into shop floor life. Few mills had a formal training program. Instead, "they would put you with someone to train you," or "your parents would take you in and train you theirself." Parents and surrogate parents took time out from their own work, which sometimes cost money out of their pockets, to help the young learn a trade. "That's the way the whole generation in Lando learned what they knowed," remembered John Guinn, "by the older generation." From the evidence of our interviews, adults did so willingly and well.

Mill managers expected children to master their jobs within a set length of time, usually about six weeks. During that period children worked for free or for a token wage. "I don't think they paid us anything to learn. But after we learnt, we got a job, a machine of our own." Some mills used this probationary period to take advantage of young people who were eager to work in the mill. Mary Thompson saw this happen in Greenville. "When I first went to work at Slater, they had boys to put up the warps on the back of the frames because they was heavy. They'd go out there in the country and get them boys and hire them and tell them they'd have to work six weeks without money. Well, that just tickled them to death, that they'd get a chance to work in a mill. And they'd work them six weeks, and they'd find something wrong with them and lay them off, and get other boys. And they run it a long time like that."

Almost all workers recalled proudly their ability to learn their jobs despite their youth. Naomi Trammell was an orphan when she went to work in the Victor Mill at Greer, South Carolina. "Well, I didn't know hardly about mill work, but I just went in and had to learn it. Really, I had to crawl up on the frame, because I wasn't tall enough. I was a little old spindly thing. I wasn't the only one, there's a whole place like that. And they had mothers and daddies [but they] wasn't no better off than I was. They had to learn us, but it didn't take me long to learn. They'd put us with one of the spinners and they'd show us how. It was easy to learn—all we had to do was just put that bobbin in there and put it up." Children learned quickly because most entry-level jobs required more dexterity than technical know-how. It took a while to be proficient, but most children could learn the rudiments of spinning, spooling, or doffing in a few weeks.

Portrait of a Jewish Immigrant Ghetto

Moses Rischin

The many immigrants that flooded America's shores in the late 1800s and early 1900s established ethnic ghettos in urban centers. Historian Moses Rischin describes one such ghetto—Manhattan's Lower East Side. Rischin writes that by the 1900s the Lower East Side housed Jews from Hungary, Galicia, Rumania, the Levantine, and the countries of Eastern Europe. He paints a vivid portrait of the tenements in which the immigrants had to live, the hardships tenement living imposed, and the major crime and violence that afflicted the area. According to Rischin, the old-world traditions and values to which the immigrants clung, the strength of their family ties, and their determined optimism helped them prosper despite the many obstacles that confronted them.

B y the first decade of the twentieth century, Manhattan's Lower East Side had become an immigrant Jewish cosmopolis. Five major varieties of Jews lived there, "a seething human sea, fed by streams, streamlets, and rills of immigration flowing from all the Yiddish-speaking centers of Europe." Clustered in their separate Jewries, they were set side by side in a pattern suggesting the cultural, if not the physical, geography of the Old World. Hungarians were settled in

---

Excerpted from *The Promised City: New York's Jews, 1870–1914*, by Moses Rischin. Copyright ©1962 by the President and Fellows of Harvard College. Reprinted with permission from the Harvard University Press.

the northernmost portion above Houston Street, along the numbered streets between Avenue B and the East River, once indisputably *Kleindeutschland*. Galicians lived to the south, between Houston and Broome, east of Clinton, on Attorney, Ridge, Pitt, Willett, and the cross streets. To the west lay the most congested Rumanian quarter, "in the very thick of the battle for breath," on Chrystie, Forsyth, Eldridge, and Allen streets, flanked by Houston Street to the north and Grand Street to the south, with the Bowery gridironed by the overhead elevated to the west. After 1907 Levantines, last on the scene and even stranger than the rest, for they were alien to Yiddish, settled between Allen and Chrystie streets among the Rumanians with whom they seemed to have the closest affinity. The remainder of the great Jewish quarter, from Grand Street reaching south to Monroe, was the preserve of the Russians—those from Russian Poland, Lithuania, Byelorussia, and the Ukraine—the most numerous and heterogeneous of the Jewries of Eastern Europe.

The leading streets of the Lower East Side reflected this immigrant transformation. Its most fashionable thoroughfare, East Broadway, bisected the district. To the north lay crammed tenements, business, and industry. To the south lay less crowded quarters where private dwellings, front courtyards, and a scattering of shade trees recalled a time when Henry, Madison, Rutgers, and Jefferson street addresses were stylish. . . .

Only after 1870 did the Lower East Side begin to acquire an immigrant Jewish cast. In the early years of the century a small colony of Jewish immigrants had lived there. Dutch, German, and Polish Jews had settled on Bayard, Baxter, Mott, and Chatham streets in the 1830's and 1840's. Shortly thereafter, German and Bohemian Jews took up quarters in the Grand Street area to the northeast and subsequently Jews of the great German migration augmented their numbers. Except for highly visible store fronts, Jews made little impress on the dominantly German and Irish neighborhood. But practically all East European immigrants arriving after 1870 initially found their way to the Lower East Side. Virtually penniless upon their arrival in the city, they were directed to the Jewish districts by representatives of the immigrant aid societies, or came at the behest of friends, relatives, or employers. . . .

Once the immigrants had come to rest on the Lower East Side, there was little incentive to venture further. Knowing no English and with few resources, they were dependent upon the apparel industries, the tobacco and cigar trades, and other light industrial employments that sprang up in the area or that were located in the adjacent factory district. Long hours, small wages, seasonal employment, and the complexity of their religious and social needs rooted them to the spot. It was essential to husband energies, earnings, and time. Lodgings of a sort, coffee morning and evening, and laundry service were available to single men for three dollars a month. Bread at two and three cents a pound, milk at four cents a quart, a herring for a penny or two, and apples at from one to five for a cent, depending on quality, were to be had. Accustomed to a slim diet, an immigrant could save much even with meager earnings and still treat himself to a bracing three-course Sabbath dinner (for fifteen cents). Thrift and hard work would, he hoped, enable him in time to search out more congenial and independent employment. Until new sections of the city were developed at the turn of the century only country peddlers were to stray permanently beyond the familiar immigrant quarters.

There was a compelling purpose to the pinched living. Virtually all immigrants saved to purchase steamship tickets for loved ones and many regularly mailed clothing and food parcels to dependent parents, wives, and children overseas. The power of home ties buoyed up the spirits of immigrants wedded to the sweatshop and peddler's pack, whose precious pennies mounted to sums that would unite divided families. Among the early comers women were relatively few, but the imbalance between the sexes soon was remedied. . . . Among the major ethnic groups of New York, only the Irish, 58 per cent female, exceeded the Jewish ratio. . . .

Old- and New-Law Tenements

Ever since the 1830's New York's housing problem had been acute. Manhattan's space limitations exacerbated all the evils inherent in overcrowding, and refinements in the use of precious ground only emphasized the triumph of material necessities over human considerations. New York's division of city lots into standard rectangular plots, 25 feet wide by 100 feet deep, made decent human accommodations impossible. In order to secure proper light and ventilation for tenement dwellers twice the space was needed, a prohibitive sacrifice considering real estate values. No opportunity was overlooked to facilitate the most economical and compact housing of the immigrant population. To the improvised tenements that had been carved out of private dwellings were added the front and rear tenements and, finally, the dumbbell-style tenement of 1879.

With the heavy Jewish migration of the early 1890's, the Lower East Side, still relatively undeveloped compared to the Lower West Side, became the special domain of the new dumbbell tenements, so called because of their shape. The six- to seven-story dumbbell usually included four apartments to the floor, two on either side of the separating corridor. The front apartments generally contained four rooms each, the rear apartments three. Only one room in each apartment received direct light and air from the street or from the ten feet of required yard space in the rear. On the ground floor two stores generally were to be found; the living quarters behind each had windows only on the air shaft. The air shaft, less than five feet in width and from fifty to sixty feet in length, separated the tenement buildings. In the narrow hallways were located that special improvement, common water closets. . . . As if the tenement abuses were not degrading enough, the absence of public toilet facilities in so crowded a district added to the wretched sanitation. It was reported that "in the evening every dray or wagon becomes a private and public lavatory, and the odor and stench . . . is perfectly horrible."

Conditions became almost unendurable in the summer months. Bred in colder and dryer climates, tenement inhabitants writhed in the dull heat. Added to the relentless sun were the emanations from coal stoves, the flat flame gas jets in lamps, and the power-producing steam boilers. Inevitably, roofs, fire escapes, and sidewalks were converted into sleeping quarters, while the grassed enclosure dividing Delancey Street and Seward Park supplied additional dormitory space. Late July and early August of 1896 were especially savage. . . .

Fire and the possibilities of fire brought added terror to the inhabitants of overcrowded tenements. "Remember that you live in a tenement house," warned insurance agents. In 1903, 15 percent of the tenements in the district still were without fire escapes. Of 257 fatalities in Manhattan fires between 1902 and 1909, 99 or 38 percent were on the Lower East Side, all victims of old-law tenements.

Few families could afford the privacy of a three- or four-room flat. Only with the aid of lodgers or boarders could the $10 to $20 monthly rental be sustained. The extent of overcrowding in the tenements, reported a witness before the United States Immigration Commission, was never fully known.

> At the hour of retiring, cots or folded beds and in many instances simply mattresses are spread about the floor, resembling very much a lot of bunks in the steerage of an ocean steamer. . . . The only way to properly determine the census of one of these tenements, would be by a midnight visit, and should this take place between the months of June and September, the roof of the building should not be omitted.

However trying tenement living proved to be for adults, for children it was stultifying, concluded a settlement worker. "The earlier years of the child are spent in an atmosphere which . . . is best described by a little girl, 'a place so dark it seemed as if there weren't no sky.'"

Evictions for nonpayment of rent and rent strikes were perennial. Uncertainty of employment, nonpayment of wages, unexpected obligations, dependents, and adversities contributed to the high incidence of evictions. . . .

Disease Takes Its Toll

Superficially, East European Jews seemed ill-prepared to contend with the demands that tenement living thrust upon them. "Their average stature is from five feet one inch to five feet three inches, which means that they are the most stunted of the Europeans, with the exception of the Hungarian Magyars." Shortest were the Galicians, tallest and sturdiest, the Rumanians. Undersized and narrow-chested, a high proportion were described as "physical wrecks." Centuries of confinement, habituation to mental occupations, chronic undernourishment, and a deprecation of the physical virtues ill-fitted them for heavy labor. . . .

Despite the trying conditions under which the immigrants lived, they showed a remarkable resistance to disease. With the highest average density of tenants per house in the city, the tenth ward had one of the lowest death rates. Indeed only a business ward and a suburban ward surpassed it in healthfulness. Dr. Annie Daniel, a pioneer in public health, volunteered her interpretation of this before the Tenement House Committee:

> The rules of life which orthodox Hebrews so unflinchingly obey as laid down in the Mosaic code . . . are designed to maintain health. These rules are applied to the daily life of the individuals as no other sanitary laws can be. . . . Food must be cooked properly, and hence the avenues through which the germs of disease may enter are destroyed. Meat must be "kosher," and this means that it must be perfectly healthy. Personal cleanliness is at times strictly compelled, and at least one day in the week the habitation must be thoroughly cleaned.

True, only some 8 percent of Russian Jewish families had baths, according to a study of 1902, and these often without hot water. Yet the proliferation of privately owned bathhouses in the city was attributable largely to the Jewish tenement population. "I cannot get along without a 'sweat' (Russian bath) at least once a week," insisted a newcomer. In 1880, one or two of New York's twenty-two bathhouses were Jewish; by 1897, over half of the city's sixty-two bathhouses (including Russian, Turkish, swimming, vapor, and medicated bathhouses) were Jewish. If standards of cleanliness were not as faithfully maintained as precept required, the strict regimen of orthodoxy, even when weakened, contributed to the immigrant's general well-being.

Nevertheless, close crowding and unsanitary conditions made all communicable diseases potentially contagious. Despite great apprehension between 1892 and 1894, Jewish immigrants did not carry to New York the cholera and typhus epidemics raging at the European ports of embarkation. But in 1899 the United Hebrew Charities became alarmed by the Board of Health's report on the mounting incidence of tuberculosis in the city. That Jewish immigrants might become easy victims of the "White Plague" was hardly to be doubted. "As many as 119 Jewish families have lived in one tenement house on Lewis Street within the past five years." Hundreds of flats had been occupied by fifteen successive families within a brief period. "Many of these houses are known to be hotbeds of disease, the very walls reeking with it." Increasingly, the dread disease with its cough and crimson spittle took its toll. . . .

Alcoholism, a prime contributor to poverty, ill-health, and mortality among other national groups, was unusual among Jewish immigrants. As Jews replaced the earlier inhabitants, the many saloons of the Lower East Side, trimmed with shields that proclaimed them "the workman's friend," declined. Those that survived drew few clients from a neighborhood addicted to soda water, "the life-giving drink"; they depended on the throng of transients that passed through the district. Jews did not abstain from drink. Yet only upon religious festivals and during the Sabbath ritual . . . did alcohol appear in the diet of most immigrants. In 1908, $1.50 a year for holiday and ritual wine seemed adequate for a family of six. "The Day of Rejoicing of the Law and the Day of Purim are the only two days in the year when an orthodox Jew may be intoxicated. It is virtuous on these days to drink too much, but the sobriety of the Jew is so great that he sometimes cheats his friends and himself by shamming drunkenness," Hutchins Hapgood noted. Jews habitually imbibed milder beverages. Russians were notorious tea drinkers. Hungarians were addicted to coffee. The less austere Galicians and Rumanians tippled mead and wine respectively. But in the New World all fell victim to the craze for seltzer or soda water with its purported health-giving powers. . . .

Neurasthenia and hysteria, however, took a heavy toll of victims. Their sickness was the result of a history of continual persecution and insecurity, intensified by the strains of settlement in unfamiliar surroundings. Diabetes, associated with perpetual nervous strain, was common. Suicide, rarely recorded among the small-town Jews of Eastern Europe, also found its victims in the tenements of New York. Despair, poverty, and the fears generated in the imagination led some immigrants to take their own lives. "Genumen di gez" (took gas) was not an uncommon headline in the Yiddish press. . . .

However desperate the straits in which Jewish immigrants found themselves, confirmed paupers among them were few. The rarity of alcoholism, the pervasiveness of the charitable impulse, the strength of ties to family . . . , and a deep current of optimism preserved the individual from such degradation. . . .

Crime and Violence Are Common

The major crime and violence in the area did not stem from the immigrants. They were its victims. The Lower East Side had always attracted much of the city's criminal element to its margins. By the last decades of the nineteenth century, it had shed the ferocity of earlier years when the "Bowery B'hoys" and the "Dead Rabbits" terrorized the area. But Mayor Hewitt's reform drive in 1887 inadvertently reinforced the district's frailties by forcing criminals and prostitutes from their accustomed uptown resorts into the less conspicuous tenements of the tenth ward, where they remained. . . .

Crime was endemic to the Lower East Side. The close collaboration between police officers, politicians, and criminals . . . had turned the district into a Klondike that replaced the uptown Tenderloin as a center of graft and illicit business. Invariably the culprits in these activities were not immigrants, but Americanized Jews learned in street-corner ways and shorn of the restraints of the immigrant generation. "It is not until they have become Americanized, have adapted themselves to the environment of the district and adopted its ways and vices, that they become full-fledged wretches," commented Dr. I.L. Nascher. In the early years of the twentieth century the effect of such conditions upon the young deeply disturbed those anxious for the public weal. In 1909 some 3000 Jewish children were brought before Juvenile Court and in the next few years Jewish criminals regularly made newspaper headlines. The appearance of an ungovernable youth after the turn of the century was undeniable and excited apprehension.

The violations of the law that characterized the immigrant community differed from the crimes of the sons of the immigrants. The former were an outgrowth of occupational overcrowding, poverty, and religious habits. Straitened circumstances contributed to the large number of cases of family desertion and nonsupport. Concentrated in marginal commerce and industry, Jews were prone to transgress the codes of commercial law. "The prevalence of a spirit of enterprise out of proportion to the capital of the community" gave rise to a high incidence of felonious larceny, forgery, and failure to pay wages. Peddlers and petty shopkeepers were especially vulnerable to police oppression for evading informal levies as well as formal licensing requirements. Legislation controlling business on Sunday found Jewish immigrants natural victims. In so congested a district, the breaking of corporation ordinances was unavoidable and the slaughtering of chickens in tenements in violation of the sanitary code proved to be a distinctly Jewish infraction.

The Bowery, way-station of derelicts, transients, and un-suspecting immigrants, attracted the less stable and wary of the immigrant girls. The dancing academies that sprang to popularity in the first decade of the twentieth century snared impetuous, friendless young women. Lured by promises of marriage, they soon were trapped by procurers for the notorious Max Hochstim Association and other white slavers who preyed upon the innocent and the un-suspecting. The appearance of prostitution, previously rare among Jewesses, alarmed the East Side.

The Lower East Side, girded by the Bowery with its un-savory establishments and Water Street with its resorts of ill-fame that catered to the seafaring trade, was surrounded by violence. Bearded Jews often were viciously assaulted by young hoodlums, both non-Jews and Jews, the area adja-cent to the waterfront being especially dangerous. . . .

A Change for the Better

Gradually the miseries and trials of adjustment were left behind. For those who had inhabited the hungry villages of Eastern Europe, the hovels of Berditchev, and the crammed purlieus of Vilna and Kovno, the factories and sweatshops of New York provided a livelihood and possible stepping-stone. Despite unsteady and underpaid employment, tene-ment overcrowding and filth, immigrants felt themselves ineluctably being transformed. The Lower East Side, with its purposeful vitality, found no analogue in the "leprous-looking ghetto familiar in Europe," commented the visiting Abbé Félix Klein. Physical surroundings, however sordid, could be transcended. Optimism and hope engulfed every aspect of immigrant life. For a people who had risen supe-rior to the oppressions of medieval proscriptions, the New York slums acted as a new-found challenge. Each passing year brought improvements that could be measured and appraised. Cramped quarters did not constrict aspirations. "In a large proportion of the tenements of the East Side . . . pianos are to be seen in the dingy rooms." And soon the phonograph was everywhere. "Excepting among the recent arrivals, most of the Jewish tenement dwellers have fair and even good furniture in their homes."

The East Europeans began to venture beyond the boundaries of the Lower East Side into other areas where employment was available on terms compatible with religious habits. Brooklyn's German Williamsburg district, directly across the East River, where Central European Jews had been established for some decades, was settled early. In the late 1880s a few clothing contractors set up sweatshops in the languid Scottish settlement of Brownsville, south and east of Williamsburg. The depression delayed further expansion for a decade despite the extension of the Fulton Street El in 1889. Then the tide could not be stemmed. Between 1899 and 1904 Brownsville's population rose from ten thousand to sixty thousand. Land values soared as immigrants came at the rate of one thousand per week. Lots selling for two hundred dollars in 1899 brought five to ten thousand dollars five years later. As the real estate boom revolutionized land values, many a former tailor was suddenly transformed into a substantial landlord or realtor who disdained all contact with shears and needles of bitter memory.

The mass dispersion of Jews from the Lower East Side to other parts of the city was in full swing in the early 1890's, as the more prosperous pioneers hastened to settle among their German coreligionists in Yorkville between 72nd and 100th streets, east of Lexington Avenue. For many a rising immigrant family in this period of swift change, it was judged to be a ten-year trek from Hester Street to Lexington Avenue.

The unprecedented flow of immigrants into the old central quarter, exorbitant rents, and the demolition of old tenements incidental to the building of parks, schools, and bridge approaches drastically reduced the area's absorptive capacity and spurred the search for new quarters. The construction of the Delancey Street approach to the Williamsburg Bridge in 1903 displaced 10,000 persons alone. The consolidation of the city and the growth and extension of rapid transit facilities connected what were once remote districts with the central downtown business quarters. In the new developments, cheaper land made possible lower rents that compensated for the time and expense of commuting. On Manhattan Island, the construction of underground transit opened to mass settlement the Dyckman tract in Washington Heights and the Harlem flats. The new subway also opened the East Bronx to extensive housing development. In Brooklyn, in addition to the heavy concentrations in Brownsville, Williamsburg, and South Brooklyn, Boro Park with "tropical gardens" and "parks" became increasingly accessible. Even distant Coney Island was brought into range by improved transit facilities.

With 542,061 inhabitants in 1910, the Lower East Side reached peak congestion. Thereafter, a decline set in. By 1916 only 23 percent of the city's Jews lived in the once primary area of Jewish settlement, compared to 50 percent in 1903 and 75 percent in 1892. By the close of the first decade of the twentieth century the Lower East Side had lost much of its picturesqueness. In tone and color, the ghetto was perceptibly merging with the surrounding city. East European Jews had scattered to many sections of the city and were swiftly becoming an integral, if not as yet a fully accepted, element in the life of the community.

Confronting the Elements: The Galveston Hurricane of 1900

Stephen Fox

One of America's deadliest disasters took place in the barrier island city of Galveston, Texas, in 1900, when a hurricane struck. According to historian and biographer Stephen Fox, Galveston's geography and location helped make it vulnerable to disaster. Fox recounts the horrific experiences during and after the storm of several Galveston families, all of whom suffered major losses. When the storm subsided, writes Fox, about one-third of the city was gone, torn and naked bodies were everywhere, and everyone and everything seemed to be in a state of chaos. Fox believes the storm should serve as a reminder to people not to underestimate the power of nature.

The dedicated weatherman and the terrible storm collided during the first week of September 1900. Isaac Cline, head of the U.S. Weather Bureau station in Galveston, Texas, was tracking a hurricane headed northwest through the Caribbean. Cline was fascinated by the young science of meteorology; after 18 years in the Weather Bureau, the last 11 in Galveston, he knew his field well. He expected this particular tropical cyclone, once it passed across Cuba, to run up the Eastern Seaboard of the United States. But it hit a stubborn high-pressure block over Florida and

Excerpted from "For a While . . . It Was Fun," by Stephen Fox, *Smithsonian*, September 1999. Reprinted with permission from the author.

veered west. The last information Cline received placed the storm south of Louisiana as it screamed across the Gulf of Mexico toward Galveston.

In the roll call of America's deadliest disasters, the body count becomes a grim Richter scale. Think of the 250 people killed in the Chicago fire of 1871, the 1,182 in the forest fire at Peshtigo, Wisconsin, in that same year, the 503 in the San Francisco earthquake of 1906, and then, even worse, the 1,836 lost in the Florida hurricane of 1928, and the 2,209 in the Johnstown flood of 1889. Yet the total deaths from these five catastrophes, taken together, amount to thousands fewer than the toll inflicted by the Galveston hurricane. . . .

Galveston: A Place Apart

It seemed obvious, afterward, that Galveston was vulnerable to calamity. The city perched on the eastern end of a barrier island—an exaggerated sandbar—a few miles off the Texas coast. Its main street, Broadway, bisected the city along the island's spine from northeast to southwest. At only 8.7 feet above sea level, Broadway offered the highest land in Galveston. Facing the Gulf, a wide, level beach ran the length of the island—27 miles of glistening white sand. To improve beach access, protective sand dunes up to 15 feet high had been removed along the city's edge. A traveler approaching Galveston from the Gulf first glimpsed its buildings seemingly floating in water, miragelike, with no land in sight.

Geography had made the place both attractive and dangerous. Constant sea breezes kept its summer weather more temperate than on the neighboring Texas mainland, drawing thousands of visitors. On the north side of town, on Galveston Bay, a new deepwater harbor promised a prosperous future. The federal government had recently spent $7 million on dredging and building jetties to deepen the channel from the Gulf into the bay. The harbor's cotton and grain exports had made Galveston, linked by railroad bridges to the mainland, the major banking and financial center between New Orleans and San Francisco. Impressive Victorian mansions were sprouting along Broadway, and new residential areas were spreading to the south and west, toward the unsheltered beach.

As resort, port and mercantile center, Galveston radiated a cosmopolitan ease. It included many citizens of German, French, Jewish and Italian ancestry, the first synagogue in Texas, and the seat of the state's oldest Roman Catholic diocese. The three leading Galveston merchant families were Protestant, Protestant, and Jewish. About 22 percent of the population was black. With power so diffused, nobody really dominated. The Artillery Club, formal and exclusive, lay adjacent to the fanciest whorehouse in town. People came to Galveston to enjoy themselves amid the oleanders and public gardens. Young swells took to oyster roasts, boat sails and fishing parties. For other tastes there were a dozen public gambling houses and many unregulated saloons that never closed. Bathhouses and refreshment stands lined the beach. Nude bathing, popular with both men and women, was restricted by city ordinance to late at night.

It was a place apart. Insularity bred both pride and complacency. At regular intervals, and particularly in 1875 and 1886, high water had swept over Galveston. These "overflows" were accepted as part of the island's uniqueness; with no great damage done, residents mopped up, cracked jokes and went on as before. Sensible proposals to build a protective dike around the city had gone nowhere. The famous beach sloped off to deep water so gradually that (it was understood) destructive waves from the Gulf would surely break and be spent before reaching shore.

A Warning Is Sounded

Isaac Cline, not a native, had his doubts. Thirty-eight years old at the time of the storm, he had grown up on a Tennessee farm and after college joined the agency that would become the Weather Bureau. While rising through various postings, he also earned a medical degree in order to study weather's effects on the human body, published and edited a newspaper, campaigned for temperance, and finished another doctorate, in philosophy and sociology. Cline met his wife, Cora, at the Baptist church where she served as organist. They had three young daughters, and Cora was well into her fourth pregnancy. Given Galveston's history of overflows and hurricanes, Isaac Cline had built his family an exceptionally strong frame house a few blocks from the beach, with the first floor built above the high water mark of 1875.

On Friday, September 7, he scanned the sky over the Gulf. For several days, he had been receiving storm-warning advisories from the Weather Bureau's headquarters in Washington, D.C. He had not observed, however, any of "the usual signs which herald the approach of hurricanes," he later wrote in a report on the storm.

He saw no "brick-dust sky," usually a reliable clue to approaching hurricanes in that area. Barometric pressure had fallen only slightly. The first real harbinger, a heavy swell from the southeast, arrived in the afternoon and continued through the night. The tide rose unusually high despite fighting strong opposing winds from the north and northwest.

At 4 o'clock Saturday morning, Cline's younger brother Joe, who roomed with the Clines and also worked at the weather office, awoke with an inexplicable sense of impending disaster. The backyard, he saw, was flooded. Alerted by his brother, Isaac drove his horse and wagon to the Gulf, where he timed the swells, and then went to his office in the city's commercial section. He found the barometer had dipped only a tenth of an inch since 8:00 P.M. the night before. He returned to the beach to gauge the tide and swells again before sending a telegram to Washington: "Unusually heavy swells from the southeast, intervals one to five minutes, overflowing low places south portion of city three to four blocks from beach. Such high water with opposing winds never observed previously." Again he went back to the beach, warning people to move inland to find shelter.

Light showers fell during the forenoon but didn't prevent thousands of people in fancy clothes from visiting the beach to watch the booming, crashing surf. Some even went swimming. Children played with driftwood boats in the flooded streets. "For a while," Louisa Christine Rollfing recalled, "even ladies were wading in the water, thinking it was *fun*. The children had a grand time." A holiday spirit persisted until the bathhouses, extended into the Gulf on pilings, broke apart. Then the streetcars stopped running. Moods and skies began to darken. ("Then it wasn't fun any more," Rollfing noted.)

The Hurricane Bears Down on Galveston

A heavy, persistent rain started around noon as the barometer plummeted and winds grew stronger. The hurricane was aiming dead at Galveston. All bridges to the mainland were underwater. Boats were useless in such conditions. No one could leave the island. The city's telephone, electric and gas utilities blinked out. People waded and swam away from the encroaching surf toward the slightly higher ground midtown. "The Gulf," Katherine Vedder Pauls said years later, "looked like a great gray wall about 50 feet high and moving slowly toward the island." Finally sensing danger, with the hurricane bearing down on them, Galvestonians were trapped on their sandbar.

At midafternoon Isaac Cline waded nearly two miles to home. The air was filled with flying bricks, masonry, roof slates, timbers, even entire roofs. Dodging those missiles, Cline also skirted downed electric wires, some sputtering and burning like long, sulfurous snakes. At home he found the water around his house waist deep. About 50 neighbors crowded in, drawn by the house's sturdy construction. When Joe arrived, the brothers stepped outside. Should they seek shelter inland? Isaac was loathe to move Cora, pregnant and ill at the time. Aside from the wind and water, the airborne debris might harm his three little girls. The house was built to stand. A sudden rise in water forced the decision to stay put.

Thousands of desperate individual dramas unfolded. Henry Johnson, a black laborer recently arrived in Galveston, took refuge in his boardinghouse near the center of town. The wind rocked the house back and forth "like a barrel," Johnson remembered. When the back porch collapsed, with the house likely to follow, he fled outside. Neighborhood men helped people leave by pushing clumps of debris out of the way with long poles. White or black, Johnson said later, it made no difference; everyone was treated alike in the crisis. Someone took him to the Union Railroad Passenger Depot, a substantial public building. It was already crowded with refugees and their animals. For hours people kept straggling in, many naked and bleeding, with broken arms, some crying a wild gibberish. Windows broke but somehow the depot itself held.

Giuseppe and Concetta Rizzo, immigrants from Italy, lived near the beach in the east end of town. Their grandson, Jimmy La Coume, a lifelong Galvestonian now 71 years old, recounts the story as it has passed down through the family. One of Giuseppe's brothers came to the house in a rowboat. He only had room for Concetta and her daughter, Jimmy's mother, then 7 years old. "OK," said Giuseppe, "come back for me." Before the boat could return, the house was swept away and Giuseppe was lost. Concetta and her daughter went to the nearby Sacred Heart Church, where the dome soon collapsed, and then to Saint Mary's University where, on the second floor, they rode out the storm, wondering about Giuseppe's fate.

The Hurricane Crests

Terrifying sounds came in relentless waves and pulses. The wind shrieked and whistled, driving the rain and groundwater. Whitecapped waves six feet high coursed up Broadway. The slanting rain, cold and sharp, felt like needles or glass splinters in the face. When slate shingles were torn off a roof, to the people cowering inside, it sounded like a freight train passing over the house. The buildings themselves seemed to be crying amid the cacophony of breaking glass, falling walls, rattling tin roofs, and wooden rain cisterns rolling and tumbling. The spire of St. Patrick's Church, the tallest structure on the island, rocked and swayed for hours, then fell in a wind gust so loud that nobody heard the tower crash. In momentary lulls even more terrible sounds became audible: cries for help, usually unanswered and unanswerable, from the dying and drowning.

The storm leveled all social distinctions, but it could not erase all cultural differences. The wife of Clarence Ousley, editor of the *Galveston Tribune*, had never truly accepted her neighbors the Niccolinis because—as Ousley's daughter Angie later put it—"they spoke English with difficulty and also used a trifle too much garlic in their cooking." The Niccolinis, "all extremely vocal," arrived seeking shelter. The Ousleys gave them a bedroom of their own.

A few blocks from Isaac Cline's house, the Ursuline Convent and Academy took in nearly a thousand refugees. When part of the north wall fell in, about a hundred blacks started to shout and sing in "camp meeting" style. Whites unaccustomed to this kind of worship grew restive and irritated. Tempers, drawn so taut, started fraying. Mother Superioress Joseph rang the chapel bell, hushed the crowd, and told them that God would hear their silent prayers, from their hearts, even through the hurricane. Everyone settled down to endure the storm together.

Shortly after 5 o'clock, the anemometer at the Weather Bureau recorded gusts of 100 miles an hour, then blew away. Isaac Cline later guessed the wind peaked at 120 miles an hour. George McNeir, captain of the sloop *Cora Dean* in Galveston Harbor, was sure it actually hit 150 miles an hour. When McNeir went aloft to clear mastheads in the ship's rigging, a tremendous gust of wind tore his feet from the lines and hung him out horizontally, like a pennant, until the gust subsided and he could continue climbing.

The hurricane crested in the early evening. "As darkness came on," Walter Davis later wrote his mother, "the Terror increased." With the storm roaring at its height, and no electricity or gas, people relied on candles and kerosene lanterns—

and occasional flashes of lightning—to see by. Otherwise the blackness was complete, adding visual isolation to already-desperate straits. The wind shifted to northeast and then east, reinforcing the building tide from the Gulf. A massive storm wave broke on the island. At 8:30 the barometer bottomed out at 28.48 inches, the lowest pressure recorded up to that time at any Weather Bureau station.

One Family's Ordeal

Floating clumps of wreckage, joining and separating, careened around and slammed into buildings. The Cline house held up under this fearsome battering until Isaac, bunkered with his family on the second floor, saw a long piece of streetcar trestle crash squarely against the side of his home. The house creaked, tipped over into the water and started breaking into pieces. Joe Cline, holding his two older nieces by their hands, turned his back toward a window, pushed from his heels, and broke through the glass and storm shutters. They found themselves floating on a piece of the house. No other survivors could be seen.

Isaac, Cora and their youngest daughter were thrown against a chimney, then into the bottom of the wreckage. Isaac, pinned down, expected to die. "It is useless to fight for life," he remembered thinking. "I will let the water enter my lungs and pass on." He lost consciousness; but by some mysterious shifting of the ruins he was propelled upward and came to with his body wedged between heavy floating timbers. During a flash of lightning he caught sight of his youngest girl on wreckage a few feet away. A few minutes later, another flash revealed Joe and the other children. Cora was gone, somewhere down below. The surviving Clines struggled onto the best piece of flotsam they could find.

For the next three hours they drifted out of control, switching from clump to clump as their fragile rafts broke apart. Placing the children in front of them, the men turned their backs to the wind, holding up planks for puny shelter. Still they were repeatedly hit and bloodied. An especially heavy blow would knock them into the water and they would struggle back to the children.

At one point, by a miracle beyond explanation, the family dog—a fine hunting retriever—appeared from nowhere and clawed his way onto the wreckage. The dog frantically smelled each of the Clines and, unsatisfied, dashed to the edge. To Joe it seemed that he was looking for Cora. The dog poised to jump and resume his hopeless search; Joe shouted and lunged for him, but he darted away and was gone. "I can almost believe to this day that animals have superhuman senses in time of danger," Joe wrote years later. "We never saw him any more."

Both humans and animals performed heroic feats under pressure. Daniel Ransom, a paperhanger and a strong swimmer, spent 2½ hours in the water, leading and carrying 45 people to safety at a large brick building. At Saint Mary's Infirmary, Joseph Corthell, a harbor pilot, and his brothers used a lifeboat to ferry more than 150 people from the neighborhood to the hospital—until their boat sank. Also at Saint Mary's, a medical student, Zachary Scott, carried more than 200 patients from outbuildings to the main structure, wading through water that eventually reached a depth of six feet.

Each hero had to make the essential fateful decision: whether to hang back in self-preservation or dare the howling maelstrom, at grave personal risk, to try to save others. Harry Maxson, 14 years old, lived with his family on the west side of town. Their house was the last remaining refuge in the neighborhood. Late that night, during a lull, Harry raised a kitchen window and listened. "I heard what I didn't want to hear," he wrote years later, "a woman yelling 'for God Sake come and save us, our home is falling to pieces.' I shut the window as quickly as I could and tried to forget that woman's voice. It was awful so far away and still so penetrating; it made me shake all over." In the next lull he opened the window again and heard the voice cry, "I can see the lights in your house." That brought it home: he had to go.

Harry told his father but could not bear to say goodbye to his mother, and set out with another man. They rode the waves toward the woman's house, which was floating and breaking apart. Inside were 13 children and 23 adults. Harry shouted that they would take the kids first, calling on each man in the house to accompany them with one child. "The longest silence I ever heard," Harry recalled, "but no one came out or even said 'boo.'. . . The men in the house were paralyzed with fear." At last a large black man appeared with a white baby, followed by the other men carrying children and some of their wives. They struggled single file, each man holding on to the next, to the Maxson house. Harry and several men undertook another trip to rescue those who remained.

The Clines drifted out to sea. They saw no houses, lights or people for two hours. Then the wind shifted to the south and blew them back to shore; they landed only 300 yards from where they had started. All were frightfully bruised; one of the girls was barely alive. They dragged themselves into a house with no roof or ceiling, and collapsed for the night, bone-weary and hurting.

A Devastating Aftermath

Sunday arrived with a beautiful sunrise and calm ocean. As survivors crawled out, looked around and got their bearings, the magnitude of the disaster was slowly revealed. It was too much to take in quickly. "There was little talk," Katherine Vedder Pauls recalled. "All were stunned by the catastrophe." About one-third of the city, mostly in sections near the Gulf, was completely gone: no houses or even streets were left, only scoured sand. Along the upper edge of that vast emptiness, a three-mile windrow of wreckage, up to two stories high and 100 feet thick, had been formed: a mass of lumber, debris and mangled corpses. In the rest of the city, hardly a building was left undamaged, and many had disappeared altogether. More than 3,600 houses were destroyed.

The retreating water left a thick slime, rank and penetrating. In the harbor, the steamship *Roma* had torn loose from its mooring, crashed into two large piers, smashed broadside through all three railroad bridges and lay stranded in mud. Docks, warehouses and grain elevators were wrecked or severely damaged. Boats of all sizes were scattered around. With telephone and telegraph wires down, one of the few boats still seaworthy was dispatched to the mainland bearing the first grim news.

Bodies, torn and naked, were everywhere: in yards and streets, caught in trees and random structures, floating in the bay. "Put your foot down," Henry Johnson recalled, "an' you put it on a dead man." Some kept their children indoors to avoid the searing sights. In one house, 13 of 15 people had died. One family lost 28 relatives; another, 42. "Every one here seems *stunned*," Eleanor Hertford wrote her future husband, "and you never see any emotion displayed of any kind, every one is perfectly calm! We all seem to have gone through so much, that we seem beyond tears!" Survivors told each other matter-of-factly of crushing family losses. "All gone," they said, all gone.

The first estimate on Sunday was 500 dead. Bodies were borne on stretchers to temporary morgues. As corpses kept turning up, the estimate went to 3,000. The saturated ground prevented mass burial. Polite formalities had to be suspended; bodies were piled on wagons without ceremony, taken to barges and dumped at sea. When they floated back to shore, immediate cremation became necessary. (In the 80-degree weather, the foul stench of putrefying flesh quickly became overwhelming.) For a month, about 70 bodies a day were found among the piles of wreckage. Most of them were simply doused with oil and burned on the spot with the debris. The soundest contemporary estimate placed the final toll at 6,000 in Galveston, a thousand elsewhere on the island, and another thousand on the mainland: a total of at least 8,000 dead, a figure accepted in recent years in studies published by the National Oceanic and Atmospheric Administration.

In the immediate chaos that followed the storm, some

looting took place. Giuseppe Rizzo's body was found with $500 missing from his money belt. An emergency guard force was soon overwhelmed. Robbers pillaged through property, staged daylight holdups, and cut the ears and swollen fingers from corpses for the jewelry. Looters were shot on sight: perhaps a dozen, perhaps scores. No records were kept. "Tuesday I went round with a pistol," Sarah Davis Hawley wrote her mother, "as so many people had been killed while trying to protect their things. Ah you can never realize the awfulness of it all." Gunfire punctuated the nights. Reports of looting continued until Thursday, five days after the hurricane, when martial law was officially imposed to restore order to the city.

Life Goes On

Several days after the storm, Ella Sealy Newell heard a boy whistling. "We all stopped to listen," she noted. "It was the first joyous sound we had heard; anything gay or bright in dress, or manner, seems utterly out of place." As time passed, most Galvestonians absorbed their losses, picked through the debris and resumed living. Isaac Cline, with Cora still missing, went back to work with his head bandaged and a foot poulticed. In his formal report, he recounted his own experiences in flat, declarative tones. "Among the lost," he wrote, "was my wife." As to the future, "I believe that a sea wall, which would have broken the swells, would have saved much loss of both life and property." Cora's body was found a few weeks later, identified by her engagement ring.

Over the next decade, a seawall was finally built and most of the city's grade was raised. Hurricanes have continued to pound Galveston every now and then but without the disastrous losses of the 1900 storm. That dreadful catastrophe reminds us of the folly of underestimating the power of nature, even in the most modern of circumstances. Its upshot also suggests the stubborn resilience of human will in the face of calamity.

CHAPTER 3

Politics and Reform

AMERICA'S DECADES

Roosevelt in Charge

A.E. Campbell

In the view of historian A.E. Campbell, author and long-time fellow of Keble College, Oxford, England, Theodore Roosevelt was quick to grasp the essence of presidential power and knew just how to use it to his best advantage. Roosevelt, he contends, believed in scientific government and in reform but was not as dangerously radical as the conservatives of his time thought him to be. Campbell attributes Roosevelt's strong reputation in foreign affairs as much to the inactivity of Roosevelt's predecessors as to his actual accomplishments. Some historians believe that Roosevelt's accomplishments were more public relations than models for change. Campbell does not disagree totally but argues that perhaps Roosevelt gave the people what they wanted—"a voice in the world"—no more and no less.

Roosevelt did not spring up at once as the leader of a fully recognised Progressive movement. His position in 1901 was quite different. He had come to the presidency by accident; he had not won it in his own right. His political credit was less for that reason—nobody owed him anything. Moreover, the presidency was far from being the central office it has since become. Members of both houses of Congress cherished their independence, their leaders were powerful political figures, and the techniques of co-

Excerpted from *America Comes of Age: The Era of Theodore Roosevelt*, by A.E. Campbell (New York: American Heritage, 1971). Copyright ©1971 by A.E. Campbell. Reprinted with permission from the author.

operation between the White House and Capitol Hill were primitive. Convention, indeed, forbade too close an intimacy. No President since Jefferson had addressed Congress in person, a convention not to be broken until Woodrow Wilson's time. And, while the President could propose and even draft legislation, the amount of direct support he could give to his proposals was not great.

The two houses of Congress were very different in character, more so than they have since become, and they maintained a lively rivalry, in which the Senate, unlike most other upper chambers, more than held its own. The members of the House of Representatives were chosen by direct popular elections; the members of the Senate were not. Until 1913, when a reform which was one of the last achievements of the Progressive movement changed the rule, they were elected by state legislatures. This had the effect—as the framers of the Constitution had intended—of removing the Senate from the influence of democracy, to some extent at least. It made it easier for powerful and wealthy men to find their way to the Senate without fighting their way up through the lower reaches of politics, and easier to stay there when they arrived. The politics of small groups is significantly different from the politics of large ones, and the Senate was a small group. It was also an undisciplined group. Presided over by the Vice-President, who was not a member, the Senate had a long tradition of egalitarianism. It was easy to frustrate business and hard to expedite it. A handful of leading and influential Senators dominated the proceedings by agreement among themselves, and one gained influence by conforming to and manipulating the rules of this club. Senators were individualists more than party regulars. They were also generally deeply conservative. The conservatism of the Senate was a powerful obstacle to reform by legislation.

The House of Representatives could hardly have been more different. Its membership was much larger, directly elected, and subject to re-election every two years. The business of the House would have fallen into chaos under rules as lax as those of the Senate. It was presided over by a Speaker, ordinarily chosen by the members of the majority party. The post-war period, during which major issues of principle were hard to find, paradoxically increased the pressure for party regularity, and two Speakers gave it institutional form. T.B. Reed of Maine—'Tsar Reed'—formulated the rules which gave virtually autocratic power to the Speaker and to the chairmen of committees, who were also nominees of the majority party. When Reed retired from the Speakership and from the House of Representatives (on a point of conscience; he was unwilling to preside over a party which was committed, he believed, to imperialism), he was succeeded by Joseph Cannon—'Uncle Joe'—of Illinois. Cannon, who held office as Speaker from 1901 to 1911, had even more power than Reed, and he used it more and more ruthlessly as his own highly conservative views became increasingly out of tune with his times. In 1910 a revolt in the House by a combination of Democrats and Radical Republicans deprived the Speaker of much of his power, and no Speaker since has achieved Cannon's importance. But, whether because Reed prized procedure and party regularity above all, or because Cannon was a cunning, ruthless conservative, the House in the first decade of the 20th century was not an easy body through which to pass reform measures. It was not by accident that the demand for reform of Congress came to rank high on many a Progressive list of reforms.

On Roosevelt's side it may be questioned how great his own faith in legislation was. In a country so various as the United States, the charge that any piece of legislation was 'special', in the sense that it benefited a certain group rather than the people or the nation as a whole, was easily made and damaging. It was a charge to which the Democratic Party had, perhaps, become more sensitive than the Republican, but in the years before Roosevelt took office more of a President's time was taken in vetoing private bills than in constructing positive legislation. All his life Roosevelt was apt to place more faith in the co-operation of honest men than in legislative rules. At any rate it was clear to him that legislation could not be his first resort. First he had to win the confidence of Congressmen, or some power with which to impress them, or both.

Roosevelt Tames the Tycoons

Roosevelt's claim to political stature rests on the speed with which he grasped the essence of presidential power, the ways in which it could be exploited, and the occasions on which it could be successfully used. One such occasion arose in 1902. The railway systems running out of Chicago across the Northwest had been steadily consolidated, until by 1900 they consisted of two great groups, one controlled by James J. Hill, with the support of John Pierpont Morgan, the other by E.H. Harriman. Hill and Harriman were among the greatest names in the railway world. Morgan was supreme in finance. A furious battle developed between the two groups for control of the entire system, a battle which ended in a compromise. All the railways would be brought together under a holding company—the Northern Securities Company—and the contestants would share control and profits.

In its nature this deal was no different from many that had taken place successfully in the past. What made it different, as Roosevelt grasped, was its scale, the size and reputation of the financial interests involved, and the fact that the public were particularly sensitive to railway mergers. It was Roosevelt's merit to see that the very scale of the merger made the parties involved more vulnerable, not less. There was in existence a law against such mergers—the so-called Sherman Act of 1890. It was a weak law, and it had largely fallen into disuse under Cleveland and McKinley. Roosevelt instructed his Attorney-General to bring an action against the Northern Securities Company, and when the case came before the Supreme Court he won a narrow victory. By a vote of five to four, the Justices decided against the company. (Justice Holmes wrote the minority opinion, the first of his famous dissents, and a promising friendship with Roosevelt came to an end.) The financial world was outraged, but the public applauded. It is doubtful whether the practical effect of this decision on the conduct of the railways was great. It is even doubtful whether that conduct had been particularly bad. Both Hill and Harriman, whatever their defects, were dedicated railway men, and Morgan personified the rigid, upright tradition of conventional banking. These men were not freebooters; they *were* too powerful. What Roosevelt accomplished, all he needed to accomplish, perhaps all he wanted to accomplish, was to demonstrate that trusts must take notice of the national interest, and that they could be held to account by a sufficiently active and courageous President.

Yet Roosevelt was not anxious to undertake suits. His real desire, increasingly so as he remained in office, was to control the trusts, not to break them up. He had a keen sense of the value to the country of the energy and skill of big businessmen. He did not fear or hate or even particularly distrust them. He believed that they needed control, and that they would yield to control only when they saw that they could do nothing else. It was above all the task of the President to make that plain. Yet when it was made plain, the practical business of devising means of control remained. Roosevelt's preferred means was the development of control commissions staffed by non-political experts. Here he reflected one element in the Progressive movement: the belief in scientific government. He believed that independent commissions, staffed by men who knew their jobs and were respected both by the public and by industrialists, would be the best means of controlling industry, and he did so because he believed that the experts would agree among themselves. The social scientist's belief that if you accumulate more facts they will lead openminded men towards agreement was apparent here.

The scope of his legislative success shows the limitations which were still felt by most people to be important. He achieved passage of a law giving workmen's compensation to all government employees—but government employees were debarred from the right to strike, and so, it could be held, needed special protection. He pushed through a factory inspection law and a child labour law in the District of Columbia—but the nation's capital was a federal enclave in which laws could only be made by Congress; hence the law implied no enlargement of federal power. He obtained a law compelling the use of safety appliances on the railways—an exercise of federal control over interstate commerce which roused the public interest in a special way, for almost anyone might be a railway passenger.

Roosevelt Takes Independent Action

Roosevelt found it hardest to achieve what he most wanted: the ability to intrude in the activity of major industries before they had done harm and not afterwards. His demand for legislation broke on the rock of Senate conservatism. His only resource was to continue with prosecution under the Sherman Act, sometimes with formal success, but not always with practical effect. Something, however, could be done when industry wanted the support of government. The railways, for example, were suffering from the ability of powerful customers to demand rebates on the rates for freighting their goods; so, of course, were the smaller customers with less bargaining power. With the support of many railway leaders, the Elkins Act of 1903, which forbade rebates, was passed. Though it was not very effective, it did something to show that the front of big business was not entirely solid, and so helped to allay public alarm. Moreover, when it was shown not to be effective it was made more so by the passage of the Hepburn Act of 1906. The passage of one act made the passage of the next easier.

There were limitations also in Roosevelt's own ideas of what was necessary. We should not attribute to him ideas that are more modern than his time. Although he was regarded as dangerously radical by conservatives in his day, he did not, for example, support the campaign led by Senator Beveridge for a national law governing the hours and conditions of child labour. Outrageous though the exploitation of child labour was, in this his instinct may have been sound. The various circumstances in which children were employed in different areas of the country at different stages of economic development would have made an effective, or even a just, national law almost impossible to draft.

On occasion the President had an opportunity for independent action. In 1902 a prolonged strike broke out in the anthracite mining region of Pennsylvania and the neighbouring states. . . . The mines were in the hands of many small owners, loosely held together in a variety of agreements with the railways that took their coal to East Coast markets, railways which themselves owned some of the mines. The miners had hitherto never been adequately organised, and when John Mitchell, the outstanding leader of the United Mineworkers of America, moved into the anthracite regions, the owners resisted strongly.

Roosevelt's strategy was to confer with both sides, and even to bring them together—not formally, for the owners would not admit Mitchell's right to speak for their employees, but under the guise of a fact-finding exercise. He succeeded in having the dispute turned over to an arbitration commission, which worked out a suitable compromise. There can be no doubt of Roosevelt's considerable success. He gained the credit for ending the strike, he had set a useful if modest precedent for his preferred method of 'impartial' adjudication of industrial disputes, he had shown himself undaunted by 'big labour' as earlier by 'big business', and he had got across the image of himself as the guardian of the public interest, the effective spokesman of the whole nation. The identification of Roosevelt with the cause of national unity had been enhanced.

The Conservation Reforms

The sense of national unity both as essential for itself and as essential if many other purposes were to be achieved, was central to much Progressive thinking. No doubt a defensive element played an important part. If action were not taken quickly, certain possibilities would be closed for ever. This was a cry which rallied a larger body of support than any single reform could do. In no area was it more effective than in one with which Roosevelt's name is especially connected—conservation. At the end of the 19th century, men first became conscious that the natural resources of the United States were not inexhaustible, and also that there were rival demands on them. At that time the most obvious problems were those of water and forests. As early as 1873 the American Association for the Advancement of Science had drawn attention to the squandering of forest land. In 1891 the

President Theodore Roosevelt

Forest Reserve Act was passed, which authorised the President to set aside public forest land as not for sale. Some forty-five million acres of land were withdrawn by Harrison, Cleveland, and McKinley. Roosevelt withdrew 150 million acres, and added another eighty-five million in Alaska and the Northwest, withdrawn until their resources had been surveyed by the government. Equally important, he had the national forests transferred from the Department of the Interior to the Department of Agriculture, where the Forest Bureau, under the father of modern conservation, Gifford Pinchot, administered them on scientific lines. Here, as so often, Roosevelt's chief contribution was to give encouragement and publicity and effective support to men already active in the field. If public concern had not already existed he could have done nothing. But he could and did tip the balance against exploitation and in favour of conservation. His successors were to show how the movement could flag lacking that steady support from the man at the heart of government.

Water was perhaps a more tricky problem even than forests. Much of the timber land of the country had fallen into the hands of big lumber companies. These had little concern for national amenities, but out of concern for their own livelihood they had some regard for replanting where they felled. Lumber companies became scientific foresters out of mere self-interest. Farmers are less farsighted. By the time the conservation movement became effective, much permanent damage had been done to arid regions. It was in the West that the need for control was greatest; but the West was also the home of intransigent individualism. Fortunately, this was a matter where different interests worked against each other, and so a matter in which Roosevelt could intervene. For example, cattle men, who deeply distrusted government intervention to restrict their use of grazing land, needed government help with their water problems. The Carey Land Act of 1894 had been the first attempt to deal with the problem. It allowed states in desert areas to sell land for purposes of reclamation and irrigation; but the act only succeeded in demonstrating that this was a problem too large for private enterprise. Roosevelt took the next step in pushing the Reclamation Act of 1902, which provided that irrigation should be paid for by the proceeds of public land sales, and that it should be under federal government control. The great dams of the American West, supplying and controlling water for several states, were built under this act. At the same time Roosevelt was active in the establishment of a whole range of national parks and nature reserves. But perhaps most important in this field of activity was that he set up the government machinery—the bureaux within the Departments of Agriculture and the Interior—which could be used and developed by his successors.

Roosevelt Plays Mediator

Foreign policy is by its nature the President's preserve and it was one in which Roosevelt took a lively interest. Certainly treaties with foreign powers must be approved by the Senate, and so become a matter of party politics. . . but not all foreign policy is a matter of treaties. . . . Here it is worth noting that the international position of the United States was still one of such security that the President, in many respects, had large scope for activity—or, of course, inactivity. It was because his predecessors had become so inactive that Theodore Roosevelt was able to make so much of a mark in foreign affairs. In the Western hemisphere, shrewdly judging that there would be no effective European reaction, he acted strongly, largely at the expense of Britain and Canada, even while he protested—sincerely no doubt—his devotion to the idea of Anglo-Saxon solidarity. He pushed through the acquisition of the Panama Canal Zone by the United States, and set in hand the building of the canal; but he also insisted that it should be American-controlled, and that Britain should relinquish any share in its control.

Elsewhere his activities were more circumscribed, but just because the United States was yet seen to be remote from international politics, the President's role as a mediator and arbitrator could be enlarged. What could be done to enlarge it, Roosevelt did. At the end of the Russo-Japanese War he invited the two countries to conduct their negotiations in the United States, he was lavish with advice to both, and he took much credit for the Treaty of Portsmouth, New Hampshire, which finally ended the war. When an international crisis developed over Morocco in 1905, he sent a delegation to the conference that settled the quarrel—as he was entitled to do but need not have done—and his influence with the German Kaiser contributed to a peaceful outcome. In all this, active though he was, Roosevelt was taking no risk for his country. The United States was put neither to danger, nor to expense. What was at risk was Roosevelt's reputation and that of his office, and these he succeeded in protecting and enhancing.

A Final Analysis

The charge most often brought against Roosevelt is that his successes were not real. They were merely in the field of public relations. They left nothing behind. Still further, Roosevelt was interested in public relations more than in accomplishment. For all his vigorous speeches, he seldom committed himself to a battle not easily won. There is something in the charges, but it may be that what the American people most wanted then was not change, but a voice in the world; and a voice Roosevelt gave them.

In his day the convention established by George Washington that a President may not hold office for more than two terms, was still only a convention. It remained a convention until Franklin Roosevelt broke it; but was so powerful a convention that Theodore Roosevelt did not even consider breaking it, although his first term had been incomplete and not won by election. Inevitably, therefore, he suffered the decline of power that afflicts presidents when their tenure is known to be nearly over. But his departure from office in 1909 was welcomed by conservatives with a sense of relief. That single fact perhaps defines his stature as a reformer.

America's Workforce: The Impoverished in a Wealthy Society

John M. Blum, William S. McFeely, Edmund S. Morgan, Arthur M. Schlesinger Jr., Kenneth M. Stampp, and C. Vann Woodward

In the early years of the 1900s, America experienced a great deal of growth—in the economy, in the population, in industry, and in confidence. And, as the historians who authored the following selection explain, so did the gap between the workers and the business elite. Organized labor grew, the authors write, but the unions did little to help African Americans, women, or the scores of immigrants flowing into the country daily. According to the authors, fear of losing jobs to these groups heightened prejudice against Asians, African Americans, and southern and eastern Europeans and helped foster racial segregation and restrictions on immigration.

John M. Blum, professor of history at such universities as Yale in New Haven, Connecticut, and Cambridge and Oxford in England, is the author and editor of numerous books about several different periods of American history. William S. McFeely is an academician, historian, and critically acclaimed author. He won the Pulitzer Prize in biography for *Grant: A Biography*. Scholar and writer of American history Edmund S. Morgan is a recognized expert on the Puritans and the Revolutionary War period of America.

Excerpted from *The National Experience: A History of the United States Since 1865*, part 2, 8th edition, by John M. Blum, William S. McFeeley, Edmund S. Morgan, Arthur M. Schlesinger Jr., Kenneth M. Stampp, and C. Vann Woodward. Copyright ©1993 by Harcourt, Inc. Reprinted by permission of the publisher.

Popular historian Arthur M. Schlesinger Jr. has served as special assistant to two American presidents and has been associated with numerous universities and institutes. He won the Pulitzer Prize in history for his books *The Age of Jackson* and *A Thousand Days: John F. Kennedy in the White House*. Kenneth M. Stampp has held professorships at a number of universities in the United States and abroad and has authored and edited several successful books. Pulitzer Prize winner C. Vann Woodward is a well-known historian of the American South. One of this century's foremost scholars in his field, he is best known for his work *Mary Chestnut's Civil War*.

When the twentieth century began, the prodigious material developments of the preceding several decades had transformed society. Yet almost all of those in positions of authority or influence in government, industry, the professions, even labor and farm organizations had been born during the years before the Civil War when the United States was still primarily a rural country. By 1901 the nation had changed profoundly, as had its problems, which were often perplexing to men and women who had grown up in an earlier age. Some Americans were nostalgic for that past as they remembered it. Others rejoiced in modernity but were eager to control its course and effects. Both of those attitudes pointed, though in different ways, to the desirability, even the exigency, of altering conditions as they had become.

As Americans were increasingly aware, they had yet to accommodate to the social and cultural changes stimulated by industrial and urban growth. They had yet to adjust their laws and their techniques of government to an age of large and complex private organizations. Americans had yet to recognize the international implications of their national wealth. They had yet to fulfill their national promise of individual liberty, opportunity, and dignity for all men and women.

The unprecedented productivity of the economy made comfort potentially available to all Americans. That possibility in turn highlighted the striking contrasts between the few and the many, the white-skinned and the dark, the urban and the rural—the striking contrast between national aspiration and national achievement. Out of an awareness of that contrast, out of the tensions of material development, out of a consciousness of national mission, there emerged the efforts at adjustment and reform that constituted the progressive movement, a striving by men and women of goodwill to understand, improve, and manage the society in which they lived.

A Time of Growth and Prosperity

During the first two decades of the twentieth century, the number of people in the United States, their average age, and their average per capita wealth all increased. In that period total national income almost doubled, and average per capita income rose from $450 to $567 a year. Though by the standards of the 1990s about 40 percent of Americans were then poor, growth in and of itself gave confidence to a generation who tended to measure progress in terms of plenty.

There were some 76 million Americans in 1900. . . . Advances in medicine and public health, resulting in a declining death rate, accounted for most of the increase. It was accompanied by a continuing movement of people within the United States. In the West the rate of growth was highest—along the Pacific slope, population more than doubled. But growth occurred everywhere, especially in the cities, where it proceeded six and a half times as fast as in rural areas. The cities, in the pattern of the past, absorbed thousands of rural folk as well as almost all of the 14.5 million immigrants who came largely from central and southern Europe in the years 1900–15. Usually swarthy and often unlettered, ordinarily Catholics or

Jews, these newcomers differentiated the cities further and further from the patterns of life that rural America remembered and revered. . . .

Spurred by the pace of private investment, the nation recovered from the depression of the 1890s. During the first two decades of the century, capital investment rose over 250 percent and the total value of the products of industry rose 222 percent. But not all groups shared equally in national wealth. Though unemployment became negligible, the richest 2 percent of Americans in 1900 owned 60 percent of the nation's wealth, a condition that persisted with little change for two decades.

Those families were at once the agents and the beneficiaries of the process of industrial expansion and consolidation. Corporate mergers and reorganizations had given a dominant influence to a few huge combinations in each of many industries—among others, railroading, iron and steel and copper, meat packing, milling, tobacco, electricals, petroleum, and, by 1920, automobiles. As early as 1909, 1 percent of all the business firms in the nation produced 44 percent of all its manufactured goods. The consolidators had become the richest and in some ways the most powerful men in the United States. They guided the process of investment. They controlled the boards of directors of the great American banks and industries. They interpreted the startling growth of industry as a demonstration of their own wisdom and their optimism about the economic future of the United States. Beyond all that, they were developing, as were the experts whom they hired and consulted, an identification with the entirety of the national economy—the enormous national market, the need for national corporate institutions to reach it, the consequent need for energetic, professional management on a vast scale. Those insights contrasted with the parochialism of smaller institutions and of rural America, and with the traditional (and rewarding) faith of the American folk in their own ability to run their affairs and in their own local institutions. The growth of the great corporations raised questions about scale and control as troublesome as were the questions raised by the related problems of poverty and wealth.

America's Less Privileged

The magnificence of American wealth contrasted sharply with the sorry lot of the American poor, whom society, as the poet Vachel Lindsay put it, had made "oxlike, limp, and leaden-eyed." In 1910 the nonagricultural laboring force consisted of more than 30 million men and 8 million women, most of whom worked too long and earned too little. Between one-third and one-half of the industrial population lived in poverty. Their children ordinarily left school to find work—only one-third of the American children enrolled in primary schools completed their courses; less than one-tenth finished high school.

Work for men, women, and children was arduous. Those engaged in manufacturing were on the job between 44 and 55 hours a week—on the average more than 52 hours. Industrial accidents were common and conditions of work unhealthy and sometimes despicable. Usually workers had to suffer their disasters alone. Employer-liability laws, where they existed, were inadequate. There was no social insurance against accident, illness, old age, or unemployment, nor were there child-care centers where women workers could safely leave their children. Indeed child labor remained common throughout the country. And the slums, where most workers lived, were as bad as they had been in the 1890s.

New kinds of mobile slums were developing, the slums of migratory workers—some immigrants, including Asians, some Native Americans, some black workers, and Chicanos. Many were leaving submarginal small farms to follow the wheat harvest north from Texas or to pick fruits and vegetables along the West Coast. So, too, the mining and lumbering camps of the South and West offered to workers only a life of drudgery, brutality, danger, and poverty. Life was equally dreary for the thousands of Chinese, Japanese, Koreans, and Filipinos who worked on the sugar plantations of Hawaii.

The inequities in American society evoked a variety of responses ranging from the complacent to the outraged. Most of the well-to-do—the business élite and the profes-

The Poor of New York City

Jacob Riis's observations in this excerpt from the Introduction to How the Other Half Lives, *his 1890 exposé of the dreadful living conditions of New York City's poor, rang just as true at the turn of the century as it had ten years earlier. Conditions like the ones Riis describes helped fuel the movement for reform that characterized the first decade of the twentieth century.*

To-day three-fourths of [New York's] people live in the tenements, and the nineteenth century drift of the population to the cities is sending ever-increasing multitudes to crowd them. The fifteen thousand tenant houses that were the despair of the sanitarian in the past generation have swelled into thirty-seven thousand, and more than twelve hundred thousand persons call them home. . . .

What the tenements are and how they grow to what they are, we shall see. . . . The story is dark enough, drawn from the plain public records, to send a chill to any heart. If it shall appear that the sufferings and the sins of the "other half," and the evil they breed, are but as a just punishment upon the community that gave it no other choice, it will be because that is the truth. The boundary line lies there because, while the forces for good on one side vastly outweigh the bad—it were not well otherwise—in the tenements all the influences make for evil; because they are the hot-beds of the epidemics that carry death to rich and poor alike; the nurseries of pauperism and crime that fill our jails and police courts; that throw off a scum of forty thousand human wrecks to the island asylums and workhouses year by year; that turned out in the last eight years a round half million beggars to prey upon our charities; that maintain a standing army of ten thousand tramps with all that that implies; because, above all, they touch the family life with deadly moral contagion. This is their worst

sional men who identified with them and served them—believed as they long had that success was a function of virtue and poverty evidence of sin. As the century turned, they

---

crime, inseparable from the system. That we have to own it the child of our own wrong does not excuse it, even though it gives it claim upon our utmost patience and tenderest charity.

What are you going to do about it? is the question of to-day. . . . The first legislative committee ever appointed to probe this sore went deeper down and uncovered its roots. The "conclusion forced itself upon it that certain conditions and associations of human life and habitation are the prolific parents of corresponding habits and morals," and it recommended "the prevention of drunkenness by providing for every man a clean and comfortable home." Years after, a sanitary inquiry brought to light the fact that "more than one-half of the tenements with two-thirds of their population were held by owners who trade the keeping of them a business, *generally a speculation*. The owner was seeking a certain percentage on his outlay, and that percentage very rarely fell below fifteen per cent, and frequently exceeded thirty. The complaint was universal among the tenants that they were entirely smeared for, and that the only answer to their requests to have the place put in order by repairs and necessary improvements was that they must pay their rent or leave. The agent's instructions were simple but emphatic: 'Collect the rent in advance, or, failing, eject the occupants.'" Upon such a stock grew this upas-tree. Small wonder the fruit is bitter. The remedy that shall be an effective answer to the coming appeal for justice must proceed from the public conscience. Neither legislation nor charity can cover the ground. The greed of capital that wrought the evil must itself undo it, as far as it can now be undone. Homes must be built for the working masses by those who employ their labor; but tenements must cease to be "good property" in the old, heartless sense. "Philanthropy and five per cent" is the penance exacted.

Jacob A. Riis, *How the Other Half Lives: Studies Among the Tenements of New York* (hypertext edition). New York: Charles Scribner's Sons, 1890.

---

were satisfied with existing conditions, and they remained fixed in their belief in minimal government. Other self-respecting men and women of the comfortable middle class harbored some anxieties about their own futures but few doubts about the merit of American institutions.

But a minority alike of the rich and of the comfortable were receptive to the messages of protest and the efforts at particular social remedy that characterized the early years of the new century. That receptivity reflected in part a dread of drastic change and of the kind of radical agitation that had punctuated the 1890s. Reform, in that view, was preferable to revolution. Further, the center of American consciousness was slowly acquiring a new conscience. It produced a growing understanding of the efforts of some of the less privileged to improve their lot, a sympathy for the protests of the best informed against the inequities of American life, and, though rarely, a tolerance for the out-rage of that small minority of Americans who were com-mitted to rapid and radical social improvement.

At Odds: Organized Labor and Minorities

The craft-union movement, well launched in the 1890s, made significant gains during the early years of the twenti-eth century. Membership in the affiliates of the American Federation of Labor (AFL) rose from 548,000 in 1900 to 1,676,000 in 1904 and, in the face of strong resistance from employers, to about 2,000,000 by 1914, though even then some 90 percent of industrial workers remained un-organized. The unions and the railroad brotherhoods con-tinued to strive for bread-and-butter objectives. . . .

The craft unions were effective but in some respects self-ish agencies of change. Though they excited opposition from business managers not yet prepared to grant labor any voice in industrial decisions, they had little quarrel with the concentration of industrial power. The American Federation of Labor did demand the right to organize workers into national trade unions, consolidations that would parallel the consolidations of capital. In order to organize, labor needed to be unshackled from state and federal prohibitions on the strike and the boycott—and needed, too, state and federal protection from anti-union devices. The unions welcomed legislation setting standards of safety and employer liability, but otherwise they preferred to rely on their own power, rather than on the authority of the state, to reach their goals. They continued to distrust the federal government, for it had so often in the past assisted in breaking strikes, and they were eager to enlarge their own power even at the expense of those they had no intention of organizing. . . .

Collective bargaining, even when possible, assisted only union members, and the craft unions were generally unconcerned with the unskilled bulk of the labor force. Indeed, . . . labor leaders looked down on the unskilled, particularly on those who were women or immigrants. Craft leaders feared that management would hire unskilled and unorganized immigrants and black laborers to replace skilled workers (though in fact skilled workers were competing less with the unskilled than with an advancing technology and mechanization). This fear intensified prejudices against Asians, black Americans, and southern and eastern Europeans—prejudices that fed growing sentiments for the restriction of immigration and for racial segregation. . . .

Scorned alike by management and by the unions, the immigrants swelling the American labor force had to learn to help themselves. They continued, as in earlier decades, to receive unsystematic assistance in finding employment from urban political machines eager for their votes. Further, each new wave of immigration brought to the United States candidates for the meanest jobs. Their availability permitted their predecessors to climb a notch higher in the hierarchy of the workplace. So it was during the first decade of the century in the needle trades in New York City where men and women from southern Italy took over some of the underpaid and arduous piece work that had fallen in the 1890s to eastern European Jews who moved up to become cutters or other skilled workers with accompanying increases in pay. The experience of those immigrant Jews revealed the need of every immigrant group to organize for its own self-protection and mutual benefit. The Jewish families in New York were able to survive financially only if wives and sometimes children added their earnings to those of husbands and fathers, and to survive emotionally only because of the support they derived from their culture and their community. Their language and religion set them apart, to be sure, but also provided them with a world of their own in which in time they could begin to prosper. Their own unions, especially the International Ladies' Garment Workers Union (ILGWU), fought for their rights. They provided their own theater, their own literature, and gradually their own bourgeoisie. Though they also learned older American ways, they were one part of a pluralistic society in which other cultures also flourished.

In New York City, as elsewhere, that was the aspiration, too, of Italians, Poles, Greeks, Bohemians, Chinese, Japanese, and others, outsiders all, whose labor drove American shops and factories to ever higher levels of production and profit. The large majority of workers needed extraordinary courage and stamina to face the toil, the poverty, and the prejudice of a society eager to use but loath to include them.

Within that majority were Japanese, Chinese, and Korean immigrants who were denied the chance to become citizens by the Naturalization Act of 1790, which limited that right to persons who were "white." Asian immigrants were also targets of race prejudice of particular severity on the West Coast. The children of those immigrants, citizens by virtue of their birth in the United States, suffered along with their parents. Segregated in communities of their own, Asians and Asian-Americans, with few exceptions, could find only marginal employment. That was true also of Hispanic-Americans, most of them agricultural workers in the Southwest.

There were 10 million black Americans, of whom almost 90 percent still lived in the South. In 1910 almost a third of them were still illiterate. All were victimized by the inferior facilities for schooling, housing, traveling, and working that segregation had imposed upon them. Worse still, the incidence of lynchings (over 1,100 between 1900 and 1914) and race riots remained high. . . . As racist concepts spread in the North as well as the South, American blacks experienced their worst season since the Civil War. A few black intellectuals, led by W.E.B. DuBois, a Harvard Ph.D., in 1905 organized the Niagara movement. . . . DuBois and his associates demanded immediate action to achieve political and economic equality for black Americans. . . .

With varying success women, too, intensified their struggle for political, economic, and social status equal to that of men. Sarah Platt Decker, president of the General Federation of Women's Clubs, converted the energies of that middle-class organization to agitation for improving the conditions of industrial work for women and children. That was also the objective of the Women's Trade Union League and Florence Kelley's National Consumers' League, which sponsored state legislation for minimum wages and maximum hours. In New York City, the International Ladies' Garment Workers Union, financed in part by wealthy matrons, conducted a prolonged strike in 1909 that won limited gains in spite of opposition from employers and police.

The Reality of the Muckraker

Richard Hofstadter

During the first decade of the twentieth century, reporter-reformers known as muckrakers changed the nature of journalism and captured the attention of a national audience. The muckrakers, writes the late political historian Richard Hofstadter, brought a new twist to the human-interest story. Their exposés of government corruption, urban slums, and the realities of poverty appealed to the emotions of those who were doing reasonably well, stirring up feelings of responsibility, guilt, and indignation. Hofstadter contends that even though the muckrakers actually did not set out to "expose evils or reform society," they did increase awareness and help bring about social change.

To an extraordinary degree the work of the Progressive movement rested upon its journalism. The fundamental critical achievement of American Progressivism was the business of exposure, and journalism was the chief occupational source of its creative writers. It is hardly an exaggeration to say that the Progressive mind was characteristically a journalistic mind, and that its characteristic contribution was that of the socially responsible reporter-reformer. The muckraker was a central figure. Before there could be action, there must be information and exhortation. Grievances had to be given specific objects, and these the muckraker supplied. It was muckraking that brought the diffuse malaise of the public into focus. . . .

What was new in muckraking in the Progressive era was neither its ideas nor its existence, but its reach—its nationwide character and its capacity to draw nationwide attention, the presence of mass muckraking media with national circulations, and huge resources for the research that went into exposure. The muckraking magazines had circulations running into the hundreds of thousands. They were able to pour funds into the investigations of their reporters—publisher S.S. McClure estimated that the famous articles of reporter Ida Tarbell cost $4,000 each and those of writer Lincoln Steffens $2,000—and they were able, as very few of the practitioners of exposure had been able before, not merely to name the malpractices in American business and politics, but to name the *malpractitioners* and their specific misdeeds, and to proclaim the facts to the entire country. . . .

Behind muckraking there was a long history of change in journalism, the story of a transformation in the newspaper and magazine world. The immensely rapid urbanization of the country had greatly enlarged daily newspaper circulation. In 1870 there were 574 daily newspapers in the country; by 1899 there were 1,610; by 1909, 2,600. The circulation of daily newspapers increased over the same span of time from 2,800,000 to 24,200,000. This expansion had opened up to publishers remarkable promotional opportunities, which brought in their train a number of changes in journalistic practice.

A New and Different
Exploitation of Human Interest

The newspaper owners and editors soon began to assume a new role. Experienced in the traditional function of reporting the news, they found themselves undertaking the more ambitious task of creating a mental world for the uprooted farmers and villagers who were coming to live in the city. . . . The newspaper became not only the interpreter of this environment but a means of surmounting in some measure its vast human distances, of supplying a sense of intimacy all too rare in the ordinary course of its life. Through newspaper gossip it provided a substitute for village gossip. It began to make increased use of the variety and excitement of the city to capture personal interest and offer its readers indirect human contacts. . . .

There were more politically independent or quasi-independent papers, and publishers felt more inclined to challenge the political parties and other institutions. In business terms the benefits to booming circulation of crusades and exposés far outstripped the dangers from possible retaliation. In an age when news was at a premium and when more and more copy was needed to surround the growing columns of advertisement, there was a tendency for publishers and editors to be dissatisfied with reporting the news and to attempt to make it. The papers made news in a double sense; they *created* reportable events. . . . They also *elevated* events, hitherto considered beneath reportorial attention, to the level of news occurrences by clever, emotionally colored reporting. They exploited human interest, in short. . . . Where the old human interest had played up the curious concern of the common citizen with the affairs and antics of the rich, the new human interest exploited far more intensely the concern of comfortable people with the affairs of the poor. The slum sketch, the story of the poor and disinherited of the cities, became commonplace. And it was just this interest of the secure world in the nether world that served as the prototype of muckraking. . . .

As author Theodore Dreiser, then a young reporter, recalled, reporters became alert to hypocrisy, perhaps a little cynical themselves, but fundamentally enlightened about the immense gaps between the lofty ideals and public professions of the editorial page and the dirty realities of the business office and the newsroom. And it was into this gap that the muckraking mind rushed with all its fact-finding zeal.

Muckraking—Backbone of the Mass Magazine

It was, of course, the popular magazine, not the daily newspaper, that stood in the forefront of muckraking, but the muckraking periodicals were profoundly affected by newspaper journalism. The old, respectable magazines, the *Atlantic, Harper's,* the *Century,* and *Scribner's,* had been genteel, sedate enterprises selling at thirty-five cents a copy and reaching limited audiences of about 130,000. . . . The new magazines that emerged at the turn of the century sold at ten or twelve or fifteen cents a copy and reached audiences of from 400,000 to 1,000,000. . . . They contained not only literature but features that resembled news. And like the daily press they soon began to make news and to become a political force in their own right. . . .

Neither the muckraking publishers and editors nor the muckraking reporters set out to expose evils or to reform society. Although the experience of the *Ladies' Home Journal, Munsey's,* and the *Saturday Evening Post* showed that immense circulations could be achieved without ever entering in any serious sense upon it, muckraking was a by-product, perhaps an inevitable one, of the development of mass magazines. . . .

Most of the . . . outstanding figures of the muckrake era were simply writers or reporters working on commission and eager to do well what was asked of them. A few, among them Upton Sinclair and Gustavus Myers, were animated by a deep-going dislike of the capitalist order, but most of them were hired into muckraking or directed toward it on the initiative of sales-conscious editors or publishers. . . .

If, from the standpoint of the editors and journalists themselves, the beginning of muckraking seemed to be more or less "accidental," its ending did not. The large magazine built on muckraking was vulnerable as a business organization. The publishing firm was so large an enterprise and sold its product for so little that it became intensely dependent upon advertising and credit, and hence vulnerable to pressure from the business community. Advertisers did not hesitate to withdraw orders for space when their own interests or related interests were touched upon. Bankers adopted a discriminatory credit policy, so that modest loans could not be secured even for the maintenance of a business of great value and proved stability. In one case, that of *Hampton's*, even espionage was employed to destroy the magazine. . . .

A Passion for Getting the Inside Story

The muckrakers had a more decisive impact on the thinking of the country than they did on its laws or morals. They confirmed, if they did not create, a fresh mode of criticism that grew out of journalistic observation. The dominant note in the best thought of the Progressive era is summed up in the term "realism.". . . The chief source of realism lay in the city and city journalism. . . .

It had never been customary in America to write about America, but especially not about the life of industry and labor and business and poverty and vice. Now, while novelists were replacing a literature bred out of other literature with a genre drawn from street scenes and abattoirs or the fly-specked rural kitchens of Hamlin Garland's stories, the muckrakers were replacing the genteel travel stories and romances of the older magazines with a running account of how America worked. "It was not," says Robert Cantwell, "because the muckrakers exposed the corruption of Minneapolis, for example, that they were widely read, but because they wrote about Minneapolis at a time when it had not been written about, without patronizing or boosting it, and with an attempt to explore its life realistically and intelligently. They wrote, in short, an intimate, anecdotal, behind-the-scenes history of their own times. . . . They traced the intricate relationship of the police, the underworld, the local political bosses, the secret connections between the new corporations . . . and the legislatures and the courts. In doing this they drew a new cast of characters for the drama of American society: bosses, professional politicians, reformers, racketeers, captains of industry. Everybody recognized these native types; everybody knew about them; but they had not been characterized before; their social functions had not been analyzed. At the same time, the muckrakers pictured stage settings that everybody recognized but that nobody had written about—oil refineries, slums, the red-light districts, the hotel rooms where political deals were made—the familiar, unadorned, homely stages where the teeming day-to-day dramas of American life were enacted. . . ."

The muckraking model of thought had brought with it a certain limiting and narrowing definition of reality and a flattening of the imagination. . . . Reality now was rough and sordid. It was hidden, neglected, and off-stage. It was conceived essentially as that stream of external and material events which was most likely to be unpleasant. . . .

The Progressive View of Reality

An excellent illustration of the spirit of Progressivism as it manifested itself in the new popular literature is provided by a famous editorial by S.S. McClure in the January 1903 issue of *McClure's*. In this editorial McClure stood back and took a fresh look at his publication and suddenly realized what it was that he and his writers were doing. He observed that his current issue, which was running an article muckraking Minneapolis by Lincoln Steffens, another on Standard Oil by Ida Tarbell, and still another by Ray Stannard Baker on labor, showed a striking and completely unplanned convergence upon a central fact in American life: a general disrespect for law on the part of capitalists, workingmen, politicians, and citizens. Who, he asked, was left in the community to uphold the law? The lawyers? Some of the best of them made a living from advising business firms how to evade it. The judges? Among too many of them the respect for law took the form of respect for quibbles by which they restored to liberty men who on the evidence of common sense would be convicted of malfeasances. The churches? "We know of one, an ancient and wealthy establishment, which had to be compelled by a Tammany hold-over health officer to put its tenements in sanitary condition." "The colleges? They do not understand." "There is no one left," concluded McClure, "none but all of us. . . . We all are doing our worst and making the public pay. The public is the people. We forget that we all are the people. . . . We have to pay in the end, every one of us."

The chief themes of the muckraking magazines are stated here. First is the progressive view of reality—evil-doing among the most respectable people is seen as the "real" character of American life; corruption is found on every side. Second is the idea that the mischief can be interpreted simply as a widespread breaking of the law. . . . If the laws are the right laws, and if they can be enforced by the right men, the Progressive believed, everything would be better. . . . Third, there was the appeal to universal personal responsibility and the imputation of personal guilt. . . .

The more the muckrakers acquainted the Protestant Yankee with what was going on around him, the more guilty and troubled he felt. . . .

In time the muckraking and reform writers seem to have become half conscious of the important psychic function their work was performing for themselves and their public, quite apart from any legislative consequences or material gains. They began to say, in effect, that even when they were unable to do very much to change the exercise of political power, they liked the sense of effort and the feeling that the moral tone of political life had changed. "It is not the material aspect of this," they began to say, "but the moral aspect that interests us.". . . McClure himself gave characteristic expression . . . when he praised Charles Evans Hughes's exposure of the New York life-insurance companies for the enormous "tonic effect of the inquiry," which, he felt, had very likely saved thousands of young men from making compromises with honor. They saw that "public disgrace" awaited evildoers, and "there is no punishment so terrible as public disclosure of evil doing."

Another paradox in the movement was that it contained an element of conservatism. In some cases the regulation of business turned out actually to be regulation *by* businessmen, who preferred regulated stability to the chaos and uncertainty of unrestrained competition. The progressive movement refers to the common spirit of an age rather than to an organized group or party. Much like the reform spirit of the 1830s and 1840s, once called Jacksonian Democracy, progressivism was diverse in both origins and tendencies. Few people adhered to all of the varied progressive causes. . . .

The Muckrakers Expose Scandal

Also important in stimulating reform activity were those social critics who publicized festering problems. The writers who thrived on exposing scandal got their name when Theodore Roosevelt compared them to a character in John Bunyan's *Pilgrim's Progress*: "A man that could look no way but downwards with a muckrake in his hands." The "muckrakers" (and TR was no mean muckraker himself) "are often indispensable to . . . society," Roosevelt said, "but only if they know when to stop raking the muck.". . .

The golden age of muckraking is sometimes dated from October 1902 when *McClure's* magazine began to run articles by the reporter Lincoln Steffens on municipal corruption, later collected into a book: *The Shame of the Cities* (1904). *McClure's* also ran Ida M. Tarbell's *History of the Standard Oil Company* (1904). McClure had set her to research on the project more than three years before. The result was a more detailed treatment than the earlier book by Henry Demarest Lloyd, but all the more damaging in its detail. Other outstanding books which began as magazine articles exposed corruption in the stock market, the meat industry, the life insurance business, and the political world.

Without the muckrakers, progressivism surely would never have achieved the popular support it had. In feeding the public's appetite for facts about their new urban-industrial society, the muckrakers demonstrated one of the salient features of the Progressive movement, and one of its central failures. The Progressives were stronger on diagnosis than on remedy, thereby reflecting a naïve faith in the power of democracy. Let the people know, expose corruption, and bring government close to the people, went the rationale, and the correction of evils would follow automatically. The cure for the ills of democracy was more democracy.

The Direct Primary and the "Gospel of Efficiency"

The most important reform with which the Progressives tried to democratize government was the direct primary or the nomination of candidates by the vote of party members. Under the existing convention system, the reasoning went, only a small proportion of the voters attended the local caucuses or precinct meetings which sent delegates to county, and in turn to state and national, conventions. While the system allowed seasoned leaders to sift the candidates, it also lent itself to domination by political professionals who were able to come early and stay late. . . .

A second major theme of progressivism was the "gospel of efficiency." In the business world during those years Frederick W. Taylor, the original "efficiency expert," was developing the techniques he summed up in his book *The Principles of Scientific Management* (1911): efficient management of time and costs, the proper routing and scheduling of work, standardization of tools and equipment, and the like. In government, efficiency demanded the reorganization of agencies to prevent overlapping, to establish clear lines of authority, and to fix responsibility. One long-held theory had it that the greater the number of offices chosen by popular vote the greater the degree of democracy, but Progressives considered this inefficient. They believed that voters could make wiser choices if they had a shorter ballot and chose fewer officials in whom power and responsibility were clearly lodged. . . .

Two new ideas for making municipal government more

efficient gained headway in the first decade of the new century. The commission system, first adopted by Galveston, Texas, in 1901, when local government there collapsed in the aftermath of a devastating hurricane and tidal wave, placed ultimate authority in a board composed of elected administrative heads of city departments—commissioners of sanitation, police, utilities, and so on. The more durable idea, however, was the city-manager plan, under which a professional administrator ran the government in accordance with policies set by the elected council and mayor. Staunton, Virginia, first adopted the plan in 1908. By 1914 the National Association of City Managers heralded the arrival of a new profession.

When America was a preindustrial society, Andrew Jackson's notion that any reasonably intelligent citizen could perform the duties of any public office may have been true. In the more complex age of the early twentieth century it was apparent that many functions of government and business had come to require expert specialists. This principle was promoted by progressive governor Robert M. La Follette of Wisconsin (1901–1906), who established a Legislative Reference Bureau to provide research, advice, and help in the drafting of legislation. The "Wisconsin Idea" of efficient government was widely publicized and copied. . . .

A Need for Corporate and Labor Reform

Of all the problems facing American society at the turn of the century, one engaged a greater diversity of reformers, and elicited more—and more controversial—solutions than any other: the regulation of giant corporations, which became a third major theme of progressivism. . . .

The problem of economic power and its abuse offered a dilemma for Progressives. Four broad solutions were available, but of these, two were extremes which had limited support: letting business work out its own destiny under a policy of laissez-faire, or adopting a socialist program of public ownership. At the municipal level, however, the socialist alternative was rather widely adopted in public util-

ities and transportation—so-called gas and water socialism—but otherwise was not seriously considered as a general policy. The other choices were either to adopt a policy
of trust-busting in the belief that restoring old-fashioned
competition would best prevent economic abuses, or to accept big business in the belief that it brought economies of
scale, but to regulate it to prevent abuses.

Efforts to restore the competition of small firms proved
unworkable, partly because breaking up large combinations was complex and difficult. The trend over the years
was toward regulation of big business. To some extent regulation and "stabilization" won acceptance among businessmen who, whatever respect they paid to competition in
the abstract, preferred not to face it in person. In the long
run, although it was not at first apparent, regulation posed
the problem raised in an old maxim that would become rel-
evant to American politics in the 1970s and 1980s: Who
will guard the guards? Regulatory agencies often came
under the influence or control of those they were supposed
to regulate. . . .

A fourth important feature of the progressive spirit was
the impulse toward social justice, which motivated diverse
actions from private charities to campaigns against child
labor and liquor. The settlement house movement of the
late nineteenth century had spawned a corps of social
workers and genteel reformers devoted to the uplift of slum
dwellers. But with time it became apparent that social evils
extended beyond the reach of private charities and demanded the power of the state. Progressives found that old
codes of private ethics and accountability scarcely applied
to a complex industrial order. One sociologist observed in
1907: "Unlike the old time villain, the latter-day malefac-
tor does not wear a slouch hat and a comforter, breathe
forth curses and an odor of gin, go about his nefarious
work with clenched teeth and an evil scowl. . . . The modern high-powered dealer of woe wears immaculate linen,
carries a silk hat and a lighted cigar, sins with calm coun-
tenance and a serene soul, leagues or months from the evil

he causes. Upon his gentlemanly presence the eventual blood and tears do not obtrude themselves."

Labor legislation was perhaps the most significant reform to emerge from the drive for social justice. The National Child Labor Committee, organized in 1904, led a movement for laws banning the still widespread employment of young children. Through publicity, the organization of state and local committees, and a telling documentation of the evils of child labor by the photographer Lewis W. Hine, the committee within ten years brought about legislation in most states banning the labor of underage children (the minimum age varied from twelve to sixteen) and limiting the working hours of older children. Closely linked with the child-labor reform movement was a concerted effort to regulate the hours of work for women. Spearheaded by Florence Kelley, the head of the National Consumers League, this progressive crusade promoted the passage of state laws to ameliorate the distinctive hardships that long working hours imposed on women who were wives and

Two young girls labor in a clothing factory in Tennessee. Photographs like this one by Lewis W. Hine helped bring about legislation banning the use of underage children in mines, shops, and factories.

mothers. Many states also outlawed night work and labor in dangerous occupations for both women and children. But numerous exemptions and inadequate enforcement often virtually nullified the laws.

The Supreme Court pursued a curiously erratic course in ruling on state labor laws. It upheld a Utah law limiting the working day in mining and smelting to eight hours as a proper exercise of the state police power to protect the health and safety of workers. The Court even referred to the unequal bargaining power of workers and employers as a justification for state action. In *Lochner v. New York* (1905), however, the Court voided a ten-hour day because it violated workers' "liberty of contract" to accept any terms they chose. Justice Oliver Wendell Holmes, Jr., dissented sharply. "The 14th Amendment does not enact Mr. Herbert Spencer's *Social Statics*," he said, meaning it did not enact Spencer's laissez-faire dogmas. Then in 1908 the high court upheld a ten-hour law for women largely on the basis of sociological data which Louis D. Brandeis presented regarding the effects of long hours on the health and morals of women. . . .

One of the most important advances along these lines was the series of workmen's compensation laws enacted after Maryland led the way in 1902. Accident insurance systems replaced the old common-law principle that an injured worker was entitled to compensation only if he could prove employer negligence, a costly and capricious procedure from which the worker was likely to win nothing or, as often happened, excessive awards from overly sympathetic juries. . . .

Roosevelt Takes a Cautious Approach to Reform

Theodore Roosevelt's version of Progressive reform was a cautious one. He cultivated party leaders in Congress, and steered away from such political meat-grinders as the tariff and banking issues. And when he did approach the explosive issue of the trusts, he always took care to reassure the business community. For him, politics was the art of the possible. Unlike the more advanced progressives and the doctrinaire "lunatic fringe," as he called them, he would take half a loaf rather than none at all. Roosevelt acted in large part out of the conviction that reform was needed to keep things on an even keel. Control should rest in the hands of sensible Republicans, and not with irresponsible Democrats or, worse, the growing socialist movement.

At the outset of his presidency in 1901 Roosevelt took up President McKinley's policies and promised to sustain them. He touched base with McKinley's friend and manager Mark Hanna, and worked with Republican leaders in Congress, against whom the minority of new Progressives was as yet powerless. Republican Speaker Joe Cannon . . . was able to announce on one occasion to a helpless House, "We will now perpetrate the following outrage."

Roosevelt, it turned out, would accomplish more by vigorous executive action than by passing legislation, and in the exercise of executive power he was not inhibited by points of legal detail. The president, he argued, might do anything not expressly forbidden by the Constitution. The Constitution, he said later, "must be interpreted, not as a straight jacket, not as laying the hand of death upon our development, but as an instrument designed for the life and healthy growth of the Nation." He was even credited with asking "What's the Constitution between friends?" but that query seems to have been apocryphal.

Caution suffused Roosevelt's first annual message, delivered in December 1901, but he felt impelled to take up the trust problem in the belief that it might be more risky to ignore it. The message carefully balanced arguments on both sides of the question. "The mechanism of modern business is so delicate," he warned, "that extreme care must be taken not to interfere with it in a spirit of rashness or ignorance." A widespread belief nevertheless held the great corporations "in certain of their features and tendencies hurtful to the general welfare." The president endorsed the "sincere conviction that combination and concentration should be, not prohibited, but supervised and within reasonable limits controlled." The first essential was "knowledge of the facts—publicity . . . the only sure remedy we can now invoke.". . .

In August 1902 Roosevelt carried the trust issue to the people on a tour of New England and the Midwest. He endorsed a "square deal" for all, calling for enforcement of existing antitrust laws and stricter controls on big business. From the outset, however, Roosevelt believed that wholesale trust-busting was too much like trying to unscramble eggs. Effective regulation, he believed, was better than a futile effort to restore small business, which might be achieved only at a cost to the efficiencies of scale gained in larger operations. Roosevelt nevertheless soon acquired a reputation as a "trustbuster.". . .

Mine Workers Stand Firm

Support for Roosevelt's use of the "big stick" against corporations was strengthened by the stubbornness of mine owners in the anthracite coal strike of 1902. On May 12 the United Mine Workers (UMW) walked off the job in Pennsylvania and West Virginia, demanding a 20 percent wage increase, a reduction in hours from ten to nine, and union recognition. The mine operators, having granted a 10 percent raise two years before, dug in their heels against further concessions, and shut down in preparation for a long struggle to starve out the miners. Their spokesman, George F. Baer, the president of the Reading Railroad, helped the union cause more than his own with an arrogant pronouncement: "The rights and interests of the laboring man will be protected and cared for," he said, "not by the labor agitators, but by the Christian men to whom God in his infinite wisdom has given control of the property interests of the country."

Facing the prospect of a coal shortage, Roosevelt called a conference at the White House. The mine owners, led by Baer, attended but refused even to speak to the UMW leaders. This outraged Roosevelt, who expressed his irritation at the "extraordinary stupidity and temper" of the "wooden-headed" owners. The president also confessed a temptation to grab Baer "by the seat of his breeches" and "chuck him out" a White House window. After the conference ended in an impasse, Roosevelt threatened to take over the mines and run them with the army. When a congressman questioned the constitutionality of such a move, an exasperated Roosevelt grabbed the man by the shoulders and roared: "To hell with the Constitution when the people want coal!" Such a comment and others like it over the years led Joe Cannon, the crusty House Speaker, to note: "Roosevelt's got no more respect for the Constitution than a tomcat has for a marriage license." Militarizing the mines would have been an act of dubious legality, but the owners feared that TR might actually do it and that public opinion would support him.

The coal strike ended in October 1902 with an agreement to submit the issues to an arbitration commission named by the president. After a last-minute flurry over the operators' refusal to accept a union man on the panel, the president blithely reclassified the head of the railway conductors' union as an "eminent sociologist." The agreement enhanced the prestige of both Roosevelt and the union leader, although it produced only a partial victory for the miners. By the arbitrators' decision of March 21, 1903, the miners won a nine-hour day but only a 10 percent wage increase, and no union recognition.

Roosevelt continued to use his executive powers to enforce the Sherman Act, but he avoided conflict in Congress by drawing back from further antitrust legislation. . . .

Roosevelt Scores a Victory Again

Roosevelt's policies built a coalition of progressive- and conservative-minded voters which assured his election in his own right in 1904. He had skillfully used patronage, and his progressive policies, achieved mainly by executive action, had not challenged congressional conservatives. Nor did Roosevelt try to take on the Old Guard at the Chicago convention in June. He accepted a harmless platform which dwelt on past achievements, and the convention chose him by acclamation. The Democrats, having lost with Bryan twice, turned to Alton B. Parker who, as chief justice of New York, had upheld labor's right to the closed shop and the state's right to limit hours of work. Despite his liberal record party leaders presented him as a safe conservative, and his acceptance of the gold standard as "firmly and irrevocably established" bolstered such a view. The effort to present a candidate more conservative than Roosevelt proved a futile gesture for the party which had twice nominated Bryan. Despite Roosevelt's trust-busting proclivities, most businessmen, according to the New York *Sun*, preferred the "impulsive candidate of the party of conservatism to the conservative candidate of the party which the business interests regard as permanently and dangerously impulsive." Even J.P. Morgan and E.H. Harriman contributed handsomely to Roosevelt's campaign chest. Parker made little headway with his charge that businessmen expected favors in return.

An invincible popularity plus the sheer force of personality swept Roosevelt to an impressive victory by a popular margin of 7.6 million to 5.1 million. Parker carried only the Solid South of the former Confederacy and two border states: Kentucky and Maryland. It was a great personal triumph for Roosevelt. Amid the excitement of election night he announced that he would not run again, a statement he later had reason to regret.

Elected in his own right, Roosevelt approached his second term with heightened confidence and a stronger commitment to progressive reform. In December 1905 he devoted most of his annual message to the regulation and control of business. This understandably irked many of his corporate contributors. Said steel baron Henry Frick, "We bought the son of a bitch and then he did not stay put." The independent-minded Roosevelt took aim at the railroads first, and it was with reference to railroads that his demands most nearly approached success. . . .

Railroads took priority, but a growing movement for the regulation of meat-packers, food processors, and makers of drugs and patent medicines reached fruition. . . . Discontent with abuses in these fields had grown rapidly as a result of the muckrakers' reports. They supplied evidence of harmful preservatives and adulterants in the preparation of "embalmed meat" and other food products. The *Ladies' Home Journal* and *Colliers* published evidence of false claims and dangerous ingredients in patent medicines, what one report called "The Great American Fraud." One of the more notorious nostrums, Lydia Pinkham's Vegetable Compound, was advertised to work wonders in the relief of "female complaints"; it was no wonder, for the compound was 18 percent alcohol.

But perhaps the most telling blow against such abuses was struck by Upton Sinclair's novel *The Jungle* (1906). Sinclair meant the book to be a tract for socialism, but its main impact came from its portrayal of filthy conditions in Chicago's meatpacking industry: "It was too dark in these storage places to see well, but a man could run his hand over these piles of meat and sweep off handfuls of the dried dung of rats. These rats were nuisances, and the packers would put poisoned bread out for them, they would die, and then rats, bread, and meat would go into the hoppers together." Roosevelt, an omnivorous reader, read *The Jungle*—and reacted quickly. He sent two agents to Chicago and their report confirmed all that Sinclair had said: "We saw meat shovelled from filthy wooden floors, piled on tables rarely washed, pushed from room to room in rotten box carts, in all of which processes it was in the way of gathering dirt, splinters, floor filth, and the expectoration of tuberculous and other diseased workers."

The Meat Inspection Act of June 30, 1906, required federal inspection of meats destined for interstate commerce and empowered officials in the Agriculture Department to impose standards of sanitation. The Pure Food and Drug Act, enacted the same day, placed restrictions on the makers of prepared foods and patent medicines, and forbade the manufacture, sale, or transportation of adulterated, misbranded, or harmful foods, drugs, and liquors.

CHAPTER 4

Technology
and Discovery

The Wright Brothers' Incredible Flying Machine

Walter Lord

The first decade of the 1900s was a time of new inventions and discoveries. In 1900 two mechanics from Dayton, Ohio—brothers Orville and Wilbur Wright—tested their first flying machine—a glider they had designed and built. Instead of stopping with this achievement, explains author-historian Walter Lord, the Wright brothers persevered and several years later built and flew their "whopper flying machine." Their invention, writes Lord, attracted little or no attention. He contends that Americans were only excited by simpler inventions like the safety razor—inventions they could understand. Walter Lord gained international recognition for his 1995 best-seller *A Night to Remember,* which chronicles the sinking of the *Titanic,* and his 1957 work, *Day of Infamy,* a retelling of the 1941 attack by the Japanese on Pearl Harbor.

With the whole nation absorbed in the drama of "bear" raids and cornered shorts, it was quite natural for the co-proprietor of a small bicycle business to use Wall Street terminology in writing a cheerful postcard to his shop mechanic.

"Flying machine market has been very unsteady the past two days," scribbled Orville Wright at Kitty Hawk, North Carolina, on October 20, 1903. The card, addressed to

Excerpted from *The Good Years: From 1900 to the First World War,* by Walter Lord (New York: Harper & Row, 1960). Copyright ©1960 by Walter Lord. Reprinted with permission from Sterling Lord Literistic, Inc.

Charlie Taylor back home in Dayton, Ohio, continued: "Opened yesterday morning at about 208 (100% means even chances of success) but by noon had dropped to 110. These fluctuations would have produced a panic, I think, in Wall Street, but in this quiet place it only put us to thinking and figuring a little."

Orville and his brother Wilbur had been "thinking and figuring" about flying machines for a long time now. In 1899 they had built a big box kite incorporating some of their theories. Its most novel feature was a method of warping the wings to get lateral balance. It flew beautifully.

In 1900 they took the next step—a man-carrying glider. To test it, they picked Kitty Hawk, which offered a steady wind, wide-open beaches and plenty of privacy. Here they tinkered with the machine for five weeks, but it wasn't until the last day that they dared go up in it. It too flew beautifully.

In 1901 they were back in Kitty Hawk with a bigger glider. Now their flights were bolder and longer—280 . . . 300 . . . 335 feet. Clearly they were getting quite good—that much was obvious to anyone who took the trouble to watch.

But few did. The taciturn people of Kitty Hawk had their own problems to worry about. They knew, of course, that the Wrights were experimenting at Kill Devil Hills, four miles down the beach, but it was a mighty long walk. And when you got there, often there was no flying to see. . . .

The Wrights fully reciprocated the natives' indifference. Even in this isolated community they lived a world apart. They visited little, kept mostly to themselves—talking, watching the birds, or puttering with their glider. Fifteen-year-old Truxton Midgett, who delivered a lot of their supplies, was especially impressed by the close way they worked together. He had a brother of his own, and he knew how hard this could be.

Without realizing it, Midgett had put his finger on the most remarkable quality about the Wrights. They were not only inseparable as brothers, but their very minds seemed to complement each other. They would bat a problem back and forth for hours, until almost invariably a solution appeared—the joint product of two brains working in perfect harmony. And so they passed the summer of 1901, returning again to Dayton late in August.

At the Drawing Board

Just about the time they arrived home, the September, 1901, issue of *McClure's* appeared with an article exploding the myth of the flying machine. Professor Simon Newcomb, the distinguished astronomer, compared it to squaring the circle. It was one of those things we would never be able to do. And in the December, 1901, *North American Review*, Admiral George W. Melville pointed out that no one had even laid the necessary groundwork: "Where, even to this hour, are we to look for the germ of the successful flying machine? Where is the preparation today?"

At this moment in Dayton, the Wrights were testing over two hundred different wing surfaces. By using a specially-built wind tunnel, they learned that a wing's front edge shouldn't be too sharp . . . that deeply cambered wings were inefficient . . . that narrow wings had relatively more lifting power. Most important, they discovered that all previous air pressure tables were hopelessly inaccurate. Page after page they jotted new figures, spelling out exactly what pressure would support different surfaces at different speeds and angles.

In 1902 they returned again to Kill Devil Hills with a new glider based on the wind tunnel data. It proved the best yet—could soar even better than the hawks. For still greater stability, they added a tail . . . then a movable rudder. With these improvements they broke all gliding records—622½ feet the week before they went back to Dayton that October.

The next step was a motor. On December 3, 1902, they wrote to ten manufacturers, seeking a 180-pound gasoline engine that could develop 8 h.p. No luck, so they built their own. Next, a propeller. It turned out that marine experience was no use at all. The approach was completely hit-or-miss; if one didn't work, shipbuilders simply tried another. But in the air this could obviously have fatal results. So again, the Wrights built their own. Now for better up-rights. Once more, tests showed past theories were invalid. Once more, the Wrights designed their own.

The "Whopper Flying Machine"

By September, 1903, they were back at Kill Devil Hills, slowly assembling the flyer. They had come a long way since 1900, but the big biplane still looked pretty much like a box kite. A spider web of struts and wires held the forty-foot wings in place. The pilot lay on a "cradle" amidship, work-ing with his hips the wires that warped the wings. In front was a horizontal elevator; in the rear a vertical tail with the new movable rudder. The engine nestled ominously along-side the pilot. It drove the two pusher-propellers by means of a clanking chain drive that reminded people of the builders' background in the bicycle business. The whole af-fair weighed an impressive 605 pounds without pilot. No wonder the Wrights proudly nicknamed it the "whopper flying machine."

As they quietly worked away, Simon Newcomb deliv-ered another blast at the whole idea of mechanical flight. Writing in the October 22 issue of the *Independent,* the professor was especially concerned with the aeronaut's problem of landing safely: "How shall he reach the ground without destroying his delicate machinery? I do not think the most imaginative inventor has yet even put on paper a demonstrative, successful way of meeting this difficulty."

The following morning the Wrights were putting the fin-ishing touches on their landing skids.

Still, they were far from being ready. All through Octo-ber and November they made endless adjustments. They mounted the engine. They trussed the wires. They tested the method of starting. They measured the air pressure on the front elevator.

And one day they learned that another man had just failed to fly. Professor Samuel P. Langley, Secretary of the Smithsonian Institution, tried to launch his plane from a barge in the Potomac, but it flopped into the river before the eyes of a derisive press. The news did not discourage the Wrights—they just studied all the data they could get on Langley's attempt.

The Wrights had their own troubles too. They broke a propeller shaft . . . sent to Dayton for another . . . broke that . . . had to dig up still another. This time Orville himself rushed to Dayton, picked up some strong steel rods, was back in Kitty Hawk by December 11.

December 14, and at last they were ready. First, a few minor repairs in the morning. Then a final check on the launching device. This was a sixty-foot monorail made by laying four fifteen-foot planks end to end. The flying machine sat on a dolly which rolled down the track. After picking up enough speed, the pilot theoretically tilted the wings and took off. Crude, but Langley had spent $50,000 for his starting equipment, while this cost only $4.

The Wrights' device had the added virtue of being portable. On a windy day they could lay the track on the level beach and take off from there. On a calm day, like this one, they could take it to Big Hill, or one of the other nearby dunes, and lay it on the slope for extra speed.

An Unsuccessful Attempt to Fly

Of course, all this required manpower, and assistance came from an unexpected source. The men at the Kill Devil Life Saving Station, about a mile away, liked to watch the Wrights in their spare time and volunteered to pitch in whenever called.

The signal came at 1:30 P.M., fluttering from the side of the Wrights' shed. As promised, the men drifted over. . . .

Through the bright afternoon sunlight the procession marched toward Big Hill, about a quarter-mile away. To move the flyer more easily, they put it on the track. As they pushed it along, they would pick up the last rail section and re-lay it ahead, over and over again.

Now they were on the hill, pondering the inevitable question: who should have what Wilbur called "first whack"?

The Wrights solved the problem in characteristic fashion—they tossed for it. Wilbur won and lay down at the
controls, the way a child goes sledding. A moment later
the motor roared into action. . . .

Down the track the flyer rolled, Orville dashing along-
side, trying to balance the wing tip. Wilbur pulled at the
wires, and in his excitement pulled too hard. The plane
shot up at a 20° angle, stalled, and fell back to the ground.

Anybody else would have been discouraged. But not the
Wrights. They knew exactly what went wrong. More important, they knew went right. The motor, the controls, the
launching device all worked perfectly. Next time the machine was bound to fly. That evening Wilbur wrote his father and sister Katherine, "There is now no question of
final success." Next morning he followed up with a wire:
". . . Success assured. Keep quiet."

Why so secret? The answer seems to lie in the complex
personalities of the Wrights themselves. In a way they were
visionaries, but they also had a sharp eye for patent rights.
They wanted recognition, but they also had a small-town
suspicion of big-city newsmen. They were confident of success, but they dreaded the taunts if anything went wrong.

The 15th and 16th were spent quietly, making further adjustments. By the second night all was ready for another try.

Twelve Seconds of Success

Thursday, December 17, dawned cold and cloudy. A strong
wind blew from the north at twenty to twenty-five miles an
hour. A thin glaze of ice coated the puddles about the
camp. A poor day, but the Wrights were anxious to get on
with it.

At 10:00 A.M. the men at the life-saving station saw the
signal. Another try would be made. Those who were free
dropped over. . . . Then W.C. Brinkley of Manteo turned
up; he was another of the local residents who had begun to
take an interest in the Wrights. Finally, came Johnny
Moore, a carefree, seventeen-year-old who lived about
three miles down the beach. . . .

Soon they were again hauling the plane to the starting point. But now the job was easy, for there was no need to use the hill on a windy day like this. The track was simply laid on level sand about one hundred feet from the Wrights' shed. Here the men placed the machine on the dolly, which rested as before on the monorail. Orville set up a camera and pointed it at the spot where he expected the plane to take off. . . .

The motor sputtered, then roared. The chain drive clanked away and the two pusher-propellers whirled around. The flyer trembled all over.

It was Orville's turn now, and at 10:35 A.M. he lay down in the cradle amidships. He too looked like a boy out sledding, but in another sense he looked like a misplaced businessman. As always, he wore a starched collar, tie, and dark suit. Wilbur, dressed the same way, took his stand by the right wing, to help balance the machine as it started on

On December 17, 1903, Wilbur and Orville Wright successfully flew this airplane over the sands of Kitty Hawk, North Carolina. Despite the importance of their achievement, few people took notice of the historic moment.

its way. Near his feet lay a shovel . . . a can of nails . . . a hammer sticking in it. Not very spectacular equipment, but somehow symbolic of two mechanically gifted men who didn't pretend to be scientific geniuses.

Orville released the wire that anchored the machine to the end of the monorail. Slowly—then faster—it lumbered down the track into the teeth of the wind. Wilbur ran alongside, holding the forward upright of the right wing. . . .

About forty feet down the track Orville jerked the front elevator wires. Up . . . up it rose, bobbing and wobbling through the air ten feet above the ground. It stayed up only twelve seconds, it went only 120 feet—but it certainly flew.

There couldn't have been less excitement. Wilbur and Orville knew it would work all along. The five spectators were pleased but not especially surprised. They had watched the Wrights gliding for three years—this seemed pretty much the same, except that this time the machine had a motor.

Into the Air Again

They hauled it back to the starting point and prepared for another flight. First, though, they had to warm up. Everyone pushed into the Wrights' little shack and crowded around the faithful carbide-can stove. Overhead were the "patent" beds, looking a little like Pullman upper berths. Along the unpainted walls were cans of food, pots, plates, and the bread pan which Orville used to bake rolls. It didn't look the like sort of place to solve the eternal problem of flight.

Nor was the conversation now about flying. Looking under the plain wooden table, Johnny Moore spied a bucket of eggs—more eggs in one place than he had seen before in his life. The people of the Outer Banks scratched along as best they could; when they did any feasting at all, it was invariably fish. This then was amazing.

He asked one of the life-saving crew where they all came from. The man reminded Johnny of a scrawy hen that was flapping around just outside the shack. "Well," he explained, "that chicken lays eight to ten eggs a day." Now here was something interesting. Moore bolted out to study the hen.

Convulsed with laughter they all trooped out to the machine again. It was Wilbur's turn. At 11:20 A.M. he took off, and again the plane bobbed along about ten feet above the ground. This time it went about 175 feet before slamming down into the sand. At 11:40 Orville tried again and got 200 feet.

It was exactly noon when Wilbur took off on the fourth flight. Again the flyer bounced along uncertainly for 100 feet or so. But now he understood the controls better. Even more important, he had the intuitive sense of balance that could only come from four years' experience flying gliders above the sands of Kitty Hawk. He knew just what to do and the machine responded perfectly. Two hundred . . . 300 . . . 600 . . . 852 feet it flew before an unexpected gust finally brought it down. It had been in the air for 59 seconds.

Just Another Piece of Sporting Equipment

That afternoon the Wrights turned to the pleasant task of informing the world of their triumph—but it seemed that the world wasn't interested. A wire telling their father to "inform press" produced nothing even in their home-town paper, the Dayton *Journal*. Some editors agreed with Simon Newcomb—a flying machine was impossible. Others confused airplanes with airships. Everyone knew that the great Santos-Dumont could keep his dirigible up an hour, make it circle the Eiffel Tower, do all sorts of things. Unless an aviator could match this, there was no story.

Only Editor Keville Glennan of the Norfolk *Virginian-Pilot* really understood. He had first heard of the Wrights in 1902, while covering a shipwreck on the Carolina coast. He instinctively realized it would be a great story if they ever got off the ground. Through a leak in the local telegraph office, Glennan now learned it had happened. He bannered the news across his front page.

But attempts at the *Virginian-Pilot* to sell the story elsewhere fell flat—only five papers bought the item and gingerly ran it the following day. When others finally picked it up later, the news proved quite a challenge to the city desk. No one knew quite how to handle the Wrights' achievement. The New York *Tribune* solved the problem in the neatest fashion. It carried the item on the sports page—just underneath the account of a sandlot football game in Brooklyn.

That seemed the best place, even after the new invention was better understood. Many of the most ardent enthusiasts thought of it only as a piece of sporting equipment. As late as 1907, a speaker at the International Aeronautical Congress thought that at best the flying machine might someday prove "useful in explorations of otherwise inaccessible places, such as mountain tops, swamps, or densely wooded regions."

All agreed it had little commercial future. The Wrights didn't think anyone would fly at night. And most authorities felt no one would ever build a machine large enough to carry a payload. Even in 1911, aviation expert W.B. Kaempffert believed that the invention would probably remain "a racing machine for gilded youth." Mr. Kaempffert also felt that the machine had little use in war: "that wholesale destruction of life and property which would seem obviously to follow from the mere existence of military flying-machines, freighted with bombs and grenades, is not to be looked for."

The reason? Kaempffert went back to a homely analogy: Every small boy knew how hard it was to drop a snowball on someone from a third-story window. Well, it would be all the more difficult to hit anything from a machine flying thirty-five miles an hour.

Acknowledgement at Last

The Wrights themselves thought that their invention would be a great force for peace. Through aerial reconnaissance each side could learn what the other was doing and wouldn't dare start anything itself. Their friend Octave Chanute agreed. Writing them in 1905, he even went a step further. He thought that the invention "will make more for peace in the hands of the British than in our own, for its existence will soon become known in a general way, and the knowledge will deter embroilments."

If so, Chanute had cause for hope. In 1904 the Wrights didn't go to Kitty Hawk, flew instead from Torrance Huffman's pasture near Dayton. By October they had made over fifty flights without attracting their neighbors, much less anybody in Washington. Then one day a letter unexpectedly arrived from Lieutenant Colonel J.E. Capper of the Royal Aircraft Factory at Aldershot. He would like very much to meet them.

The colonel and his wife proved charming guests. He knew a good deal about the Wrights. In fact, that was why he was here. Would the Wrights care to propose terms toward supplying their machine to His Majesty's Government?

The Wrights said they would think it over, and in January, 1905, wrote a letter still marking time. Eight days later they launched a serious campaign to interest Washington. For a long while they got nowhere. Twice, in fact, they received from the War Department virtually the same form letter of refusal.

Ultimately, there was the appropriate, happy ending. The British negotiations fell through; Washington saw the light. But not until 1907—after the Wrights had enjoyed nearly four years of successful flying.

Inventions That "Really Count"

It wasn't that Americans were oblivious of progress. They were enchanted when they understood. But the inventions that carried real meaning—that made life so exciting—were the simple things. A steady stream of them poured out these days . . . touching one and all, enriching the life of everyone: the safety razor, the "perpetual pencil," the subway, the long-distance telephone that now reached from New York to Omaha. With wonders like these, there seemed no end to the possibilities. Nobody even blinked at the advertisement for "Best-Light," a mysterious method that gave six times more light than electricity and cost only two cents a week.

The home especially seemed to take on new attractiveness from these inventions that "really counted." For the first time plumbing was coming into its own. "The luxury and pleasure of a shower bath," declared the Standard Sanitary ad, "is a revelation to those not already acquainted with its charming delights."

Entertainment too broadened in scope and meaning. There was, of course, the new Victor Talking Machine that played disks instead of the usual cylinders. But what especially intrigued people was the Kinetoscope, or Vitagraph—it had a dozen names—that projected moving pictures on a screen. It had been the tag end of vaudeville shows since the late '90s, but now it was suddenly coming into its own. First, little theatres, and now in 1903 a film with a plot—*The Life of an American Fireman*—that instantly promised a whole new field of diversion.

The automobile also was drawing closer to daily reality. It was even getting reliable. In the late summer of 1903, as the Wrights prepared their power-flyer, the whole nation cheered E.T. Fetch and M.C. Krarup, the dauntless pair who made the first coast-to-coast auto trip. They drove their Packard "Pacific" from San Francisco to New York in fifty-two days, but the press assured the public that, despite this fast time, they had many difficulties along the way. One stretch, according to *Popular Mechanics*, "made the autoists think they had certainly strolled beyond the domains of human aggression. An indefatigable perseverance and determination, however, successfully steered them out of this unearthly region." It turned out that the editor was referring to Utah. . . .

The afternoon after Theodore Roosevelt won the 1904 presidential election Wilbur and Orville Wright dragged their "whopper flying machine," out of its weather-beaten shed in the Huffman pasture near Dayton. Wilbur climbed aboard and took off on a three-mile flight that lasted over five minutes. It was their longest to date, and flown specifically in honor of what they called "the phenomenal political victory."

As usual they drew no headlines. But in the end this was perhaps inevitable. For the Wrights remained simple, unostentatious mechanics. Basically, they were still the proprietors of a small-town bicycle shop—they never pretended to be anything else. And the activities of such men, however talented, enjoyed little popular interest. These were the days before the emergence of the scientist and inventor—or even the sport and movie star—as a public personality. For the vicarious glamour that enriches drab lives, people turned invariably to the dazzling world of Society and fashion.

Henry Ford and His Motorcar for the Masses

Stewart H. Holbrook

In 1903, Henry Ford organized a new company in Detroit—the Ford Motor Company. Author Stewart H. Holbrook relates how Ford, whom Holbrook calls the "great
tinker," turned his company into a billion-dollar operation
and revolutionized the American way of life in the process.
Holbrook writes about how Ford overcame all opposition
and designed and produced the Model T, or "Tin Lizzie,"
the first motorcar that the average working person could afford to buy. In Holbrook's view, the Model T became the
nation's "sensational gadget." Before he became an editor
and author of numerous successful works about Americans
and American history, the late Holbrook had a varied career
as a semi-pro baseball player, a reporter, an actor, and a log-
ger in Canadian lumber camps. Holbrook also was a lecturer for several years at Harvard University in Cambridge,
Massachusetts, and at Boston University in Massachusetts.

Two unrelated events of 1909 marked the twilight of one
era for Americans and the dawn of another. In the same
year that saw the passing of Edward H. Harriman, the great
railroader, Henry Ford launched his Model T automobile.

Ford's announcement contained as little grace as the

thing he was talking about. "I will build a motorcar for the great multitude," he said pompously. He went on to remark that the Model T was to be so low in price it would be within the means of everyone; and wound up with a reference to Deity and a resounding cliché. Everyone and his family, concluded Ford, could, with his new car, "enjoy the blessing of hours of pleasure in God's great open spaces."

The professional advertising men may have gagged, as well they might, but in the next nineteen years Ford made and sold fifteen million copies of his Model T and stamped his name indelibly on an era.

Ford had nothing to do with inventing the internal combustion engine, or even with the assembly-line method of manufacture, which was already old when Ford was born. What he did was to take both the invention and the method and tinker them into near perfection. He did more than that. His theory in regard to wages . . . created, or rather forced, a new philosophy that Ford's contemporary manufacturers found hard to accept.

The Dawn of the Horseless Carriage

The great tinker or the "divine mechanic," as he has been called, was born on a farm in 1863. He did not want to be a farmer, though his gaunt face and angular frame were considered characteristically rustic and he did not like big cities or big-city people. As soon as he was able he left his father's acres, where his only interest had been farm machinery and cheap watches, and went to Detroit to work in a powerhouse. His spare time was spent wholly in tinkering, mostly with a gasoline engine of his own contrivance.

Other Americans were tinkering with similar engines which they were attaching to buggies. Still other Americans were applying electric power to buggies. And the traditionalists were using steam power for the same purpose. In the summer of 1893, Charles Duryea braved ridicule by running his little gasoline machine up and down the streets of Chicopee Falls, Massachusetts. A year later, a horseless carriage built by Elwood Haynes and the Apperson brothers,

Elmer and Edgar, made the Fourth of July memorable at Kokomo, Indiana.

Meanwhile Henry Ford had put together a machine that would run pretty good. Only lack of money prevented him from taking it to Chicago in 1895, where an endurance run for horseless carriages had been sponsored. In that year there were approximately three hundred motor vehicles in the United States, mostly homemade affairs. (England had more than twice as many.)

Possibly the first motorcar made specifically for sale in the United States was a job by Alexander Winton, marketed in 1898. After that, things began to happen rapidly. The fast-money boys were quick to sense a new opportunity for stock issues. During the first four months of 1899, at least eighty concerns were formed, allegedly to make one or another type of motorcar. Their stock issues totaled $338,000,000, and though few of the companies made many cars, and some made no cars at all, the amount of stock offered for sale indicated that Americans, who had been bilked with canal stocks, bilked again with railroad stocks, were positively gluttons.

Then, on Christmas Day, 1900, occurred an omen of the great new age in the making, when in New York City, a "young woman was knocked down and fatally injured while crossing Broadway by an automobile vehicle." The Ford era had arrived, even though the Ford Motor Company was three years in the future.

Henry Ford's Motor Company

Henry Ford tinkered on. Finally he put together a car that would run like the very wind and drove it himself in a number of the early races. In 1903, with twelve partners who put up a total of $28,000, the Ford Motor Company was organized in Detroit.

Parts for the cars were to be made under contract by several different companies. Space for an assembly plant was rented for seventy-five dollars a month. Ten men were hired at $1.50 a day. Ford thought that the outfit, of which he was manager and tinker general, could make ten cars daily.

There was plenty of competition. Buick had just been incorporated. Apperson, Franklin, Pierce-Arrow, and Stearns had been in business for two years or more. Cadillac, Overland, and Packard had been making cars for more than a year. The older firms, all dating from the 1890s, included Haynes, Locomobile, Oldsmobile, and Studebaker. There was also a host of others, possibly as many as five hundred, which came and went, most of them leaving stock certificates to go into attic trunks along with yellowing certificates of shares in canals that were never dug and railroads that were never built.

The new Ford Motor Company progressed steadily through the usual lean periods and hard times customary with most business enterprises. In five years it increased output about fivefold. During this time Ford had tried eight different models, which varied from two to six cylinders. Both chain drive and shaft drive were used. One model had the engine behind the driver's seat. The output had grown to one hundred cars a day. Ford himself was still the boss mechanic, seldom far from the bench and the drafting board.

Five of Henry Ford's original partners were afflicted with shortsightedness. They wanted to get out. Ford was glad to buy their stock, which gave him majority control of the company. Now he could go ahead with an idea that had been brewing in his mind, namely, to make one thousand cars a day. A car that would sell for no more than the price of a horse and a buggy.

A Great Innovation—The Model T

Ford's remaining associates were solidly against 1,000 cars a day. They were "inexpressibly shocked" and even contemplated court action to stop the madness. But Ford went ahead to design, then to announce Model T, the one and only model that was to occupy him for the next two decades.

There may be Americans who have never seen a Model T, but they cannot be many and their lives have been singularly circumscribed. It was a stark, almost a grim affair, this black mechanical monster that was to change life in America in so many ways, this new god of Henry Ford's countrymen.

Its appearance interested Ford no more than did the nuances of grammar. He meant that this thing, this vehicle, should *run*, that its owner could repair it with haywire or, if seriously injured, with new parts supplied cheaply by Ford dealers all over the country. He meant that its first cost and its upkeep should be within the means of those who, just a little later, were to be familiarly known as the lower third or the "little people."

In 1909 Ford's idea was revolutionary. In that era motorcars were generally considered to be the ostentatious toys of the wealthy. Dr. Woodrow Wilson, president of Princeton University, saw the deepest social aspects in the automobile, and said publicly that the motorcar presented "a picture of the arrogance of wealth, with all its independence and carelessness." He felt that more than anything else it had "spread socialistic feelings" among Americans.

Henry Ford's Model T stopped any such socialistic feelings in their tracks. Within a few years the lowest proletarians were seeing America, or at least getting around, in Ford cars; and one-gallus sharecroppers had something besides procreation to amuse them. Yet, the motor era which Ford did so much to usher in also brought a new caste system that was founded on neither birth nor wealth nor brains, but simply the make of car a man owned. Vestiges of it are still to be seen. . . .

General Motors Is No Great Competition

Ford got Model T into production not a moment too soon. A promoter named William Durant was putting together what he hoped would be an automobile trust similar to U.S. Steel and Standard Oil. He called it General Motors. Into it went Buick, Cadillac, Oldsmobile, and lesser concerns. (Durant also wanted the Maxwell Company, and Ford, but failed to get them.) Durant tried to get capital from J.P. Morgan & Company, boasting to the bankers that half a million cars could be made and sold every year.

The House of Morgan dismissed Durant as visionary and otherwise unstable.

Promoter Durant at last got from the banking houses of Lee Higginson and J. & W. Seligman a five-year loan of fifteen million dollars. These bankers considered motor making so risky that General Motors had to pay them two and a half million in cash and some four million in securities. The loan not only came high, but the bankers also insisted on a first mortgage and forced Durant to surrender leadership of the company to the bankers' representative. The high-priced loan was used for plant expansion and to buy materials.

Henry Ford's Model T was meanwhile becoming the sensational gadget of the United States. Selling for a little under a thousand dollars in 1909, its price dropped spasmodically over the years to low as $295. "Watch the Fords Go By" was more than a slogan. Almost every other car on the dusty highways was a Model T. It was the only automobile that went into folklore. Cartoonists, gagsters, vaudeville comedians, and the anonymous fraternity that invents off-color stories went to work on the Ford car with enthusiasm. It was the Tin Lizzie, and more things happened to Tin Lizzie than ever happened to the farmer's daughter of legend. The Ford Motor Company had a conventional advertising appropriation, though it was not needed. No American gadget ever received so much free advertising as Model T.

In 1914 approximately two hundred and fifty thousand Model T cars were made and sold. They accounted for forty-five per cent of all automobiles made in the United States that year. . . .

An Embarrassment of Riches

During its first quarter century the Ford Company profits came to one billion dollars. Henry Ford was in no manner astonished. He told his friend, Garet Garrett, that "a business absolutely devoted to service will have only one worry about profits. They will be embarrassingly large."

The Ford profits *were* embarrassingly large, yet of all of America's very wealthy men, Henry Ford almost alone seems to have escaped the charge of being a bloated capitalist, as the popular phrase had it. This may have been due in some part to the fact that he neither looked nor acted nor thought like a J.P. Morgan or a John D. Rockefeller, or even a Jim Hill. His was a bucolic figure, and at heart he was a rustic. He hated banks and bankers. He abhorred idle people. Again and again he denounced the profit motive, and for all his immense fortune, one is prepared to believe that Ford really did not care for money.

If he ever thought of himself as the champion of anything, it was as the champion of the man with the hoe, or the hammer. Far from being classed with the moneybags of the nation, Ford was considered a radical, perhaps a revolutionary. . . .

At the time of his death, which came in 1947, Henry Ford was eighty-four years old. The Ford Motor Company was still a family affair. What Ford himself was "worth" in money is impossible to know. Statements appeared in financial pages saying that a billion dollars would not be far wrong. To spend the Ford personal income he had long since established the foundation that bears his name. . . .

In his later years Ford devoted much time and a great deal of money to the collection of Americana. Whether or not this was a conscious effort to live down his most celebrated remark, namely, that "History is bunk," is not to be known. It may have come to him, over the years, that his Model T had done more than any other one thing to remove the America he had known in his youth, known even as a man of forty. It had eliminated the old-fashioned farm isolation. It had radically changed hamlets and villages. It had done something to large cities.

Peary Conquers the North Pole

Donald B. MacMillan

For years, controversy surrounded Arctic explorer Robert Peary's claim to have discovered the North Pole in 1909. Many experts found flaws in Peary's accounts of his expedition. In the following selection, Arctic explorer Donald B. MacMillan describes the hardships Peary experienced on his various Arctic expeditions in the late 1800s and early 1900s. In MacMillan's view, Peary was a great leader, whose perseverance and leadership qualities gained him the respect and loyalty of his men. MacMillan argues that Peary was the first to arrive at the North Pole and contends that those that doubted Peary did not give enough consideration to the all-important facts he identifies in the selection. Donald B. MacMillan was a member of Peary's 1909 expedition and led his own Arctic expedition from 1913–1917.

"Stars and stripes nailed to the Pole!"

The accomplishment of that which had been declared repeatedly to be the impossible, that which our strongest nations had striven to do for more than three hundred years, at the cost of many lives and the expenditure of millions of dollars, demanded great leadership.

What manner of man was this who persuaded the polar Eskimos to penetrate to the interior of the great *ser-mik-suah*, the abode of evil spirits; induced them to leave their

Reprinted from Donald B. MacMillan, "Peary as a Leader," *National Geographic*, April 1920.

homes and journey seven hundred miles due north; to travel out over the drift-ice of the Polar Sea so far that they declared that they would never again see their wives and children? . . .

We find the key to Rear Admiral Robert E. Peary's character in his reply to the late ex-President Roosevelt upon the presentation of the Hubbard Medal of the National Geographic Society upon the explorer's return in 1906 from the world's record of "Farthest North," when he said:

"The true explorer does his work not for any hopes of reward or honor, but because the thing which he has set himself to do is a part of his being and must be accomplished for the sake of its accomplishment.

"To me the final and complete solution of the polar mystery, which has engaged the best thought and interests of some of the best men of the most vigorous and enlightened nations of the world for more than three centuries, and which today stirs the heart of every man or woman whose veins hold red blood, is the thing which should be done for the honor and credit of this country, the thing which it is intended that I should do, and the thing that I must do.". . .

An Expedition to Greenland

On the 15th of July, 1886, far in on the back of the great ice-cap of Greenland, at an altitude of 7,525 feet, lay two forms huddled in the snow. For forty-eight hours they listened to the sullen roar of wind and drifting snow across their bodies. . . .

At the first peep of dawn of the long Arctic day we find Peary accepting the challenge and assembling his forces at the edge of the ice-cap. On Independence Day the American flag was unfurled at Navy Cliff, some six hundred miles to the north.

When, weeks later, he struggles toward home over that apparently endless white waste, with inflamed eyes, frostbitten and sunburnt face, dropping dogs, and food nearly gone, he looks up into the clear heavens and declares that "man was not born to die beneath such a sky.". . .

Peary Refuses to Succumb

Six years later, contrary to all Arctic precedent, he dared to harness his dogs, leave his ship frozen in the ice, and sledge northward in the middle of the big Arctic night.

With the thermometer at fifty and sixty below zero, not a particle of food in his sledges, he groped his way along the eastern shores of Ellesmere Land, around Cape Baird, and into Lady Franklin Bay, searching for the headquarters of the Greely Expedition, abandoned sixteen years before.

He stumbled through the door with both feet frozen to the ankles. Nothing could be done here to relieve his suffering. Toe after toe sloughed off. Finally he was lashed to a sledge and carried through the broken ice of bays and inlets and along the ice foot back to his ship, two hundred miles to the south. And with him, to aid in the amputation of the stumps of eight toes, went a can of anesthetic, found there in the house and brought into the Arctic regions in 1881.

Now a cripple? Within thirty-seven days following the final amputation was headed north again, equipped with crutches!

The antagonistic elements of the Northland should have submitted meekly and bowed humbly, as this plucky little caravan wound its way up through Kennedy and Robeson channels with the great unknown as its objective point.

The *Roosevelt* Sets Sail

Two years later we find this intrepid man encamped on the bleak shores of Cape Sabine, surrounded by his loyal Eskimos, patiently perfecting his equipment and preparing for that hazardous trip of eight hundred miles to the top of the earth. . . .

Four years he remained in the North, and returned scarred and temporarily beaten, but with a knowledge of why he was beaten—the secret of final success. His staunch friends believed in him and gathered around him, and in the fall of 1904 they saw the sturdy *Roosevelt* beginning to take shape under the skillful hands of Maine shipbuilders.

With engines throbbing under high pressure and smoke belching from her funnel, Peary and Captain Bob Bartlett fairly hurled this first American-built Polar ship around Cape Sheridan and into the Polar Sea, farther north than any other ship had ever steamed. She had done what she was planned to do; she had justified her existence; and there she lay, on the northern shore of Grant Land, panting like an athlete at the end of the race. . . .

Long before the sun returned, the ninety-mile trail to Cape Columbia was patted down with the feet of more than two hundred dogs. From that point to the Pole the course lay straight out over the drift-ice of the Polar Sea for 413 miles. . . .

With the ever-repeated "Huk! Huk!" and the snapping of whips, men, dogs, and sledges were swallowed up in the rough sea ice. And again silence reigned along the shore, along the face of the cliff, and in and about the deserted snow village.

The Pole Eludes Peary Again

All went well for a few days, which is but a friendly ruse of the Arctic to inspire confidence, and then it happened—a six-day blizzard, obliterating the trail, smashing up the ice of the Polar Sea, scattering and destroying caches of food, and driving all . . . 60 miles to the east. . . .

One by one the various divisions struggled shoreward; but Peary and his men, although knowing that no relief could be expected from the rear, that all food supplies were gone, deliberately turned their backs toward home and their faces toward their objective point and plodded on until they stood at the world's record of "Farthest North," 174 miles from the Pole.

Weeks later that tired little band climbed feebly up over the ice foot on the northern coast of Greenland, burned their last sledge for fuel, ate one of three dogs, and began their long walk back to the ship, frozen in the ice at Cape Sheridan. Within two weeks this indomitable man was heading west along the northern shores of Grant Land, in a thousand-mile trip to the northern shores of Axel Heiberg Island!

Such a journey immediately following such an experience in the Polar Sea was so improbable and apparently impossible so late in the year that many were inclined to doubt Peary's claim to have reached that distant point. . . .

In 1906 Peary arrived in America, reporting that he had failed to reach the Pole, but declaring that he would make another and last attempt. . . .

A Final Attempt for the Pole

We entered upon this enterprise with no misunderstanding. We knew what we were facing, for we had followed him in our reading for years. We knew that this was probably his last attempt, and that he might go beyond the limit of safety, but, if so, then we all wanted to be with him and were eager for the start.

As we steamed along the Labrador coast and out into the ice of Baffin Bay, we began to know our commander and were drawn strangely toward the man whom we recognized as one thoroughly versed in ice technique—a master of his profession. We often recalled the parting words of President Roosevelt at Oyster Bay: "Peary, I believe in you, and if it is possible for man to get there, I know you'll do it!". . .

Decks were cleared for our battle in Melville Bay. Holds were carefully restored: necessary food and equipment made readily accessible: boats supplied with provisions, rifles, and ammunition for a retreat following a possible loss of our ship. . . .

Those happy days of wending our way northward in and out between floes and icebergs passed all too quickly. Finally that day arrived when we passed in under the big hills of Meteorite Island and heard the glad cry of those Far North natives upon beholding "Peary-ark-suah" (Big Peary) back again.

Let there be no doubt as to Peary's popularity in the Far North. Absolutely honest and square in all his dealings with these black-haired children of the Arctic, firm but ever just and kind in all his relations, he remains to them as the great "Nalegak," a leader or chief among men.

We can never forget this reception at Cape York—kayaks darting about the ship, the shouts of his former dog drivers, men who had starved with him on the Polar Sea, others on the shore standing at the water's edge ready to grasp the bow of our boat, women laughing, babies crying, and half-grown children with that look of mingled fear and animal curiosity.

How happy they were to see him back and how eagerly and how impatiently they awaited the word to pack their world's goods and transfer all to the deck of the *Roosevelt* for the long voyage northward.

And so it was at every village: the best men in the whole tribe awaited his call. . . .

The Push Northward Continues

Some three weeks later, with decks almost awash and black and fuzzy with dogs and Eskimos, the saucy-looking *Roosevelt* swung around Sunrise Point and into the heavy ice of Smith Sound, her destination the northern shores of Grant Land, far up at the edge of the Polar Sea.

Behind us, upon the shores of Foulke Fjord, was a reserve of coal and food, to which Peary and his men could retreat if their ship was crushed. Such wise precaution was the result of his years of labor in the North and his repeated failures.

The successful negotiation of this last dangerous stretch Peary considered as the crucial link in the long chain of success. That no opportunity for advance should be lost was very evident from his almost constant vigil on the bridge, in the main rigging, or in the crow's nest. . . .

Together Captain Bob Bartlett and Peary drove their ship farther northward than any other ship ever steamed. Boats were ready for immediate launching: food lined the rail; emergency bags were packed.

Once in our winter quarters, Peary again displayed his qualities of leadership by removing from the ship everything absolutely needed for the attainment of the Pole and the retreat southward, if the vessel should be crushed, carried away by the ice, or burned.

In spite of the loss of the *Roosevelt*, the work would have been carried out as planned. Even houses were built to shelter the large contingent of seventy-five men, women, and children.

Preserving the Enthusiasm

With the Arctic night now coming on, the problem presented itself of how to preserve the health and happiness and good spirits until the time of our departure out over the ice of the Polar Sea five months later. . . .

Peary's men were away with a crack of whip and laughter and enthusiasm almost as soon as our keel touched bottom at the edge of the Polar Sea, and they continued to come and go throughout the year, far into the interior of Grant Land, in quest of musk-oxen, caribou, and Arctic hare; for Peary, who never had a single case of scurvy on any of his expeditions, fully appreciated the value of fresh meat as an antiscorbutic. . . .

These excursions were not merely to keep us in good health and contentment: every move was directed toward the success of the expedition, geographically and scientifically. There were no schools between decks for the men, as in olden days; no weeks of preparation for farce or drama; no weekly or monthly periodical published; no roped promenade from berg to berg; no long hours in bed between meals.

We were either away with our dog teams among the mountains of Grant Land hunting reindeer, musk-oxen, or Arctic hare or were one hundred miles up or down the coast, living in snow houses, engaged in taking tidal observations, or at the ship working upon our equipment for the Polar dash.

If one word was written large upon the face of every man and upon the walls of every little stateroom in the steamship *Roosevelt*, it was the word *enthusiasm*. . . .

The Importance of Equipment

Certain items [of equipment] were so far superior to anything yet devised for Arctic work that their value, even to a novice, was obvious. Such were perfected by Peary following years of repeated struggle. . . .

As an illustration, previous to the 1908 trip the most satisfactory stove for Arctic sledge-work was the so-called Primus, which converts cracked ice at 60 below zero into a gallon of tea in about 20 minutes. Peary reasoned that the more rapid his stove, the more sleep for his men at the end of the long march. He thereupon devised a stove which is so economical in fuel consumption and so quick in its action that many are almost inclined to doubt the fact that we had our gallon of tea in *nine* minutes from the time that the match was applied.

Our clothing, that of the Smith Sound Eskimo, could not be improved upon. Our food was amply sufficient for the maintenance of health and strength. Our sledges were modeled by Peary for the rough ice of the Polar Sea and skillfully fashioned by our master mechanic, Matt Henson. Our equipment was without a doubt the most nearly perfect yet devised for Polar work.

Peary's plan for advance and attack upon the Pole, based upon his experience and failure in 1906, was unique and a large factor in his final success.

From the time when one leaves the northern shores of Grant Land or Greenland, one must depend wholly upon the food on the sledges for sustenance of men and dogs. An occasional bear or seal might be secured, but such would be the exception. . . .

To feed Peary and his men until he was within striking distance of the Pole and selfsupporting for the five hundred miles of the return trip was the work assigned to the so-called supporting parties under the command of Henson, Bartlett, Marvin, Borup, Goodsell, and myself.

Every five days a white man and his Eskimos were to return to land with an amount of food equal to one-half consumed in the outward trip, with orders to double march, and if held up by open water to eat the dogs. The work of this division was done: it was no longer needed in a task where one's life might depend upon ounces, not pounds; where every additional particle of food is a synonym for miles of travel, and where the last ounce might mean the last mile and success in one's life-work.

The Urgency of Success

In general, the American people have minimized the dangers of travel on the Polar Sea and have overestimated the narrow margin of safety of even a small party five hundred miles from land.

The presence of one man not absolutely needed in the work endangers the lives of all, for that man must be fed and must receive an equal amount of the last bite. . . .

Every man realized what the success of this trip meant to Peary, and each man knew that the sooner he returned to land after he had finished his work, the better the chances of Peary reaching his goal. . . .

Weeks later the little band of six returned, clearly revealing the terrible strain and anxiety during that rapid dash to land over ice fields which threatened to be rent asunder by the high tides of the approaching full moon. In fact, the work was *too* well done, as many a doubt as to Peary's achievement was based upon the time of his return.

Peary Was the First

During the days of that most unfortunate controversy [over Peary's claim to have reached the Pole] enough consideration was not given by the public to the following all-important facts:

First. Peary's supporting parties placed him at nearly the 88th parallel.

Second. The observations at this point were taken and signed by Captain Bartlett, of the *Roosevelt*.

Third. From this point on Peary had five well-provisioned sledges, five of the best men of 25, 48 of the best dogs of 250, and only 120 miles to go.

Fourth. The trail to land was well marked and broken ends knit together by the retreat of the various divisions.

Fifth. All expeditions for a half century have double-marched and even triple-marched on the return trip.

How often have I heard the assertion that Peary told none of his men that he had reached the Pole until he learned of Dr. Frederick Cook's attainment! Far up on the northern shores of Grant Land, at the edge of the Polar Sea, there stands a cairn, Peary's announcement of the attainment of his life's work, built there *twelve weeks* before we reached civilization. He did not forget his men. The names not only of his assistants, but of every man on board the *Roosevelt*, are written there and placed under glass as a protection against the weather. . . .

Naturally eager to steam southward to proclaim to the world the news of his discovery after so many years of hardship, yet Peary felt that his first duty was toward his Eskimos, those natives who made it possible for him to win out. And there we remained, killing walrus and supplying them with food for the long winter night to come. . . .

Fond and Sad Memories

We steamed southward from Indian Harbor, and upon our arrival at Battle Harbor our Commander was met by a flood of telegrams from the press and from various geographical and scientific societies at home and abroad. . . .

As we steamed southward on our last lap with this great explorer, we often reviewed the year that had gone so quickly, and our relations with our leader. . . .

I well remember falling through the ice at 59 below zero. With sealskin boots filled with water and rapidly stiffening clothes, I arrived at our encampment of snow houses. Peary beat the ice from my bearskin pants, pulled off my boots, and wiped my feet and legs with the inside of his warm shirt. And when covered with blood, a heavy 40-82 bullet having passed through my arm, into my shoulder, and out through the back, and clipping the side of one finger, he remarked: "I would much rather had that thing happen to me than to you!"....

Is it any wonder . . . that we as assistants, when we heard the blowing of the whistles of Sydney, N. S.; beheld the line of craft circling out to escort us into the harbor; saw waving flags and docks black with people, should be almost sorry that he had won out?

We knew that never again would we have the honor and the pleasure of serving under such a leader.

CHAPTER 5

Beyond American Boundaries

The Rise of American Imperialism

Warren Zimmermann

Former U.S. ambassador to Yugoslavia Warren Zimmermann shares his views on America's imperialism during the late 1800s and early 1900s. He contends that, contrary to popular belief, America was not at all isolated in the late 1800s. By then, Zimmermann writes, the United States was already a "would-be imperialist power." He attributes the rise of American imperialism to popular theories on social Darwinism, the development of a larger navy, and the influence of the press and powerful politicians. During the early 1900s, Americans had a new and stronger sense of mission brought to the forefront and kept there by such politically astute and determined leaders as Theodore Roosevelt.

I n 1898, America's role in the world changed forever. A country whose power and influence had been largely limited to the continent of North America suddenly acquired a global reach that it would never relinquish.

The march of events behind this transformation has the staccato urgency of an old Movietone newsreel. On April 25, 1898, two months after the sinking of the USS *Maine* in Havana Bay, the United States goes to war with Spain over Cuba. On May 1, some 8,000 miles away in the Philippines, Admiral George Dewey destroys the Spanish fleet off Manila. On June 21, the U.S. Navy seizes the tiny,

Excerpted from "Jingoes, Goo-Goos, and the Rise of America's Empire," by Warren Zimmermann, *The Wilson Quarterly*, Spring 1998. Reprinted with permission from the author.

Spanish-held island of Guam, with its fine Pacific harbor, 1,000 miles east of Manila.

The zigzag pattern of conquest continues, from the Caribbean to the Pacific and back. On July 1, Lieutenant Colonel Theodore Roosevelt, attired in a brass-buttoned uniform just bought from Brooks Brothers, leads his Rough Riders in an exuberant charge—on foot—up San Juan Hill in eastern Cuba. Routing a poorly armed Spanish force, Roosevelt's troops take the heights overlooking Santiago Bay, where, two days later, the U.S. Navy wins the battle for Cuba by capturing an entire Spanish squadron. On July 7, President William McKinley, exulting in the expansionist fervor, annexes Hawaii, under de facto control of American sugar planters since 1893. On August 13, Manila falls to Dewey. The next day, the U.S. Army takes control of the Spanish island colony of Puerto Rico after an efficient nine-day campaign launched almost as an afterthought to the action in Cuba. On December 10, by the Treaty of Paris, Spain cedes to the United States the Philippines, Guam, and Puerto Rico, none of which had been important prewar American objectives. Spain also renounces sovereignty over Cuba, which *had* been the principal U.S. objective, thus opening the island to American military rule.

America Becomes an Empire

And so, by force of arms, America in only a few months' time had gained territorial possessions on both the Atlantic and Pacific sides of its continental mass. Nor did imperial expansion end with 1898. In an 1899 division of Samoa with Germany, the United States acquired the strategic deep-water harbor off Pago Pago. A jagged line of bases, or "coaling stations" as they were called in the age of steam, now ran from California to Hawaii to Samoa to the Philippines. This chain of possessions made possible the extension of American political and economic influence to China—an opportunity Secretary of State John Hay's Open Door Policy of 1899 was designed to seize. The new imperialism culminated in the linking of America's Atlantic and

Pacific holdings via a canal across the narrow waist of Central America. President Roosevelt set this project in motion in November 1903, subverting the government of Colombia to produce an ostensibly revolutionary Panamanian government willing to sign the requisite treaty.

By 1903, America's role in the world had been transformed. Throughout the 19th century the country had expanded steadily, but its growth had been overland—to the Hispanic south, to the sparsely populated west, even to noncontiguous Alaska. Now, however, the nation expanded overseas—indeed, all its new acquisitions were islands. This burst of offshore conquests, compressed into the last two years of the old century and the first three of the new, made the United States a genuine empire.

The United States would never again acquire as much territory as it did during those eventful years, but that half-decade marked a turning point in the way America related to the world. It gave Americans and their leaders self-confidence, a sense of their own power, and an abiding belief that they could shape international life according to their values. Thus, it foreshadowed the often awesome ambiguities of America's waxing and waning global involvements during the whole of the 20th century. . . .

The Forces Behind the New Imperialism

Why did America launch itself so abruptly upon an imperialist course? Wasn't this a nation that had taken to heart George Washington's admonition against "foreign entanglements," a nation, moreover, that had spent most of the 19th century in an isolation guaranteed by two wide oceans and the protection of the British navy? No less a man than Secretary of State John Quincy Adams, a principal author of the 1823 Monroe Doctrine, which asserted U.S. hemispheric authority, had said, "America does not go abroad in search of monsters to destroy."

The answer is that this picture of isolation was never quite accurate. By the early 19th century, the United States was already a would-be imperialist power. . . .

Cuba had long been a special attraction. No fewer than four American presidents before McKinley, beginning with Polk in 1848, tried to buy the island from Spain. The settlement of the Pacific coast also stirred President Polk to negotiate with Colombia to open the way for an isthmian canal. Secretary of State William Henry Seward, who acquired Alaska in 1867, also sought the Virgin Islands, as well as British Columbia and Greenland. President Ulysses S. Grant's efforts to annex Santo Domingo in 1870 got as far as a tie vote in the Senate. Canada was a perennial target of American imperialists; Theodore Roosevelt was not the first American president to cast covetous eyes on it.

The Pacific, for which no Monroe Doctrine existed, was not exempt from American designs. Hawaii, where Americans had fishing and missionary interests early in the century and lucrative sugar plantations later, was always considered the most delectable morsel. . . .

For the most part, America's early imperial gestures went nowhere. Clearly, something had changed during the last decades of the century to make the United States a more decisive player in the imperial game.

One change was the exhaustion of the territorial frontier after the Civil War, combined with a surge of wealth that made the United States the world's largest economy by the 1890s. These facts of historical geography and economics diverted restless energies overseas. Official attention to Cuba and Hawaii was largely stimulated by American sugar interests there. Senator Henry Cabot Lodge equated trade with territory: "We must not be left behind. . . . In the economic struggle the great nations of Europe for many years have been seizing all the waste places, and all the weakly held lands of the earth, as the surest means of trade development."

A second factor was a new sense of mission that dominated the latter part of the century, an idealistic fervor that partook equally of Darwin and God. . . .

The Darwinian notion of racial competition fit nicely with the American doctrine of Manifest Destiny, by which the West had been conquered and the Indians subdued. The most enthusiastic proponent of both was Theodore Roosevelt, who took a racialist, if not exactly racist, view of history. "All the great masterful races," he claimed, "have been fighting races, and the minute that a race loses the hard fighting virtues, then . . . it has lost its proud right to stand as the equal of the best. . . . Cowardice in a race, as in an individual, is the unpardonable sin.". . .

Third, these moral and biological arguments were reinforced by the development of an American imperial strategy calling for a large navy, Pacific bases, an isthmian canal, and, above all, an assertive role for a growing world power bound for rivalry with Great Britain, Germany, and Japan.

Finally, the new imperialism was stimulated by a phenomenon that remains with us today—the influence of the press. William Randolph Hearst and Joseph Pulitzer realized that a war with Spain over Cuba would sell newspapers. . . . Hearst and his rival Pulitzer shamelessly invented Spanish atrocities against Cuban revolutionaries. And when the *Maine* blew up, Hearst's *New York Journal* sprang to accuse the Spanish. "THE WARSHIP *MAINE* WAS SPLIT IN TWO BY AN ENEMY'S SECRET INFERNAL MACHINE," it blared, though it had no evidence (and none was ever found) that the Spanish were responsible. . . .

The last decade of the 19th century brought to a climax, and ultimately decided, a battle between those who urged American expansion and those who opposed it. The conflicting passions provided a valuable and sometimes eloquent debate over basic American traditions and values. Less benign were the calumny, insult, and invective that often marked the rhetoric. From the safe distance of his expatriate life in London, Henry James called Roosevelt "a dangerous and ominous jingo." (The word comes from a London music-hall ballad: "We don't want to fight/ But by Jingo if we do,/ We've got the ships, we've got the men,/ We've got the money too!") Roosevelt dismissed James as a "miserable little snob." His generic epithet for his anti-imperialist opponents was "goo-goos," a contemptuous reference to self-proclaimed advocates of "good government."

The Fathers of Modern Imperialism

The role of powerful personalities working in opposition and in concert is often as important as that of impersonal forces in shaping world-historical developments. One way to understand the cause, consequences, and character of America's imperial breakout is to look closely at the men most responsible for it. While a list of "jingoes" would be long, five figures stand out: John Hay, secretary of state under McKinley and Roosevelt, and the only one of the five whose political career spanned the entire period between the Civil War and the Spanish-American War; Alfred T.

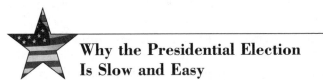

Why the Presidential Election Is Slow and Easy

The two candidates in the presidential election of 1900 were the incumbent, William McKinley, and the man he had beaten in the last election—William Jennings Bryan. Most Americans did not get too worked up about the election, in which a main issue was American imperialism. The author of this editorial, which appeared in Overland Monthly *magazine two weeks before the election, offers one explanation of why the campaign has been "so tame."*

Although there are but two more weeks until election day, the campaign still drags along in a lifeless way, without much apparent interest to anybody. The oratory seems to be left to William Jennings Bryan on the one side, and to Roosevelt and Hanna on the other. Illinois and Indiana are being stirred up considerably, because it is conceded that anything is possible in those two States. McKinley carried Illinois by 148,000 majority over Bryan last time, but then the Gold Democrats were out for blood and got it. Illinois was [John] Palmer's own State and his candidature played havoc with Bryan's chances. It must be remembered that Cleveland's majority in the State in 1892 was over 80,000. It is in order for the pendulum to swing back this year. The conditions are all favorable for the change. The labor conditions are bitter

Mahan, a naval officer and military philosopher of genius; Elihu Root, a New York corporation lawyer who, as secretary of war under McKinley and Roosevelt, was responsible for the administration of the Philippines and Cuba; Henry Cabot Lodge, the devious junior senator from Massachusetts, for whom American imperialism was close to a sacred creed; and Theodore Roosevelt himself, who towered over even these giants in his intellect, energy, and determination.

These five could fairly be called the fathers of modern American imperialism. Coming together at a critical period of American history, they helped to shape it. . . .

---

in Chicago, and will be heard from on election day. Indiana went for McKinley by 18,000 majority, for Cleveland by nearly double that number. The Bryanites expect to carry it this year. Imperialism is most unpopular in Indiana. But conceding the two States in question to Bryan, his chances of success would seem to be exceedingly slim. McKinley is believed, by the closest figures in national politics, to be absolutely sure of 258 electoral votes, which of course gives him the election. It is a curious fact that in the South both races are for Bryan. The erstwhile slave owners and slaves alike see in him the coming redeemer. If our "subjects" in Porto Rico, Hawaii and the Philippines had votes they would also cast them for Nebraska's favorite son. Mr. Bryan has been on the stump for the past four years and his sayings are widely known. Mr. McKinley's doings during all that time have been known to the people. We think that the bulk of American citizens long ago decided for one or the other, and that probably is the chief reason why the campaign is so tame. In England the men who conducted a successful war are carrying everything before them. The same thing would have happened to Mr. McKinley had he but cleared out of the Philippines. We do not doubt that he will be reelected, but his backbone will not receive the stiffening it badly needs, by the proportions of his popular majority.

Editorial, *Overland Monthly*, October 1900.

Secretary of State John Hay

John Hay, the oldest of the five, was born in Indiana in 1838, the son of a doctor who moved his family to Warsaw, Illinois, when John was three. . . .

Hay had a protean career. He was an aide to President Abraham Lincoln at age twenty-two, a best-selling poet and novelist, and for a time, editor of the *New York Tribune*. He served as a diplomat in Paris, Vienna, and Madrid before becoming ambassador to the Court of Saint James. . . .

Hay did not become secretary of state until September 1898, after the Spanish had been defeated in Cuba and the Philippines. He was thus an implementer rather than an initiator of the new imperialism. Though an imperialist, he was a reluctant one. As the American navy steamed to victory in Santiago and Manila bays, Hay from the embassy in London wished Cubans, Puerto Ricans, and Filipinos autonomy or independence, not colonization by the United States. A letter to Theodore Roosevelt containing the famous phrase, "It has been a splendid little war," can actually be read as cautionary, since he added, "[The war] is now to be concluded, I hope, with that fine good nature, which is, after all, the distinguishing trait of the American character." Only weeks later, he praised Andrew Carnegie for an article attacking imperialism. But Hay was an Anglophile, and the spectacle of Britain's decline probably moved him toward his eventual acceptance of a kind of imperialism. "The serious thing," he wrote to Adams in 1900, "is the discovery—now past doubt—that the British have lost all skill in fighting; and the whole world knows it, and is regulating itself accordingly."

Military Philosopher Alfred Thayer Mahan

Alfred Thayer Mahan (1840–1914) was a brilliant misfit in an organization with little tolerance for misfits. Of impeccable military lineage, he was the son of the dean of faculty at West Point and an Annapolis graduate himself. He preferred writing and research to sea duty, provoking one superior officer to call him a "pen-and-ink sailor." Yet it was on a cruise to France at the age of 23 that he discovered the idea that shaped his life's work. The French army's occupation of Mexico City convinced Mahan that the Monroe Doctrine was no stronger than the capacity of a U.S. fleet to support it. . . . "I am an imperialist," he said, "because I am not an isolationist."

Mahan's great work, *The Influence of Sea Power upon History, 1660–1783* (1890), remains a masterpiece of clarity, analysis, and fine prose. Its thesis is that a great nation must be a strong sea power, and that this requires "a widespread healthy commerce and a powerful navy.". . . He held that the United States had an obligation to expand so that its civilization, culture, and religion could be spread abroad for the benefit of the more backward nations. . . .

Roosevelt had in fact preceded Mahan in arguing in print that the United States needed a stronger navy. In his book *The Naval War of 1812,* begun at Harvard and published in 1882 when he was only 24, Roosevelt contended that the United States had won the war because of the quality of a navy that had since been allowed to decline. Roosevelt praised *The Influence of Sea Power upon History* to his cosmopolitan intellectual coterie, inadvertently ensuring that it became a required text in the rival navies of Germany, Japan, and Great Britain. Thus Mahan became the dominant strategist not just of the American navy but of many of the major navies of the world.

Secretary of War Elihu Root

Elihu Root (1845–1937) enjoyed the early career of a conventionally brilliant member of the minor eastern establishment. . . . As a young lawyer representing big corporations, he had the pushiness and arrogance of one to whom everything came easy. . . .

Root, like Hay, was a grudging imperialist. Following the sinking of the *Maine,* he wrote to a friend, "I deplore war. I have earnestly hoped that it might not come. I deny the obligation of the American people to make the tremendous sacrifices which it must entail. . . . I prefer that we should not do it; I don't think we are bound to do it; I would prevent it if I could." But being above all a pragmatist, Root supported the war once it was joined. He accepted President McKinley's offer of the War Department in July 1899 for the purpose of administering the islands taken from Spain. "So I went to perform a lawyer's duty upon the call of the greatest of all our clients, the Government of our country.". . .

Roosevelt called Root "the greatest man that has arisen on either side of the Atlantic in my lifetime, . . . the brutal friend to whom I pay the most attention." The compliment was not all hyperbole. Root grew in his job, combining mental acuity, directness, and managerial genius with a sense of fairness in the governing of America's new colonial subjects.

Senator Henry Cabot Lodge

Of the five men considered here, Henry Cabot Lodge (1850–1924) was the one who most deserved the title of "jingo.". . . He was an obsessive writer and published biographies of Alexander Hamilton, Daniel Webster, and George Washington before he was 40. He was also a determined politician, who lost three elections in Massachusetts before winning a seat in Congress in 1886 and then being elected to the Senate in 1892. Lodge's experience in politics, both winning and losing, helped make him the supreme political tactician of his time. . . .

Lodge may have come to his view of the world through his family. He was the heir to a shipping fortune, and his wife was the daughter of an admiral. From the platform of the Congress, he spoke out early and often for the annexation of Cuba and a permanent naval presence in Hawaii, and he conspired with Roosevelt for the seizure of the Philippines. He wrote in 1895, "From the Rio Grande to the Arctic Ocean there should be but one flag and one country. . . . Every consideration of national growth and national welfare demands it." Lodge was driven by the conviction of America's superiority and its right to "conquest, colonization, and territorial expansion." His views were more than a little bigoted. His activism in the Congress against new immigrants was directed mainly against Chinese, Italians, Russians, and Eastern Europeans. "We are at this moment," he claimed, "overcrowded with undesirable immigrants.". . .

President Theodore Roosevelt

Theodore Roosevelt (1858–1919) was close to Mahan, Hay, Root, and Lodge, and he admired all four. But for all his contradictions, he was a bigger man than any of them. It is striking how early and often he was spotted for greatness—by family friends, Harvard cronies, politicians, and cowboys. His extraordinary memory, his multiple enthusiasms, his supreme self-confidence, and his unbounded energy made him a force of nature. He is "pure act," said Henry Adams, who was no act. Roosevelt held major positions at startlingly early stages of his life: minority leader of the New York State Assembly at 24, U.S. civil service commissioner at 31, New York City police commissioner at 36, assistant secretary of the Navy at 38, governor of New York at 40, vice president and president of the United States at 42. . . .

Roosevelt came to his imperialist views through the expansive energy of his character and his particular understanding of American history. Like Mahan, he was a big-navy man; like Hay, he was an Anglophile who believed that America had to replace a faltering Britain in maintaining the balance of power. In *The Winning of the West* (1889), his stirring account of America's territorial expansion, he showed indecent contempt for the rights of Indians: "The most righteous of all wars is a war with savages, though it is apt to be also the most terrible and inhuman. The rude, fierce settler who drives the savage from the land lays all civilized mankind under debt to him." Then, shifting to a global canvas: "American and Indian, Boer and

Zulu, Cossack and Tartar, New Zealander and Maori,—in each case the victor, horrible though many of his deeds are, has laid deep the foundations for the future greatness of a mighty people."

With views such as those, it was only a step to the two principles that guided Roosevelt during his first foreign-policy assignment at the Navy Department. First, he believed that the spread of the more advanced peoples (preferably English-speaking) over the less advanced benefited mankind as a whole. Second, he maintained that when American interests clashed with those of another state, the former had to be defended. Roosevelt did put some limits on his imperial rapacity. To Carl Schurz, a dedicated anti-imperialist, he wrote, "Unjust war is dreadful; a just war may be the highest duty." And in theory, if not always in practice, he took a moderate view of the Monroe Doctrine. He saw it as an "Open Door" in South America: "I do not want the United States or any European power to get territorial possessions in South America but to let South America gradually develop its own lines, with an open door to all outside nations."

Roosevelt rejected "imperialism" as a description of his approach. He tolerated "expansion." The word he preferred was "Americanism." The author of heroic tales of America, the doer of heroic deeds, he saw his country as truly beneficent toward the lesser nations. Even before he came into positions of policy responsibility, he would sit in the Metropolitan Club with his allies Mahan and Lodge and plan ways for the United States to wrest the imperial baton from ineffectual, corrupt, unworthy Spain. Long before he became president, Roosevelt was the most influential advocate of America's new imperialism. . . .

From 1898 to 1903, Roosevelt, Lodge, and Mahan were involved in virtually every action that transformed the United States into an imperial power. Hay and Root came to Washington after the initial surge of conquest, but they helped carry it forward even as they sought to temper its excesses. . . .

Imperialism Casts a Long Shadow

Americans like to pretend that they have no imperial past. What was done in their name in Cuba, Puerto Rico, Samoa, Guam, Hawaii, the Philippines, and Panama—all in the space of five years—proves them wrong. American acquisitiveness may have been less extensive than the global foraying of Britain, France, Spain, and Portugal, but it was just as indifferent to the interests of local populations. . . .

In the taking of colonies, America was no different (except in scale) from the major European powers engaged in the late-19th-century struggle for empire. In the administration of its acquisitions, however, America's record has been largely positive. Hawaii has become a state. The Philippines were promised, and finally received, independence, and relations between the two countries remain close. Puerto Ricans consistently voted for close ties with the United States, with no significant popular sentiment for independence. Theodore Roosevelt's America became a classic imperialist power, but it went on to become a moderate and generally effective colonial governor.

The five-year period in which America became an imperial state unleashed forces that have affected its entire subsequent history. For the first time, the United States had used its armies overseas. With two smashing naval victories, it had proven the value of a powerful navy. With the republic on the way to becoming a global military power, Americans were coming to believe, with Roosevelt, that the world was interdependent and that America must play a major role in it. In entering on the world stage, America had exercised its peculiar propensity to join narrow interests with messianic goals, to combine raw power with high purpose. The events and debates of 100 years ago have left their mark on American leaders and their actions ever since. . . .

With the hindsight of 100 years, it seems clear that the actions of Roosevelt and his friends helped to change the way America has viewed the world and acted in it. One of Roosevelt's Harvard professors, William James, who detested the imperialism practiced by his former pupil, wrote of 1898: "We gave the fighting instinct and the passion of mastery their outing . . . because we thought that . . . we could resume our permanent ideals and character when the fighting fit was done." But the fighting fit did change our ideals and our character. Today, for better or worse, we still live with the consequences—and under the shadow—of the imperial actions taken a century ago.

The Philippines and Imperialism—
An Issue of Debate

Barbara W. Tuchman

As the late Pulitzer Prize–winning author-historian Barbara W. Tuchman explains in the following selection, the treaty signed with Spain ending the Spanish-American War of 1898 changed America forever. The treaty itself was an issue of debate between Imperialists—those who believed that America should be a colonial power—and anti-Imperialists—those who maintained that America should not impose its sovereignty over other lands and peoples. The author paints a vivid portrait of the price of war in the Philippines and the uncertainties of the American people regarding making the Philippines an American territory. According to Tuchman, American imperialism became a major political campaign issue, with both the anti-Imperialists and the rebel leader of the Filipinos hoping that the election would end the war raging in the Philippines. Barbara Tuchman was a prominent historian popular for her writing style. She wrote narrative histories that the average person could read and understand.

P resident William McKinley, after soul-searching and prayer, had arrived at the decision desired by his advisers and popular with his party: the Philippines must be kept. In Paris, Spain's commissioners were given to under-

Excerpted from *The Proud Tower: A Portrait of the World Before the War, 1890–1914*, by Barbara W. Tuchman (New York: Ballantine Books, 1966). Copyright ©1966 by Barbara W. Tuchman, renewed 1994 by Lester Tuchman. Reprinted by the permission of Russell & Volkening as agents of the author.

stand that the time for dickering was over; possession talked. They would have to yield or face renewal of the war. A token payment of $20,000,000 was offered to grease acceptance of the inevitable. On December 10, 1898, the Treaty of Paris was signed, transferring sovereignty of the Philippines to the United States, with the $20,000,000 to follow upon ratification. "We have bought ten million Malays at $2.00 a head unpicked," remarked Speaker of the House Reed acidly, and in the most prescient comment made by anyone at the time, he added, "and nobody knows what it will cost to pick them."

Although by now it was half expected, President of the Philippine Republic Emilio Aguinaldo and his forces learned of the settlement in bitterness and anguish, many of them hardly able to believe that their liberators and allies had turned into a new set of conquerors. Without an organized army or modern weapons, they prepared to fight again, while waiting for a still possible default. The strong anti-Imperialist current in the United States was known to them and there was hope that the Senate would fail to ratify the treaty.

Reopening on December 5, 1898, the winter session of Congress was dominated by the fight over the treaty, more intense than that over Hawaii. Every vote counted. To gather their two-thirds, the Republicans led by Henry Cabot Lodge as chief Whip had to utilize every artifice, every argument, every avenue of pressure upon their own members and whatever Democrats might be amenable, while the anti-expansionists struggled to hold firm just enough Senators to make a third plus one. . . .

The public was not happy about the Philippine adventure and confused as to its duty. Democrats and Populists especially had felt the war in Cuba to be in the cause of freedom. Now, through some sorcery of fate, the war had turned into a matter of imposing sovereignty over an unwilling people by right of conquest. America had become the new Spain. In this unhappy moment impressive advice was offered through the combined effort of two men with the same extraordinary sensitivity to history-in-the-making. On February 1, 1899, magazine publisher S.S. McClure published in a two-page spread in his magazine an exhortation in verse by British poet/author Rudyard Kipling addressed to the Americans in their perplexity.

Take up the White Man's burden
Send forth the best ye breed,
Go bind your sons to exile
To serve your captives' need;
To wait in heavy harness
On fluttered folk and wild,
Your new-caught sullen peoples,
Half-devil and half-child. . . .

Take up the White Man's burden
The savage wars of peace,
Fill full the mouth of Famine
And bid the sickness cease. . . .

Ye dare not stoop to less—

The note of righteousness was reinstated; Kipling had struck the perfect combination of noble destiny and unselfish mission. Widely reprinted and quoted, the poem spread across the country within a week, doing much to reconcile the hesitant to the imperial task.

A Treaty in Dispute

In Washington it appeared as if opponents of the treaty might be successful, for the Republicans lacked one vote to make up the two-thirds for ratification. Suddenly, William Jennings Bryan arrived in Washington and to the amazement of his followers urged them to vote *for* the treaty. As leader of the Democratic party, he fully intended to be the standard-bearer himself in 1900, but he recognized the need of a new standard. Calculating that he could not win on a repetition of the silver issue, he was perfectly prepared to give it up in favor of imperialism, a new crown of thorns.

He was sure that retention of the Philippines would be productive of so much trouble as to make a flaming campaign issue—but it must be consummated first. Consequently, he told his party, it would not do to defeat the treaty. . . .

At this point, with the vote scheduled for February 6, 1899, with the outcome uncertain, with each side anxiously canvassing and counting every possible aye and nay, the Filipinos rose in their own war of independence. Their forces attacked the American lines outside Manila on the night of February 4, 1899. In Washington, although the news intensified the frenzied speculation, no one could be certain what effect it would have. A last-minute petition signed by ex-President Grover Cleveland, President Eliot of Harvard and twenty-two other men of national prominence was addressed to the Senate, protesting against the treaty unless it included a provision against annexing the Philippines and Porto Rico. "In accordance with the principles upon which our Republic was founded we are in duty bound to recognize the rights of the inhabitants . . . to independence and self-government," it said, and pointed out that if, as McKinley had once declared, the forcible annexation of Cuba would be "criminal aggression by our code of morals," annexation of the Philippines would be no less so. Its text was unanswerable but it offered no judgeships, political futures or other coin that Lodge and Bryan were dealing in.

When the Senate voted on February 6, 1899, the treaty won by 57–27, with a one-vote margin. It was "the closest, hardest fight I have ever known," said Lodge. In the aftermath one thing on which all agreed was that Bryan had swung the deciding votes. By the time the vote was counted 59 Americans were dead and 278 wounded and some 500 Filipinos were casualties in the Philippines. The cost of picking Malays was just beginning to be paid.

"The way the country puked up its ancient principles at the first touch of temptation was sickening," wrote William James in a private letter. Publicly, to the Boston *Evening Transcript*, he wrote, "We are now openly engaged in crushing out the sacredest thing in this great human world—the attempt of a people long enslaved" to attain freedom and work out its own destiny. The saddest thing for men such as James was the parting with the American dream. America, [Charles Eliot] Norton wrote, "has lost her unique position as a leader in the progress of civilization, and has taken up her place simply as one of the grasping and selfish nations of the present day."

To many others the knowledge of American guns firing on Filipinos was painful. The anger of the Anti-Imperialists deepened and their membership increased to half a million. . . ."We are false to all we have believed in," wrote journalist Moorfield Storey. "This great free land which for more than a century has offered a refuge to the oppressed of every land, has now turned to oppression." Still unwilling to give up, he hoped for leadership from Speaker of the House Thomas B. Reed, whom Roosevelt had called "the most influential man in Congress." Writing to Senator Hoar, Storey begged him to "persuade Mr. Reed to come out as he should. He is very sluggish and lacks aggression in great matters. If he would come out I think he might really be the next President."

It was too late. Reed's sluggishness was that of a man for whom the fight has turned sour. Others whose main interest lay in non-political fields could feel as deeply without being shattered. Reed's whole life was in Congress, in politics, in the exercise of representative government, with the qualification that for him it had to be exercised toward an end that he believed in. His party and his country were now bent on a course for which he felt deep distrust and disgust. To mention expansion to him, said a journalist, was like "touching a match" and brought forth "sulphurous language." The tide had turned against him; he could not turn it back and would not go with it. . . .

At War in the Philippines and at Home

Military operations in the Philippines swelled in size and savagery. Against the stubborn guerrilla warfare of the Filipinos, the U.S. Army poured in regiments, brigades, divisions, until as many as 75,000—more than four times as many as saw action in Cuba—were engaged in the islands at one time. Filipinos burned, ambushed, raided, mutilated; on occasion they buried prisoners alive. Americans retaliated with atrocities of their own, burning down a whole village and killing every inhabitant if an American soldier was found with his throat cut, applying the "water cure" and other tortures to obtain information. They were three thousand miles from home, exasperated by heat, malaria, tropical rains, mud and mosquitoes. They sang, "Damn, damn, damn the Filipino, civilize him with a Krag . . ." and officers on occasion issued orders to take no more prisoners. They won all the skirmishes against an enemy who constantly renewed himself. A raiding party which missed Aguinaldo but captured his young son made headlines. . . .

Aguinaldo fought for time in the hope that anti-Imperialist sentiment in America would force withdrawal of the forces already sickening of their task. The longer the war continued, the louder and angrier grew the Anti-Imperialist protests. Their program adopted at Chicago in October, 1899, demanded "an immediate cessation of the war against liberty." They collected and reported all the worst cases of American conduct in the Philippines and all the most egregious speeches of imperialist greed and set them against the most unctuous expressions of the white man's mission. They distributed pamphlets paid for by Andrew Carnegie, and when the League's executive head, Edward Atkinson, applied to the War Department for permission to send the pamphlets to the Philippines and was refused, he sent them anyway.

Anxious to end the war and placate the "new-caught sullen peoples" and govern creditably, the Administration sent various committees to investigate the atrocities, to find out what the Filipinos really wanted—short of self-government, which they said they wanted—and to report on what form of civil government to give them. In April, 1900, the shy, kindly, three-hundred-pound Judge William Howard Taft was sent out to set up a civil government, armed with a charter drawn up by the new Secretary of War, Elihu Root, which granted the Filipinos a liberal degree of internal autonomy. Since neither they nor the Americans were ready to give up fighting, the attempt was premature, but Taft stayed on, determined to govern in the interest of "the little brown brother" as soon as he was given a chance. When friends at home, concerned for his welfare, sent anxious queries about his health, he cabled Elihu Root that he had been out horseback riding and was feeling fine. "How is the horse feeling?" Root cabled back.

Despite difficulties there was no re-thinking or hesitancy among the dominant Republicans about the new career upon which America was launched. The bill for constructing the Nicaragua Canal was in the Senate and so was Albert Beveridge, more closely allied with the Almighty than ever. "We will not renounce our part in the mission of our race, trustees under God, of the civilization of the world," he said on January 8, 1900. He informed Senators that God had been preparing "the English-speaking and Teutonic peoples" for this mission for a thousand years. . . .

Imperialism Is a Campaign Issue

As the war passed its first anniversary with the American forces deeply extended, there was one event ahead that might yet bring it to an end: the coming Presidential election. In this the Anti-Imperialists and Aguinaldo placed their hopes. Its earliest oddity was a boom for Admiral Dewey, partly inspired by the desperation of some Democrats to find any candidate other than Bryan. Having concluded after some study of the subject that "the office of President is not such a very difficult one to fill," the Admiral announced he was available but as his wording did not inspire confidence and he seemed vague as to party, his candidacy collapsed. Bryan loomed.

The Anti-Imperialists were caught in an agonizing dilemma. McKinley represented the party of imperialism; Bryan in Carl Schurz's words was the "evil genius of the anti-imperialist cause," loathed for his betrayal in the matter of the treaty and feared for his radicalism. Schurz met with Carnegie, Gamaliel Bradford and Senator Pettigrew at the Plaza Hotel in New York in January, 1900, in an effort to organize a third party so that the American people would not "be forced by the two rotten old party carcasses to choose between two evils.". . .

Campaigning on imperialism as he had planned, Bryan ranged the country as strenuously as before. He was tarnished, but his magnetism, his passion and his sincerity-of-the-moment still reached through to the people and even across the Pacific. In Bryan, but for whom the Treaty of Paris would have been defeated, the Filipinos placed their faith. "The great Democratic party of the United States will win the next fall election," Aguinaldo promised in a proclamation. "Imperialism will fail in its mad attempt to subjugate us by force of arms." His soldiers shouted the war cry, "Aguinaldo-Bryan!"

In their Chicago platform, anticipating the election, the Anti-Imperialists had said, "We propose to contribute to the defeat of any person or party that stands for the subjugation of any people." There was nothing to do, as a friend wrote to ex-President Cleveland, but "to hold your nose and vote" for Bryan. The modified rapture of such people for the Democratic candidate won them the name thereafter of the "hold-your-nose-and-vote" group. So distasteful to the *Nation* were both candidates that it refused to support either, preferring, as a dissatisfied reader complained, to "sit on a fence and scold at both."

The Republicans had no such difficulties. Although they preferred to be called expansionists rather than Imperialists, they were proud of the condition whatever its name, and believed in its goals. Forthright as usual, Lodge said, "Manila with its magnificent bay is the prize and pearl of the East; . . . it will keep us open to the markets of China. . . . Shall we hesitate and make, in coward fashion, what Dante calls the 'great refusal'?" Secretary Hay having pronounced the Policy of the Open Door, China's markets were much on men's minds. During the summer of the campaign, the siege of the legations at Peking by the Boxers and the American share in the relief expedition pointed up the far-flung role the country was now playing. Its most convinced and vocal champion was McKinley's new vice-presidential nominee, Theodore Roosevelt, who took the President's place as chief campaigner. Unsure of victory, for the "full dinner pail" was more a slogan than a fact, he campaigned so vigorously and indefatigably that to the public and cartoonists the Rough Rider with the teeth, pince-nez and unquenchable zest appeared to the be the real candidate. He derided the specter of militarism as a "shadowy ghost," insisted that expansion "in no way affects our institutions or our traditional policies," and said the question was not "whether we shall expand—for we have already expanded—but whether we shall contract."

America Moves into the Twentieth Century

The country listened to thousands of speeches and read thousands of newspaper columns raking over every argument for and against imperialism and every aspect of the war in the Philippines. It learned, thanks to the efforts of the Anti-Imperialists, more about the conduct of its own troops than the public usually does in wartime. Dumdum bullets, so thoroughly disapproved (except by the British) at The Hague Peace Conference the year before, were found to have been issued to some American troops. In the end the American people, like the British in their Khaki election of the same year, approved the incumbents. What a people thinks at any given time can best be measured by what they do. McKinley and Roosevelt were elected by 53 per cent of the votes cast and with a greater margin over Bryan than had been received in 1896. Expansion and conquest were accepted and the break with the American past confirmed. Still at war in the Philippines, America moved into the Twentieth Century.

For Aguinaldo, after the election, there was nothing more to hope for. Retreating into the mountains, still fighting, he was captured by trickery in March, 1901, and in captivity in April signed an oath of allegiance to the United States together with a proclamation to his people calling for an end to resistance: "There has been enough blood, enough tears, enough desolation."

Professor Norton voiced the elegy of the Anti-Imperialists. "I reach one conclusion," he wrote to a friend in the month of Aguinaldo's capture, "that I have been too much of an idealist about America, had set my hopes too high, had formed too fair an image of what she might become. Never had a nation such an opportunity; she was the hope of the world. Never again will any nation have her chance to raise the standard of civilization."

Six months later came Czolgosz's shot and McKinley's place was taken by Roosevelt, "that damned cowboy," as Mark Hanna said when he heard the news. The remark was not astute. It was an architect of the new age who now became its President at forty-three.

The Panamanian Affair

Walter LaFeber

In this excerpt from his diplomatic history of the Panama Canal, historian Walter LaFeber focuses on the political maneuvering and diplomatic duplicity that resulted in U.S. control of a Panamanian waterway. He explains how a carefully engineered revolution helped ensure that the canal was built where powerful American government leaders, strong-willed American businessmen, a determined French entrepreneur, and Panamanian nationalists wanted it built. In the case of the Panama Canal, contends the author, the United States chose power over principle. LaFeber, who has lectured at universities worldwide, is the author of numerous diplomatic histories and longtime Noll Professor of History at Cornell University in Ithaca, New York.

W ith an isthmian canal virtually within his grasp, Roosevelt refused to allow those "contemptible little creatures" in Colombia [which controlled Panama] to frustrate his grand plan. But TR could not decide how to deal with the Colombians. He apparently held little hope the deadlock would be broken by a successful Panamanian revolt. As the President searched desperately for alternatives, Bunau-Varilla and the Panamanian nationalists were devising a solution. That solution, together with a 1904 agreement negotiated between Washington and Panama City by

Excerpted from *The Panama Canal: The Crisis in Historical Perspective*, updated edition, by Walter LaFeber. Copyright ©1990 by Walter LaFeber. Used by permission of Oxford University Press, Inc.

Secretary of War William Howard Taft, created the framework for sixty years of relations between the two countries. . . .

Bunau-Varilla, with considerable help from top State Department officials, took the lead in solving Roosevelt's dilemma. During September and October 1903, the Frenchman held a series of talks with Hay, Assistant Secretary of State Francis B. Loomis (whom Bunau-Varilla had known since a meeting in Paris two years before), and John Bassett Moore, a former Assistant Secretary of State, renowned international lawyer, and confidant of TR. Out of the conversations grew Bunau-Varilla's conviction that if the Panamanians tried to declare their independence the United States would use force, ostensibly to uphold its 1846 commitment to maintain transit rights across the Isthmus, but in reality to prevent Colombia from quashing the revolution. . . .

Bunau-Varilla needed no more hints after a candid talk with Hay in the privacy of the latter's home. "I expressed my sentiments on the subject some days ago to President Roosevelt," the Frenchman began, "the whole thing will end in a revolution. You must take your measures. . . ." Hay played the game perfectly: "Yes, that is unfortunately the most probable hypothesis. But we shall not be caught napping. Orders have been given to naval forces on the Pacific to sail towards the Isthmus." As Bunau-Varilla later editorialized, "It only remained for me to act."

He first contacted the head of the revolutionary junta, Dr. Manuel Amador Guerrero, a physician closely associated with the Panama Railroad, now owned by the New Panama Canal Company. Amador happened to be in New York City to obtain money and support for the plot. Bunau-Varilla contacted Amador none too soon, for the Panamanian had just discovered that Cromwell, the New Panama Canal Company's lawyer, was growing fearful that the revolution would abort and his company's concessions seized by a vengeful Colombia. . . .

Plans again moved forward on the Isthmus. The revolutionaries comprised an odd but not illogical assortment. . . . As Roosevelt understood, "You don't have to foment a revolution. All you have to do is take your foot off and one will occur."

As the zero hour approached, however, TR displayed more optimism than did people in Panama. In early October the commander of the U.S.S. *Nashville* visited Colon, then reported to Washington that although three-quarters of the people would support a leader who would build a canal, "such a leader is now lacking, and it isn't believed that in the near future these people will take any initiative steps." The junta was preparing to provide the leadership, but the timing would be crucial. Closely following ship movements in the newspapers, Bunau-Varilla learned on October 30 that the *Nashville* was leaving Jamaica for an unspecified port. He correctly guessed it was heading for Colon and would arrive in two or three days. . . . Bunau-Varilla wired this news to Amador, who had returned to the Isthmus to lead the revolt. Both men now believed the United States was moving into a position to support their revolution. Loomis, however, jumped the gun and the result was nearly farce. "Uprising on the Isthmus reported," the Assistant Secretary anxiously cabled the United States Consul in Panama on November 3. "Keep department promptly and fully informed." Maintaining his composure, the Consul replied, "No uprising yet. Reported will be in the night. Situation critical."

Late that day the Panamanians struck, quickly seizing control of the Isthmus. The governor appointed by Colombia to rule the province, José Domingo de Obaldía, had long been sympathetic to Panamanian autonomy and gladly joined the revolutionaries. For his understanding he became one of Panama's first Vice-Presidents. . . .

Commander Hubbard aboard the *Nashville* received no orders regarding the uprising until late on November 2. Roosevelt and Loomis apparently did not trust the navy with their plans. Thus when 2500 Colombian soldiers appeared off Colon on November 2 to prevent the rumored revolution, a confused Hubbard allowed them to land. James R. Shaler, the superintendent of the railway, saved the situation. He first moved his cars to the Pacific side of the Isthmus, 48 miles from Colon, so the Colombians could not use the railway. Then he talked the Colombian officers into traveling to Panama City, assuring them that their troops would soon follow. In reality, the soldiers next saw their commanders when all were packed aboard ships for the return trip to Bogotá. The next day U.S. sailors finally landed to ensure that the Colombian troops behaved. An independent Panama had already been proclaimed by Amador. A new nation the size of South Carolina was born, and the labor pains had been easy. None of the belligerents was killed. The only deaths were a Chinese citizen who had gotten trapped in some desultory shelling, a dog, and, according to some reports, a donkey.

The Rewards of Revolution

Roosevelt justified his aid to the revolutionaries by citing the 1846 commitment, a justification that had no legal or historical basis. The treaty certainly did not give the United States the right to use force against Colombia, with whom the pact had been made, in order to build a canal. Nor did it require Colombia to allow a canal to be constructed. The treaty indeed justified United States intervention in order to preserve Colombia's sovereignty on the Isthmus. TR intervened, however, to destroy that sovereignty.

But Roosevelt clung to the 1846 pact since he had little else. He was consequently interested when Oscar Straus, a New York lawyer and adviser of the President, suggested the 1846 treaty required the United States to intervene because it was not made merely with Colombia, but was "a covenant running with the land"—regardless of who happened to control the land. With delight, and doubtless a sense of relief, Roosevelt immediately ordered Hay to use this argument. The United States held to this interpretation even though John Bassett Moore (certainly the State Department's most distinguished lawyer) exploded Straus's sophistry and suggested that in TR's hands it actually amounted to a "covenant running (away!) with the land!!"

The President later argued that the seizure had been for the sake of "civilization," thereby adopting the proposition that since North American actions were justified morally they were justified legally. His Attorney-General, Philander C. Knox, offered the appropriate reply: "Oh, Mr. President, do not let so great an achievement suffer from any taint of legality." Knox's caustic advice was better than he knew, for soon Roosevelt began a campaign, backed by force, to compel Latin American governments to uphold their own legal obligations as he defined those obligations.

In one sense, TR acted quite uncharacteristically: he aided a revolution. For a man whose central political tenet was stability, and for a nation that had fought revolutionaries and secessionists at least since 1861, unleashing revolution marked an abrupt change. It was also a short-lived

Workers at Pedro Miguel install culverts for the Panama Canal's massive locks.

change. Roosevelt possessed his canal territory and recognized the new Panamanian government led by Amador, Pablo Arosemena, and Obaldía on November 6. But when the Panamanian army attempted to land at Colon to claim the city, TR stopped it. A little revolution was sufficient. Washington needed time to sort things out. The Panamanian government would have to wait a while before its army could enter the country's second largest city. In the first moments after recognition, Panama and the United States were at loggerheads.

Nor did Roosevelt try to reconcile the Colombians. On November 6 he told them he had intervened because "treaty obligations" and the "interest of civilization" required that the Isthmus not endure "a constant succession of . . . wasteful civil wars." TR urged Bogotá to recognize the new government. . . .

Bunau-Varilla Deceives Panama

TR and Hay focused on arranging the canal treaty with the Panamanians, or, more precisely, the Frenchman who had taken the opportunity to represent Panama. . . .

The new government meanwhile instructed the Frenchman that the negotiations were to be guided by three principles. First, no deals could be made that affected "the sovereignty of Panama, which [was] free, independent, and sovereign." Second, the United States should pledge to uphold the new nation's "sovereignty, territorial integrity, and public order." That clause would place North American troops, if necessary, between Panama and a vengeful Colombia. Third, a canal treaty would be drafted, but only after consultation with Panamanian leaders Amador and Federico Boyd. "You will proceed in everything strictly in agreement with them," the Frenchman was told.

The instructions did not reach Bunau-Varilla in time, nor did Amador and Boyd. The minister made certain of that. On Friday the 13th of November he began talks with Roosevelt and Hay. Bunau-Varilla emphasized that time was all-important. If the treaty was not rushed to completion, he argued, a number of events would occur, all of them bad. . . .

Hay quickly prepared a treaty draft. It was largely the Hay-Herrán agreement that Colombia had rejected. The draft explicitly recognized Panamanian sovereignty in a canal zone, and even went further than the Hay-Herrán agreement by increasing Panama's judicial authority in a zone. Panamanian troops would protect the canal, and United States forces would be used in the area only with Panama's consent. The proposed treaty would run 99 years, or until about 2002.

Then, in what proved to be one of the most momentous twenty-four-hour periods in American diplomatic history, Bunau-Varilla worked all night and all day on November 16 to rewrite Hay's paper. . . .

Hay could hardly believe his eyes. Bunau-Varilla's treaty ensured the canal's neutrality, proposed payment to Panama of an amount equal to that which the United States would have paid Colombia, and guaranteed Washington's protection of Panama's independence. The United States was to assume a virtual protectorate over the new country. But in return, the treaty gave the United States extensive powers in the Canal Zone, for Washington would have "all the rights, power, and authority within the zone . . . which the United States would possess and exercise if it were the sovereign of the territory within which said lands and waters are located to the entire exclusion of the exercise by the Republic of Panama of any such sovereign rights, power, and authority.". . .

Bunau-Varilla surrendered Panamanian judicial power in the Zone, widened the zone area from ten kilometers (or six miles) to ten miles, and lengthened Hay's 99-year lease to "perpetuity." The astonished Secretary of State made only one change (the United States "leases in perpetuity" phrase was transformed into the more direct wording that Panama "grants to the United States in perpetuity the use, occupation, and control" of a canal zone). At 6:40 p.m. on November 18, the treaty was signed by the two men. Amador and Boyd arrived in Washington three hours later.

Bunau-Varilla met them at Union Station, showed them the pact, and Amador nearly fainted on the train platform.

The Panamanian government angrily protested "the manifest renunciation of sovereignty" in the treaty. That protest echoed down through the years, becoming ever more magnified. If the new government rejected the pact, however, it faced bitter alternatives: the United States might seize the canal area without either paying for it or undertaking to protect the new republic, or Roosevelt might build in Nicaragua and leave the Panama City revolutionaries to the tender mercies of the Colombian army. In truth, the Panamanians had no choice.

They had leaped across an abyss to gain their independence, were hanging on the other side by their fingertips, and the United States held the rescue rope. Having helped put them in that position, Bunau-Varilla dictated the terms under which they could be pulled up to safety. Hay and Bunau-Varilla were too powerful and sophisticated to allow Panama to claim it accepted the treaty under duress, a claim that if declared legally valid could void the acceptance. Panama, however, did accept under duress. Having a French citizen disobey the Panamanian government's instructions, and then having no choice but to accept the Frenchman's treaty, compounded the humiliation. In the 1970s a documentary film made in Panama about the 1903 affair was entitled, "The Treaty that No Panamanian Signed."

A Mandate from Civilization

For the revolutionaries humiliation was nevertheless preferable to hanging. Throughout the negotiations Bunau-Varilla had kept them informed of rising indignation in the United States over his and Roosevelt's management of the affair. The President soon had another revolt on his hands; this one was in the Senate and the country at large.

It was not a massive revolt, but a surprising number of Senators and important newspapers condemned TR's action. . . .

Even the newspapers and public spokesmen who supported TR refused to justify his action on moral grounds. Instead, as *Public Opinion* noted in November 1903, since the majority of the country wanted "an isthmian canal above all things," it was willing to overlook moral issues in order to justify taking the canal as strictly "a business question."

Roosevelt refused to take that approach. As have most rulers who aggressively used naked force, he wanted it masked with morality. In an outspoken special message to the Senate on January 4, 1904, the President submitted the treaty and justified his actions in November on the grounds of the 1846 pact, "our national interests and safety," and the usual Rooseveltian claim of "the interests of collective civilization." He suffered no doubts that the United States had "received a mandate from civilization" to build a canal, although he could not tell exactly how that mandate had been expressed. One problem, of course, was that "the interests of collective civilization" had never been seen or defined (was Colombia, for example, a part of "collective civilization"?). Like many Rooseveltian phrases, the term better fit the President's prejudices than any international legal or moral standard.

Yet TR won. . . . The prospects of a United States–controlled canal caused flutters of patriotism in too many hearts and the prospect of rich satisfaction in too many pocketbooks. . . .

After early 1904, politicians who opposed United States control of the canal were committing political suicide. Bunau-Varilla had triumphed. Although, as the *Pittsburgh Post* remarked, TR's methods in Panama "were subversive of the best principles of the republic," the Frenchman had made the treaty so attractive that the United States, as he hoped, quickly chose power over principle. . . .

The Worsening of Relations

In May 1904 Roosevelt created an Isthmian Canal Commission to build the canal. The Commission was placed under the supervision of Secretary of War Taft. Within three months, the military members of the Commission clashed with the State Department representatives in Panama. In Panama the questions of sovereignty and the right of United States intervention coalesced to create the first major crisis between the two countries. The events of 1904 were not only a portent. They left an indelible mark on Panamanian political life. . . .

After he intervened in Panama in 1903, Roosevelt painstakingly explained his actions to the Cabinet, then demanded to know whether the explanation would silence his opponents. "Have I defended myself?" he asked. "You certainly have," replied a brave Elihu Root. "You have shown that you were accused of seduction and you have conclusively proved that you were guilty of rape." Roosevelt never understood how his policies and explanations worsened the problems in the Caribbean area that he tried to stabilize. He, Taft, and Bunau-Varilla were making Panama as well as the Canal Zone a virtual colony of the United States, but the North American leaders refused to assume even the responsibilities of enlightened colonialism, save that of using force or the threat of force to maintain order. That solution worsened, not ameliorated, Panama's problem and, consequently, Panamanian relations with the United States.

CHAPTER 6

The Eve of
a New Decade

A Placid Man in a Restless Time

Mark Sullivan

In a six-volume work published from 1926 to 1933, the late journalist Mark Sullivan offered an acclaimed social history of the first two and a half decades of the twentieth century. Highly respected contemporary journalist Dan Rather, managing editor and anchor of television's *CBS Evening News* and *48 Hours,* abridged and edited Sullivan's volumes. In the following selection from his work, Rather focuses on the presidency of William Howard Taft. He describes Taft's inclination to choose sides between conservative Standpatters and progressive Insurgents, his response to an angry controversy over conservation, and his decision to try to reverse his decline in popularity by striking out against the business trusts. According to Rather, Taft was an honorable, highly ethical, and courageous man and a good president. Rather explains that Roosevelt set expectations when he told the American people that Taft and he were alike. According to Rather, Taft's chief failing was that he was not the replica of Theodore Roosevelt that the American public expected him to be.

I n the argot of politicians and Washington correspondents, there is at the beginning of every administration a "honeymoon period," during which White House and Capitol and partisan press, abjuring politics, radiate an altogether

---

artificial and impermanent sweetness and trust and tolerance toward each other, and especially, on the part of the latter two, toward the new president. In William Howard Taft's case, the sentimental interlude was exceptionally sugary. "Never," said the *New York Sun,* "did any man come into the Presidency before with such universal good will."

A survey that probed beneath the surface would have revealed, however, that there had formed within the Republican Party an angry cleavage, an insurgency by a minority West against a majority East.

This insurgency, diverse in its origins, had one root in a feeling on the part of the West that the protective tariff, instituted to foster eastern "infant industries," had overfed those industries until they were now fat and overbearing giants; another in the resentment of the West, composed mainly of individual businesses, chiefly farming, against highly organized business in the East and its great corporations which drew much of their sustenance from the West but paid most of their profits to the East; another in the irritation of the granger West against the mainly eastern-owned railroads, which had gone on from the seventies to the passage of the Railroad Rate Act in 1906; another in the memories of the long controversy over currency, between mainly debtor West and mainly creditor East, which had lasted from soon after the Civil War until 1896; another in the feeling that the remaining free lands, in the West, especially the mineral and oil-bearing ones, were being accumulated in the private possession of eastern-owned railroads and other corporations—this one of the grievances, expressed in a movement called "conservation of natural resources," had many adherents in East as well as West.

All these roots drew sap from a deep undercurrent of American tradition, a spirit of resistance against authority, opposition against organized power, suspicion against vested interests. This truculent independence, now expressing itself acutely in insurgency against the Republican Party, was a dominant trait of the American people, as old as America itself. Politically and socially it *was* America. It had inspired the first settlement of the continent, had caused our separation from the mother country, had dictated the spirit and forms of the new government and institutions we set up. Our earliest settlers, as well as most of our immigrants, had been picked persons, selected by the law of their own natures on the basis of resentment against authority. In Europe in the seventeenth, eighteenth, and nineteenth centuries, the individual who found himself most irked by a stratified society, who most resented organized power, whether of the church or of the system of land-tenure, or of caste of inherited place—any whose instinct urged him toward independence, moved to America. In each succeeding generation, this process of natural selection on the basis of instinct for independence repeated itself. In each generation, the most restless "went West," the first wave to central New York, western Pennsylvania, Kentucky, and Tennessee; the next to Indiana, Illinois, and Wisconsin; the next to Iowa, Kansas, Nebraska, and Missouri; the next to the Rocky Mountains and the Pacific Coast. By the time of Taft's administration or earlier, the people of the West were the result of three or four successive sievings of those most independent in spirit. Also a new condition had arrived; the free land was exhausted. No longer was there any "out West" to absorb those whose nature it was to resist authority, organization, to be made restless by the ruts of settled ways. Deprived of the chance of escape from what irked them, they turned to fight it.

The condition expressed itself in a division of the Republican Party, in the country and in Congress, into mainly eastern "Standpatters" (apt word for conservative contentment with what is) and mainly western "Progressives," translated, by newspaper and popular zest for a fighting word, into "Insurgents."

A Difficult Test for Taft

Which group the new president should stand with would be in the popular mind a test of Taft's fidelity to Roosevelt and Roosevelt's policies. Partly a misleading test, for Roosevelt had not really "stood with" the Insurgents; rather, he had used this group as one element of the power which he forged from many sources. Nor had Roosevelt ever completely flouted or directly and permanently opposed the conservative East—them, too, Roosevelt had used as one of the materials out of which he fused his power. But the legislation Roosevelt had brought about was largely in the Insurgent direction, his attitude toward public questions was mainly that of the West, the mainspring of his popularity came from that section. Now the West would instinctively view Taft in the light of whether he stood with them and their representatives in Congress, whether in his official attitudes as well as his informal intimacies he would seem to associate most with the Insurgents in Congress, or with the orthodox Standpatters who held the official places of power and were a large majority of the party.

To Taft it would be a difficult test, for Taft lacked Roosevelt's vigor, which kept both factions subordinate to his own leadership; lacked Roosevelt's diversity of temperament, which used to encourage Standpatters and Insurgents alternately, as each group lent itself to Roosevelt's larger purpose of the moment. Taft lacked Roosevelt's geniality coupled with dominating vitality, which could alternately flout Standpatter or conservative—and then immediately and cheerfully lift the victim to his feet and carry him along in Roosevelt's forward surge. This variousness of temperament, this fecundity of talent for dominance, Taft lacked. Particularly did Taft lack the primitive energy which enabled Roosevelt always to ride the wave, lead the procession. Taft, with his more phlegmatic temperament, his more legalistic mind, would be prevailingly and conspicuously on one side or the other. In Taft's case the outcome of the test would make him seem all black or all white.

The static quality in Taft, his inertia, would bring it about that the label which he should finally bear would be less chosen by himself than fixed upon him by whichever side had the greater energy in surrounding him, pressing upon him, leaning against him. . . .

The Conservation Controversy

This aggressiveness of Roosevelt in behalf of conservation, his assumption, as a broad rule of practice, that the president can and should do anything in the public interest (as conceived by him) that the Constitution did not expressly forbid, gave rise to the atmosphere of angry controversy over conservation when Roosevelt was succeeded by Taft. Roosevelt's official spearhead in the fight had been James R. Garfield, who as secretary of the interior had authority over the public domain. . . . For this reason Roosevelt wished Taft to keep Garfield in the cabinet. Taft did not. From that, the rest followed.

Taft appointed Richard A. Ballinger of Seattle, Washington. Taft may readily have thought that Ballinger was an adequate appointment, for Ballinger had been, up to a few months before, a subordinate in Garfield's department, head of the General Land Office, and as such had seemed to be in sympathy with Garfield, Roosevelt, and conservation. Taft was loyal to conservation, and would not consciously have appointed a secretary of the interior who would reverse the policy.

To Roosevelt intimate conservationist Gifford Pinchot and the ardent young zealots who had gravitated around him, the dropping of Garfield was complete justification for acute distrust; in their state of mind hardly any successor whom Taft might appoint could fail to be under suspicion. Pinchot was now without the governor that Roosevelt had been to his impulses. With Roosevelt out of touch in Africa, Pinchot became what Roosevelt described him, one "who would expend his great energy in fighting the men who seemed to him not to be going far enough forward."

Ballinger (and Taft) had been in office less than six months when Pinchot put his suspicion into action. To a young subordinate in Ballinger's department, Louis R. Glavis, Pinchot gave a letter of introduction to Taft. Glavis, calling on Taft, charged that his superior, Ballinger, was improperly expediting transfer of 100,000 acres of government coal land in Alaska to a group of capitalists (composed mainly of the Guggenheim family) on claims which, Glavis charged, were in part invalid. Taft sent the charges to Ballinger. Ballinger delivered to Taft a defense and explanation—with buttressing documents it contained upward of half a million words.

Taft addressed to Ballinger a "ponderous, sweeping letter of exculpation and endorsement intended to be a permanent seal of sanctity, to refute all present charges against Ballinger and make future ones impossible." Taft told Ballinger that he had "examined the whole record most carefully" and that he had "reached a very definite conclusion." Taft's conclusion was that "the case attempted to be made by Mr. Glavis [is] without any substantial evidence to sustain his attack [and] embraces only shreds of suspicions"—this phrase, catching the public fancy, became conspicuous in the subsequent commotion. Taft authorized Ballinger "to dismiss L.R. Glavis from the service of the government for filing a disingenuous statement unjustly impeaching the integrity of his superior officers."

The Controversy Escalates

To the support of Glavis quickly came Pinchot. His support took the form in part of having some of his subordinates furnish to the newspapers information from the government files tending to support the charges Glavis had made, tending to reflect on Ballinger and, by this time, inferentially, on Taft. When this activity became known, Pinchot wrote a public letter saying that his subordinates "broke no law and at worst were guilty only of the violation of official propriety."

Pinchot's action was, of course, flagrant insubordination. Taft dismissed him from office. Now, to the support of both Pinchot and Glavis, came *Collier's Weekly,* many newspapers, practically all the cult of conservation zealots, as well as miscellaneous altruists. *Collier's* printed Glavis's charges under a headline asking "Are the Guggenheims in charge of the Interior Department?" illustrated by a giant corporate hand reaching out to seize the nation's heritage. Such journalistic exclamations were sufficient excitant to a public which never grasped, to the end of the case or since, the meaning of "clear-listing," "lieu lands," "filing" or the other technical intricacies that made up the substance of the charges and the evidence. The conservation zealots demanded that Ballinger be investigated by a committee of Congress. When the committee met, *Collier's* paid a fee of $25,000 to an able Boston lawyer and reformer, Louis D. Brandeis, to represent Glavis and in general the forces hostile to Taft.

Within the committee, a majority, Republican, reported that Ballinger was "a competent and honorable gentleman, honestly and faithfully performing the duties of his high office with an eye single to the public interest," that the charges against Ballinger "appear to have had their origin in a strong feeling of animosity created by a supposed difference in policy respecting Conservation." The minority, Democratic and Insurgent Republican, reported otherwise. About everybody agreed that Ballinger was, to put it very mildly, in that state, insecure for a holder of public office, in which his "usefulness was impaired." Ballinger, six months after the report of the committee, resigned.

Pinchot took ship for the White Nile to pour out his tale to Roosevelt, who, by this time, knew that Taft was not expert in administering the government of the United States. He knew, too, that Taft was failing in adequate support of Roosevelt's policies. But Roosevelt also knew Pinchot, knew the touch of fanaticism in him, his disposition to court martyrdom. And Roosevelt knew the rules of conducting an executive office. Remembering his own experiences with Congress, he knew the utter impossibility of having in the executive branch of the government a subordinate who would conspire with men in Congress to embarrass the president. "I am not yet sure," Roosevelt wrote, "whether Taft . . . could have followed any course save the one he did."

Roosevelt's following, however, knowing little and caring

less about the question of administrative discipline involved, thought only in terms of conservation, and of Pinchot as a disciple of Roosevelt. Conservation, they felt, had been betrayed by Taft, Pinchot humiliated. The Ballinger case was a prominent ring in the downward spiral of Taft's fortunes.

Taft Acts on Bad Advice

Taft, at this stage, did a thing of the sort that men in desperation sometimes do when they find the strength of the tide running against them too strong for their mental footing. Not Taft so much as his advisers, for it was not in Taft's nature to do a desperate thing; left to himself he would have let the tide against him go on to whatever fate it might bring him. But some of his advisers suggested that the tide adverse to Taft might be reversed, the Progressives placated, and the Democrats disarmed, by a policy of thoroughgoing prosecution of the trusts. The advice coincided with Taft's fundamental conviction that the law, being on the statute books, should be enforced. In this spirit were started a number of antitrust suits which, in the aggregate of all that were prosecuted in Taft's administration, exceeded by far the number prosecuted in Roosevelt's, or any other—made the Taft administration the outstanding one in American history for prosecution of trusts.

As a spectacular high spot in Taft's prosecution of the trusts, his attorney general, George W. Wickersham, on October 26, 1911, filed a suit for dissolution of the United States Steel Corporation, citing, as one cause for its being a monopoly, its purchase of the Tennessee Coal and Iron Company four years before, and alleging that the act of purchasing had included securing approval from Roosevelt, and that Roosevelt's approval had been procured by deceit.

That suit against the Steel Corporation, with its reflection upon Roosevelt, while it might have seemed the solution of one of Taft's present troubles, was the beginning of a future and a more serious one—was, indeed, the most disastrous act of Taft's political career, and led to the most calamitous episode in the history of the Republican Party.

The People Turn Against Taft

By the time Taft had been a year in the White House, the fat man jokes about him, which when he was secretary of war had been genial and kindly, began to take on a caustic tang—the 1907 jest about Taft being "the politest man I know because he gave up his seat in a street-car to three women," now supplanted by the 1910 one about a fat woman trying to get off a streetcar: because she was stout, she was obliged to go down the steps backward, but at each stop the conductor and the friendly passengers, seeing her facing forward, assumed she was getting on the car, and by giving her a helpful push facilitated her progress in the direction she did not want to go, so that she was carried past four stops before she could make it clear that it was off, not on, that she wanted to go.

The very things Taft had done to please the crowd . . . were now criticized. He had sat in the bleachers at a baseball game at Pittsburgh, declining to take a box, and had been praised by the press of the country—"he refuses to be exclusive," he is "one of the people." He had made tours of the country and journeys from Washington so numerous as to cause him to conclude privately that "the major part of the work of a President is to increase the gate receipts of fairs." Now, in the changed mood of the country, those excursions and his diversions were turned against him. Too much of his time was "occupied in pleasure seeking, attending baseball games in a number of different cities, frequent attendance at theatres, playing golf and riding around Washington and other places in automobiles."

Inevitably, much of the criticism, whether caustic anger or merely gentle jibing or sad disappointment, took the form of comparison with Roosevelt, as in:

Dear Teddy, I need you; come home to me quick,
    I am worried and weary and worn.
And as hope long deferred only makes the heart sick,
I am sadly in need of your potent "Big Stick";
    So, Teddy, please haste your return. . . .

Taft recognized the change in the public mood, and, though brave about it, was distressed. His family and intimate friends "felt as unhappy at the way things were going as Taft himself; I feel so sorry for him I could almost cry," wrote a faithful aide.

It was a pity, and it was unfair. Taft was not a bad president, he was a good one. He had absolute integrity. Considerably less than Roosevelt would Taft relax the highest standards of public service to name a friend to office or pay a debt to a politician. He was clear-minded and discriminating about men, too, and could on occasion exercise a unique power of characterization—one of the Insurgent senators he described as "so narrow he can see through a key-hole with both eyes at once without squinting."

Far less than most presidents would Taft practice hypocrisy, even the relatively harmless political variety, or compromise with it. Anything devious was abominable to him. In all the 330 pounds of him, not a pound nor an ounce nor a gram was deceit. Furtiveness he despised. At his desk, if a politician leaned to whisper to him, Taft's end of the conversation would rise until the windowpanes rattled. Courage he had, too, at all times the quiet kind, and, when roused, the energetic kind. Never did he yield to any organized militant minority—his scorn for that was a chief cause of his downfall.

Taft Is Not Roosevelt

All Taft's personal failings were immaterial, whether those of inertia before ill-fortune assailed him, or those of irritability later. His tragedy was merely that he was a placid man in a restless time, had a judicial temperament when the country was in a partisan mood, was a static man in a dynamic age. Under other conditions, or in many a four years of the country's history, Taft's elephantine bulk, his good-nature, his easygoing pace, might have commended him to the country, made him a hero at the time and subsequently a legend of gargantua, made him an ideal president. During any period of national quiescence Taft might have been uniquely in tune with the universe. His heartiness, genuineness, and sincerity might have been a tonic to similar qualities in the country. But the people had recently drunk deep of the very different qualities of another personality; having been stimulated by the heady wine of strenuousness, they could not be content with the tepid nectar of Taft's milder qualities.

Taft's chief failing was that he differed from Roosevelt, his chief misfortune that he followed Roosevelt in the presidency. The country had been tuned to the tempo of Roosevelt, and inevitably therefore could only be out of step with the tempo of Taft. To accent the maladjustment, Roosevelt had told the country that Taft was like himself. Taft could not live up to that picture; and to fail to live up to expectations created in others is a sure cause of failure. Taft might be an excellent president in a score of ways; all would do him no good if he was not excellent in the precise way the country had been led to expect. Pathetically, with earnest goodwill, Taft had hoped, had tried, to be what Roosevelt had said he would be. "I do nothing," he had written to Roosevelt as the latter took ship for Africa, "without considering what you would do in the same circumstances, and without having in a sense a mental talk with you over the pros and cons of the situation."

Taft had written that, in all sincerity, during his first month in the White House. He had meant to live up to it. He did not foresee that the role of trying to be Roosevelt involved a pose which his forthright simplicity would not permit him to continue. For Taft, any pose was distasteful to his character, impossible to his nature. He had to be himself. And Taft as himself, placid, easygoing, slow to decide, was a far cry from the strenuous, quick-acting Roosevelt whom the country, with some important exceptions, had come to regard as the model of what a president ought to be.

Seeds of Change

Peter Jennings and Todd Brewster

The period between 1900 and 1914 was an exciting and disturbing time in America. Broadcast journalist Peter Jennings and former *Life* magazine editor and writer Todd Brewster describe the political, social, technological, and cultural changes that characterized this period. Americans had to prepare for what they thought the future would bring, write Jennings and Brewster. They explain that immigration was a major challenge, not only in respect to the number of immigrants but to their ethnic diversity as well. In the authors' view, incorporating the immigrants into American society was a major challenge to American ideals. Peter Jennings is anchor and senior editor of ABC News's *World News Tonight*. Todd Brewster is Senior Editorial Producer of *The Century*.

The end of the nineteenth century carried . . . tension and foreboding because it coincided with the end of the absolutes that had governed life for so long. Charles Darwin's theories of evolution and natural selection, introduced in 1859 and refined in 1872, had shaken man's understanding of his origins *and* his purpose. . . . At the same time, socialism and democracy began to dominate world political thought, agreeing at least on one tenet, growing undeniable in these times: that the social order needed to be

---

amended to take power from the elites and provide it to the masses. Finally, the growth of science and industrialism in the last days of the 1800s and the first of the new century had begun to prepare people for a new relationship with their natural environment, technology promising conquest of the darkness (the lightbulb), the sky (the airplane), the horizon (the automobile), and many of the burdens of work, even as it introduced new avenues to entertainment (the phonograph, the movies) and communication (the telephone, the wireless).

The machine, it appeared, was poised to become everyman's slave, devoted and reliable, an inexhaustible ox, and a testament to man's ability to master his surroundings. Increasingly, people were even leaving the farm to live in a machine-made world, the city, knowing that it was there that the new life would emerge. Some of the biggest of these fast-growing metropolises—Paris, St. Louis, Buffalo, Atlanta, and, of course, Chicago—held turn-of-the-century fairs displaying the enormous promise of the industrial future—and this to people for whom the paved road was still a novelty. . . .

Everywhere one looked, there was the sense of being at the end of one kind of history and the start of another. By 1911 the edges of the earth had been reached—the American explorer Robert Peary tackling the North Pole, the Norwegian Roald Amundsen landing on the South. . . . But the sense of an exhausted past was not limited to geography. In the years that straddle 1900, art abandoned all pretensions to reproducing the realistic image, first shattering it into "little cubes" (as French artist Henri Matisse announced, giving the name to one of painting's newest and most violent ideologies) and going onward from there to spend the rest of the century exploring the fecund frontier of abstraction; music rejected traditional harmony for the otherworldly sounds of what composer Arnold Schoenberg called "pantonality"; literature played with the narrative; and physics, with the discovery of the electron, turned from the study of the macrocosmic forces of matter and energy that had dominated the field in the nineteenth century to the microcosmic world of subatomic particles that would lead eventually to Hiroshima. Finally, there was the 1901 funeral of Queen Victoria, all by itself an impressive piece of timing, the monarch whose name had been synonymous with the passing era now herself passing along with it.

In Europe, art and culture guided the march into *le moderne*, but in America, technology loudly announced the promise of the future, bringing the enthusiasm of discovery and the confidence that the new age would be a better age. It was American inventors whose genius thrilled the world with possibility (Edison, the Wrights) and, perhaps even more important, American industrialists (Rockefeller, Carnegie) and systems-builders (Ford, Taylor, Insull) who understood how to deliver the new technology into the lives of the masses. And who could not see the excitement in this? Design by design, piece by piece, object by object, America's crusading capitalists were replacing the natural world with a new man-made world, promising to establish a new life not just for the privileged few but for *mankind*, a world set in defiance of natural limits, a world shaped to fit man's needs, giving him comfort and pleasure and most of all freedom. And yet precisely because it *was* a defiance of nature and because it was a life with so little precedence, because it offered none of the comforts associated with tradition, the thrill of the new was received by nervous hands.

For now it was mostly anticipation. A few more years and a horrific war would pass into history before the world would finally cast off the yoke of the 1800s and enter into what some were calling nothing less than a second creation. Yet even in the years leading up to World War I, Americans found themselves anxiously making adjustments to prepare for life as they imagined it would soon be, and in the process, tentatively approaching some of the challenges that would inform their lives onward throughout the 1900s. How, for instance, to put an *American* imprint on the exciting yet foreign age that they now faced? How to fit a society conceived as a decentralized agrarian republic into a century of urban and industrial might? How to adjust a mostly white, Anglo-Saxon nation to the arrival of new immigrants from backgrounds alien to American traditions? How to reconcile competing notions of environmental and biological determinism with the American ideal of racial equality? How to execute the divine mission so many Americans believed to have been given to them as "trustees of the world's progress, guardians of its righteous peace"? Indeed, how to be an American in the alternately terrifying and exhilarating epoch unfolding before them as the twentieth century?

A New Ethnic Diversity

If the future had a shape, a logo, it was undoubtedly the skyscraper. The architectural wonder of the late nineteenth century had risen, literally, from the ashes of Chicago. The city had burned into history in 1871, then reconstructed itself not in wood or brick or iron, but in the very modern materials of steel and glass and steel-reinforced concrete laid out in a grid, so that the load was not borne by the walls, as had been previous practice, but dispensed throughout the structure, allowing it to rise toward the clouds, an urban silo. The skyscraper was almost too obvious a response to the closing of the frontier (vertical space replacing horizontal), and it became so commanding an image of the time that it inspired a Connecticut manufacturer to create one of the most durable and popular of twentieth-century toys, the Erector set. But even more important, as the new buildings began to reflect not the simple squared-off roofs that were common to the work of the great Chicago architect Louis H. Sullivan, but the striking, piercing verticality of church spires, they spoke to the aspirations of a new age dedicated to new values. By 1913, when New York City's Woolworth Building was opened, reaching for the heavens at sixty stories and 792 feet, the structure was boldly declared to be "the Cathedral of Commerce."

New York took to verticality like few other cities, the island of Manhattan being truly fixed space, and as the primary port of entry to the United States its newest buildings presented an image of upward motion to the throng of immigrants that in the century's first years pushed toward American shores. On his way to the administration center at Ellis Island, the immigrant first looked up as he passed the Statue of Liberty—an initial gesture of optimism demanded of him by his new homeland—but in fact he needed little encouragement to feel enthusiasm for the world he would now enter. For the millions making their way across the Atlantic, a new breed of immigrant from central and southern Europe fleeing pogroms and poverty, America was truly the land of opportunity.

From 1890 to 1910 nearly 13 million immigrants came to the United States, swelling the population and dramatically changing the nation from a mostly homogeneous citizenry descended from English, German, Scotch, and Irish ancestry to a population of dramatic ethnic diversity. If nineteenth-century America was white, Anglo-Saxon, and Protestant, then twentieth-century America would be white *and* black (the freed slave moving to stake his claim to a better life) *and* yellow. And it would include not only Protestants but Eastern Orthodox peoples from Russia and Greece, Latin peoples from the Catholic Mediterranean states, and Jews from Russia and Poland. The incorporation of immigrants from such vastly different backgrounds, holding vastly different beliefs and following vastly different customs, would pose one of the century's greatest challenges to American ideals.

The fresh arrivals were mostly rural peoples, but they came to the New World in search of jobs in industries that were centered in American cities and towns. And whereas they had sweated under the sun to till the earth in southern Italy, Russia, and the eastern European Slavic states, here they would work to the demands of a backbreaking foreman listening for the sound of the whistle that would announce the end of their workday. In the early years of the century, millions of new immigrants were packed into midsize American factory towns (in 1900 someone calculated

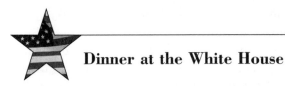

Dinner at the White House

President Theodore Roosevelt created a stir in 1901 when he invited African American educator Booker T. Washington to dine at the White House. The New York Times *was one of several newspapers to report on the incident and the president's reaction to his critics.*

Washington, Oct. 19—Quite the most exciting subject of conversation here for a day or two has been the entertainment at dinner on Wednesday by the President of Booker T. Washington. The news got out just as other announcements have been made of the guests of the President to dine, Mr. Roosevelt having adopted that method of meeting persons with whom he desired to have extended conversation.

The response that was flashed back from the South, where it was learned with something of a shock that a negro had sat at table with the President and his family, was the first intimation to the President that he had transgressed. The subject has been dealt with here by the newspapers with delicacy. The critical reports from the South have been printed, and there has been some deprecatory comment upon the resentful tone of Southern criticism. . . .

To one of his callers today, a friend who did not introduce the subject, the President is reported to have said, in referring to the dinner incident: "I do not need to give you an explanation of the Booker Washington affair, do I?" The visitor made a reply of inquiry. Then the President went on to say that he was amazed that he could be so misunderstood by those who had criticized him.

When he had declared that he did not intend to have anything to do with the white or black "scalawags" in the South, and followed that declaration by avoiding some appointments that he believed should not be made, and appointed some Democrats because he believed it to be for the best interests of the public service, he was applauded. But he considered that he had a perfect right, and that it was his duty in order to accomplish what he desired to do, to consult with white and black men who are not "scalawags."

He admired him for his character, his devotion to a cause, and for what he has accomplished.

The President does not pretend to defend himself from his assailants by entering upon a discussion of the color question. That seems to have had no weight with him in considering whether he should or should not invite Mr. Washington. The idea of a violation of Southern prejudice and tradition with the purpose of provoking and alienating his Southern friends never entered his mind. . . .

When he visited Tuskegee Institute he was the guest of Mr. Washington but did not, it is said, dine with him. This was commented upon as thoughtful regard for local opinion against social association between whites and blacks. It cannot be truthfully said that the President regards the incident and the subsequent comment as humorous, although it has been said that he did and that he proposed to get more fun out of it by asking Mr. Washington to dine with him again.

No such reckless story is believed by those who know Mr. Roosevelt. That it is regretted by many Republicans is plain enough. Maryland Democrats have seized upon the incident to turn it to account in the pending State campaign, and Republicans have admitted that it may give the State to the Democrats. The prosecution of Rear Admiral Schley has been a pretty hard load to carry, it is admitted, and would have handicapped the Republicans, and now this negro-at-dinner incident is being advertised in campaign fashion in all the leading papers of the State.

"The Dinner Incident," *New York Times,* October 19, 1901, as cited in James S. Olson, ed., *The United States in the Twentieth Century, Volume I: America 1900–1945.* New York: St. Martin's Press, 1995.

that twenty-five languages were being spoken in the textile mills of Lawrence, Massachusetts) while millions more undertook a quintessentially modern mission: the building of the big city. Weeks after he left the soil of Sardinia, a young Italian worker could find himself digging subway tunnels, laying trolley track, paving roads, constructing bridges or sewers or electrical lines, even sitting atop a steel girder erecting one of the vaunted new skyscrapers. And thanks largely to the help of such eager new Americans, the city of San Francisco, felled by a tremendous earthquake in 1906 that left 200,000 people homeless, was able to rebuild itself in less than three years, the precarious wooden structures erected during the city's days as a gold rush boomtown now wisely replaced by the kind of sturdy steel foundations that had a better chance of withstanding another tremor.

Confronting New Problems of Change

For the old-stock Americans, the ones whose parents and grandparents had arrived in previous centuries, the new immigrants and the new age came at once, and it was easy to confuse them. Many Americans were greeting the problems of big-city life for the first time, confronting the grime, corruption, disease, and overcrowding that came with such rapid, unrestricted growth, and they tended to see it not so much as a product of urban congestion as the work of foreign peoples defiling the American system. Indeed, in the century's first years, New York City had become Europe-on-the-Hudson, an amazing conglomeration of ethnicities—each group clinging to its heritage in tenement neighborhoods where there could be ten people packed in a room, more than two thousand in a city block. And the suddenness with which the character of that city and others was changing roused the voices of those who claimed the new immigrants were less in search of a new life centered around American ideals than in carrying the decadence of the Old World to American shores ("these bringing . . . unknown gods and rites . . . those, tiger passions here to stretch their claws").

The argument was, in fact, an old one. Americans had been grappling with the nativist urge throughout the nineteenth century, with some of their most distinguished political leaders lending credibility and eloquence to feelings that were at root nothing more than the coarsest form of bigotry. But the restrictionist fears at this moment were perhaps that much more vigorous for the stakes many people believed were at hand: for if the nation was remaking itself, Americans wanted to ensure that the new image retained some of the familiarity of the old.

America in 1900 was a provincial society of just 76 million citizens, a place of such innocence that it is hard for people at the end of the twentieth century to contemplate its quiet life: a nation of dirt roads and horse-drawn carriages, of tight corsets and Victorian pretensions, of kerosene lamps and outhouses, top hats and bowlers, McGuffey Readers and the *Ladies' Home Journal*. Cities were crowded with smoke-filled men's clubs and ornate wood-paneled bars like McSorley's Old Ale House in Manhattan (which prided itself on providing "good ale, raw onions and no ladies"), while country towns, which were still home to 60 percent of the nation's population, remained ensconced in the frontier ethic, villages of stark simplicity and virtue. The average American adult had but five years of schooling (and only recently had the nation made dramatic strides at reducing a substantial rate of illiteracy). Yet, even in such absence of worldly sophistication and learning, many people felt confident of two critical judgments: that America was earth's Eden, its people God's chosen. . . .

A Growing Passion for Reform

"Progress" was a word that carried a multitude of meanings at the turn of the century, and both the positive one embraced by the organizers of the 1904 St. Louis fair and the negative one New Englander Joe Knowles preached from his perch atop the birch trees of Maine in 1913 contrasted sharply with the creed of those who actually called themselves progressives. Concerned about the harsher edges of the modern workplace, these reformers directed their attention less toward the perfectibility of man than toward the perfectibility of industrial capitalism, the trimming and pruning of the economic frontier that had been heretofore governed only by the "natural" laws of the free market.

The conditions that inspired the progressives to act were, to say the least, appalling. At the turn of the century, the average industrial laborer's workweek involved fifty-nine hours on the job (in the steel industry, that could stretch to eighty-four hours). Pay was scant and many industries worked seasonally, shutting down for months at a time and leaving people without a paycheck until the factory opened again. Textile workers faced a particularly brutal situation, crammed into tiny urban garrets where many were paid not by the hour, but by the piece, an arrangement that forced them to work at a pace so frantic it would inspire a new word, "sweatshop." And coal workers—delivered by the company doctor, taught in the company school, housed in the company house, and buried in the company graveyard—lived lives but a step from the misery of indentured servitude. . . .

The key to change in the early years of the new century was the constituency that now embraced it. In the past, progressive reforms had appeared radical and un-American, smacking of socialism (and socialists would indeed gain a footing in the electorate that would peak in the presidential contest of 1912), but, in part because the nation was enjoying the kind of prosperity and stability that historically nurtures a quest for betterment, reform seemed now to excite even the middle class, inspiring millions toward compassion for those caught in the sweatshops and the mills. As Kansas newspaperman William Allen White later described it, the image of the disenchanted American had changed. He had "shaved his whiskers, washed his shirt, [and] put on a derby."

At least some of the public's willingness to address reform at this time could also be laid to its newfound faith in science as the unchallengeable Truth, the explicator of all human activity. The great age of invention (usually defined as across the years 1870–1920) fostered the heroic image of the genius-inventor, . . . the confident, self-made man who combined elements of American frontier mythology with the promise of the future. . . . But a large part of the romantic aura surrounding science also went beyond machines to systems and the growing sense that science in this form could render benefit upon *any* problem or task: improve the speed of work and the competitiveness of business, the raising of children and the management of the house, the eradication of the slum and the successful maintenance of the urban society. Social work was the most obvious outgrowth of this mind-set, as evidenced by the growing number of "settlement houses" dotting the urban landscape, each of them dedicated to the progressive belief that the immigrant's plight was a by-product of his circumstances, *not* his racial or ethnic limitations. . . .

Progressives were split on the issue of women's rights. On one side were the suffragists, who insisted that all good things would flow from the extension of voting privileges to women. Not only did these activists claim the vote as a democratic principle, they also argued that it would improve society, predicting that when women could use the vote to affect social policy, society would become more receptive to reform, leading to a lessening of crime and vice, even the elimination of war.

On the other side of the issue, however, were progressives who saw suffrage as dangerous for women in the way in which the vote might work to *overvalue* equality and make it harder to push, for instance, for special legislation protecting women and children in the workplace. . . .

By the early years of the century's second decade, suffragists had decided to put all their attention on a constitutional amendment, resorting to displays of civil disobedience to force the national leadership to comply. And indeed, with women being enfranchised in other parts of the world, an air of the inevitable entered the suffrage issue that needed only the force of the coming war and its demands upon women as laborers to become a reality.

Theodore Roosevelt: Model of the Age

The era's most famous progressive sported a prominent set of whiskers, a distinctively toothy grimace, pince-nez eyeglasses, and a jaw as solid as rock. Theodore Roosevelt was the kind of president that American historian Frederick Jackson Turner could appreciate, a New York aristocrat who by dint of his enthusiasm for the rugged life had every right to claim that he, too, was a "Western man in all but my residence." Except that TR, as he was affectionately known by the nation he led for seven years, was really most at home in a seat of power, and at that, preferably the one in the White House. . . .

Roosevelt was so much a man of his time, he embodied so many of its popular preoccupations (even some of those that seemed to be in conflict), it is hard not to think of him except as a caricature of the age. Who could better represent America's fresh sense of geographical definition than TR, who as biographer Edmund Morris points out was born of a southern mother and a northern father, yet was himself an easterner whose fascination was with the West? Who could better stand for the sometimes racially questionable declaration of a new American "breed" than this passionate follower of social Darwinism who had come to national attention with his charge up Cuba's San Juan Hill in the Spanish-American War of 1898, a triumph that helped claim, he said, the place of Americans among "the great fighting races" of the world? Who could better display America's emerging social conscience than a chief executive who believed not only in the natural right of the strong to prevail over the weak but also that the strong should, by moral purpose, work in *defense* of the weak, a president who wrote his senior essay at Harvard on "The Practicability of Equalizing Men and Women Before the Law" and who saw the government as responsible for curbing the abuses of the wealthy and standing up for the interests of both labor and the consumer? And who could better represent the modern quest for efficiency than this dynamo who by the age of forty-three had authored dozens of books and served as New York State assemblyman, United States civil service commissioner, police commissioner of New York City, assistant secretary of the navy, governor of New York, vice president, and, finally, president? . . .

Yet even as Roosevelt was initiating the nation's first tentative steps toward the social conscience that Turner had envisioned as America's next great adventure, he was also prodding the nation's attention toward what he saw as the preeminent civilization's responsibilities abroad. And while much of that was rhetoric, too, the debate that it prompted would, like most conflicts of this time foreshadow a discussion that would run throughout the century. . . .

Still, the president's interest in the world of international politics was more personal than political. Like most of the chief executives who would follow him in this century, TR's ego sought the exposure that only the grander stage of world politics could provide him. In 1905 he personally forged an end to the Russo-Japanese War (earning himself a Nobel Peace Prize), and his parade of the United States Navy fleet around the world in 1908 (done in defiance of Congress) was muscle-flexing gesture more demonstrative of the scrappy boyhood boxer's instincts that remained with Roosevelt his entire life than a popular mood. Most Americans simply did not yet want the role in international affairs that TR was ready to thrust upon them. . . .

Du Bois and Washington—Men of Reason

Just as it is hard at the end of the twentieth century to contemplate America's early-century innocence, so, too, is it hard to contemplate the nation's unashamedly high level of bigotry, a time when popular magazines regularly described blacks as "niggers" or "coons," "darkies" or "pickaninnies"; when adult black men were called "boy" and the caricatures of the time—Uncle Ben and Aunt Jemima—demonstrated the depth of understanding with which white America viewed the black personality. This was a day when the term "race riot" referred most likely to white people bringing violence down on blacks (not the opposite, as it came to mean in the latter half of the century), when a visit to the White House by black leader Booker T. Washington in 1901 was greeted with public censure ("Roosevelt Dines with a Nigger," read the headline of one paper), and when, in some places in the South, it was deemed so entertaining to see a black man suffer that theaters were reserved for lynchings. . . .

For blacks living under such conditions, life became defined by a kind of repeated duality: they were both black *and* American, free *and* enslaved, equal *and* "inferior." Writing in his landmark 1903 book, *The Souls of Black Folk*, W.E.B. Du Bois declared that the African-American's life was defined by this "two-ness—an American, a Negro, two souls, two thoughts, two unreconciled strivings, two warring ideals in one dark body, whose dogged strength alone keeps it from being torn asunder." And yet Du Bois himself, along with Booker T. Washington, defined still another "two-ness," in the way that each chose to advocate for a separate path to black progress: Du Bois, the voice of protest pushing the white power structure to grant greater freedom and ensure equality; Washington, the spokesman for self-improvement, whose philosophy had been so eloquently uttered in his speech at the 1895 Atlanta Exposition . . . , an address in which he became the first black leader to advise the African-American to acquiesce in both disfranchisement and some manner of Jim Crow and to "cast down your bucket where you are" and build a life apart from mainstream white society. . . .

Had black Americans chosen to follow Washington, the history of race relations in the twentieth century might have been very different, but Du Bois, while in agreement with Washington on some matters, eventually offered an alternative philosophy, and in the end, it was his that won the day. Anyone looking for the roots of the American civil rights movement of the latter twentieth century should start with the decision to follow Du Bois: a walking-cane and white-glove mulatto elitist who had been born into freedom in the North, was educated at Harvard, and believed that "the Negro race" could be saved by "its exceptional men.". . .

The "Big Ditch" Ushers in a New Era

In 1913, at roughly the same time that New Yorkers were scoffing at modern painting, a project more uniformly pleasing to contemporary sensibilities was nearing completion 2,300 miles south of Manhattan. The dream of uniting the Atlantic Ocean with the Pacific, of a canal bisecting the thin strip of land connecting North America to South America, had dated back to the time of Spanish exploration in the sixteenth century. Ever since gold was discovered in California in 1848, prompting the building of a Panama railroad connecting steamships on either side to rush prospectors to their dreamland and back home again, Americans had been especially frustrated by their desire to have a connecting waterway all their own, a way to move freight and passengers from coast to coast with ease. . . .

No president loved a challenge more than Teddy Roosevelt, and, just as John Kennedy would set his sights on the moon more than a half century later, TR set out to claim for America the rights to the world's greatest technological feat. America itself would dig the "Big Ditch," as it became popularly known. And by the time the canal opened in August 1914, a good six months ahead of schedule, TR, though long out of the White House, would remain the personality most associated with it. . . .

Like Roosevelt himself, the canal was a bridge between two eras. The idea belonged to the 1800s—its grandeur, its hubris, its brazen display of the colonial mentality—but its execution would have been impossible without the tools of the modern period. . . .

At almost the precise moment that America's great engineering feat became a reality, declaring in the minds of many the arrival of an age of unambiguous technological achievement, popular attention turned elsewhere, toward Europe and the event that would consume the world in darkness.

Chronology

1900

American troops sent to restore order during Boxer Rebellion in China; the International Ladies' Garment Workers Union is founded; Eastman Kodak introduces the $1 Brownie box camera; the first U.S. auto show is held.

1901

President William McKinley is assassinated by Polish-American anarchist Leon Czolgosz; forty-two-year-old Vice President Theodore Roosevelt becomes the youngest president in American history; Cuba becomes a U.S. protectorate; Booker T. Washington's autobiography *Up from Slavery* is published; President Roosevelt invites Booker T. Washington to dine at the White House, creating controversy; the largest trust of the period, U.S. Steel, is organized; the Socialist Party of America is founded.

1902

The U.S. government intervenes for the first time ever in a strike, the Great Anthracite Coal Strike; President Roosevelt prosecutes J.P. Morgan's Northern Securities Company for violating the Sherman Act.

1903

The Ford Motor Company is established; Orville and Wilbur Wright achieve the first controlled, powered flight in an airplane; the first national wildlife refuge, Pelican Island, Florida, is named; W.E.B. Du Bois's *Souls of Black Folk* is published; Jack London's *Call of the Wild* is published; the American League Boston Red Sox baseball team beats the National League Pittsburgh team in the first World Series; *The Great Train Robbery*, the first narrative film ever made, is released and becomes a box-office hit; Panama splits from Colombia and grants the United States the right to build the Panama Canal; Guglielmo Marconi sends a wireless greeting from President Roosevelt to Edward VII of Britain.

1904

Theodore Roosevelt is elected to his second term as president of the United States; the government announces the Roosevelt Corollary to the Monroe Doctrine; the Supreme Court dissolves the Northern Securities Company; Russia and Japan go to war; the World's Fair—the Louisiana Purchase Exposition—opens in St. Louis.

1905
President Roosevelt mediates the end to the Russo-Japanese War; the Industrial Workers of the World (IWW) is founded in Chicago.

1906
An earthquake and fire levels two-thirds of the city of San Francisco; a hurricane strikes Galveston, Texas, resulting in the worst recorded natural disaster in North American history; Upton Sinclair's *The Jungle* is published; construction of the Panama Canal gets underway; U.S. troops occupy Cuba to put down a revolt; Theodore Roosevelt wins the Nobel Prize for Peace for his mediation of the Russo-Japanese War.

1907
Robert Peary reaches the North Pole; President Roosevelt bars Japanese immigration to the United States; more than 360 miners are killed in an explosion in Monograph, West Virginia, the nation's worst mining disaster to that time.

1908
William Howard Taft is elected president of the United States; Henry Ford introduces the Model T.

1909
The National Association for the Advancement of Colored People (NAACP) is founded.

1910
President Taft initiates "dollar diplomacy" in Nicaragua; architect Frank Lloyd Wright completes Robie House in Chicago.

For Further Reading

Books
The 1900s

Richard Abel, *The Red Rooster Scare: Making Cinema American, 1900–1910*. Berkeley: University of California Press, 1999.

Frederick Lewis Allen, *The Big Change*. New York: Harper, 1952.

Ann Angel, *America in the 20th Century: 1900–1909*. New York: Marshall Cavendish, 1995.

Judy Crichton, *America 1900: The Turning Point*. New York: Henry Holt and Company, 1998.

Editors of Time-Life Books, *Dawn of the Century: 1900–1910*. New York: Time-Life, Inc., 1975.

———, *This Fabulous Century: Volume I, 1900–1910*. New York: Time-Life Books, 1998.

Janice Green, *Our Century 1900–1910*. Belmont, CA: Fearon Education, 1989.

John F. Kasson, *Amusing the Million: Coney Island at the Turn of the Century*. New York: Hill & Wang, 1978.

Michael Lesy, *Dreamland: America at the Dawn of the Twentieth Century*. New York: New Press, 1997.

Nancy Smiler Levinson, *Turn of the Century: Our Nation One Hundred Years Ago*. New York: Lodestar Books, 1994.

Walter Lord, *The Good Years: From 1900 to the First World War*. New York: Harper & Row, 1960.

Martin Meltzer, *Theodore Roosevelt and His America*. Danbury, CT: Grolier, 1994.

Eva Jane Price, *China Journal 1889–1900: An American Missionary Family During the Boxer Rebellion*. New York: Charles Scribner's Sons, 1989.

Dan Rather, *Our Times: America at the Birth of the Twentieth Century*. New York: Scribner, 1996.

Steven A. Riess, *Touching Base: Professional Baseball and American Culture in the Progressive Era*. Champaign: University of Illinois Press, 1999.

Jacob A. Riis, *How the Other Half Lives: Studies Among the Tenements of New York*. Mineola, NY: Dover Publications, 1985.

Orville Wright, *How We Invented the Airplane: An Illustrated History*. New York: Dover Publications, 1988.

The 20th Century

David R. Contosta and Robert Muccigrosso, *America in the Twentieth Century: Coming of Age*. New York: Harper and Row, 1988.

Bernard Edelman, *The Story of the 20th Century by the Americans Who Lived It*. New York: Farrar, Straus and Giroux, 1999.

Harold Evans with Gail Buckland and Kevin Baker, *The American Century*. New York: Alfred A. Knopf, 1998.

Peter Jennings and Todd Brewster, *The Century*. New York: Doubleday, 1998.

Geoffrey C. Ward, *Baseball: An Illustrated History*. New York: Alfred A. Knopf, 1994.

Anthologies Containing Documents Written in the 1900s

John H. Cary, ed., *The Social Fabric*. New York: HarperCollins, 1995.

J.R. Conlin and C.H. Peterson, eds., *An American Harvest: Readings in American History, Volume 2*. San Diego: Harcourt Brace Jovanovich, 1986.

John A. DeNovo, ed., *The Gilded Age and After*. New York: Charles Scribner's Sons, 1972.

Louis Filler, ed., *Contemporaries: Portraits in the Progressive Era by David Graham Phillips*. Westport, CT: Greenwood Press, 1981.

Sidney Fine and Gerald S. Brown, eds., *The American Past—Conflicting Interpretations of the Great Issues, Volume II*. New York: Macmillan, 1970.

Leon Fink, ed., *Major Problems in the Gilded Age and the Progressive Era*. Lexington, MA: D.C. Heath, 1993.

Immigration Before, During, and After the 1900s

Maldwyn A. Jones, *Destination America*. London: Weidenfeld and Nicolson, 1976.

William Loren Katz, *A History of Multicultural America: The Great Migrations 1880s–1912*. Austin, TX: Raintree Steck-Vaughn, 1993.

Norman Kotker et al., *Ellis Island: Echoes from a Nation's Past*. New York: Aperture, 1991.

L. Edward Purcell, *Immigration (Social Issues in American History Series)*. Phoenix, AZ: Oryx Press, 1995.

Moses Rischin, ed., *Immigration and the American Tradition*. Indianapolis: Bobbs-Merrill, 1976.

Ronald Takaki, *A Different Mirror: A History of Multicultural America*. Boston: Little, Brown, 1993.

Life and Presidency of Theodore Roosevelt

James Barber and Amy Verone, *Theodore Roosevelt, Icon of the American Century*. Seattle: University of Washington Press, 1999.

Lewis L. Gould, *The Presidency of Theodore Roosevelt (American Presidency Series)*. Lawrence: University Press of Kansas, 1991.

Nathan Miller, *Theodore Roosevelt: A Life*. New York: Morrow, William, 1994.

Edmund Morris, *The Rise of Theodore Roosevelt*. New York: Random House, 1980.

Major Events of the 1900s

Malcolm Barker, comp., *Three Fearful Days: San Francisco Memoirs of the 1906 Earthquake and Fire*. San Francisco: Londonborn Publications, 1998.

William Bronson, *The Earth Shook, the Sky Burned*. San Francisco: Chronicle Books, 1997.

Tim J. Fox and Duane R. Sneddeker, *From the Palaces to the Pike: Visions of the 1904 World's Fair*. St. Louis: Missouri Historical Society, 1997.

John D. Weaver, *The Brownsville Raid*. College Station: Texas A&M University Press, 1992.

Personalities of the 1900s

Bonnie Carman Harvey, *Jane Addams: Nobel Prize Winner and Founder of Hull House*. Berkeley Heights, NJ: Enslow Publishers, 1999.

Paul Joseph, *The Wright Brothers*. Minneapolis, MN: Abdo & Daughters, 1996.

Stephen Kirk, *First in Flight: The Wright Brothers in North Carolina*. Winston-Salem, NC: J.F. Blair, 1995.

David L. Lewis, *The Public Image of Henry Ford: An American Folk Hero and His Company*. Detroit: Wayne State University Press, 1988.

Milton Meltzer, *The Many Lives of Andrew Carnegie*. Danbury, CT: Franklin Watts, 1997.

Sidney Olsen, *Young Henry Ford: A Picture History of the First Forty Years*. Detroit: Wayne State University Press, 1997.

Dennis Rawlins, *Peary at the North Pole: Fact or Fiction?* Washington: Robert B. Luce, 1973.

Richard L. Taylor, *The First Flight: The Story of the Wright Brothers*. New York: Franklin Watts, 1990.

John Edward Weems, *Race for the Pole*. New York: Henry Holt, 1960.

Progressivism and Reform During the 1900s

John D. Buenker and Edward R. Kantowica, ed., *Historical Dictionary of the Progressive Era, 1850–1920*. Westport, CT: Greenwood Press, 1988.

Steven Dennis Cashman, *America in the Age of Titans: The Progressive Era and World War I*. New York: New York University Press, 1988.

David R. Colburn and George E. Pozzetta, *Reform and Reformers in the Progressive Era*. Westport, CT: Greenwood Press, 1982.

Steven J. Diner, *A Very Different Age: Americans of the Progressive Era*. New York: Hill and Wang, 1998.

Leon Fink, ed., *Major Problems in the Gilded Age and the Progressive Era*. Boston: Houghton-Mifflin, 1993.

Lewis L. Gould, *The Progressive Era*. Syracuse, NY: Syracuse University Press, 1994.

Arthur S. Link and Richard L. McCormick, *Progressivism (The American History Series)*. Wheeling, IL: Harlan Davidson, 1983.

Otis Pease, ed., *The Progressive Years*. George Braziller, 1962.

Dorothy Schneider and Carl J. Schneider, *American Women in the Progressive Era, 1900–1920*. New York: Anchor/Doubleday, 1994.

Periodicals and Newspapers

Mark C. Carnes, "Little Colonel Funston," *American Heritage,* September 1998.

Lane Hartill, "Muckrakers Dug Up Dirt on Big-Business," *Christian Science Monitor,* March 16, 1999.

Wally Herbert, "Did Peary Reach the Pole?" *National Geographic,* September 1988.

Paul Andrew Hutton, "T.R. Takes Charge," *American History,* August 1998.

Sandy Marvinney, "Theodore Roosevelt, Conservationist," *New York State Conservationist,* June 1996.

Janet Reitman, "The Muckraker vs. the Millionaire," *Scholastic Update,* November 2, 1998.

Linda Simon, "Muckraker in Chief," *The World & I,* April 1999.

Bernard A. Weisberger, "Righteous Fists," *American Heritage,* May/June 1997.

Richard Young, "The Brownsville Affair," *American History Illustrated,* October 1986.

Warren Zimmermann, "Jingoes, Goo-Goos, and the Rise of America's Empire," *The Wilson Quarterly,* Spring 1998.

Index